Working Images

Visual methods such as drawing, painting, video, photography and hypermedia offer increasingly accessible and popular resources for ethnographic research. In *Working Images*, prominent visual anthropologists and artists explore how old and new visual media can be integrated into contemporary forms of research and representation. Drawing upon projects undertaken both 'at home' in their native countries and abroad in locations such as Ethiopia and Venezuela, the book's contributors demonstrate how visual methods are used in the field, and how these methods can produce and communicate knowledge about our own and other cultures. As well as focusing on key issues such as ethics and the relationship between word and image, they emphasise the huge range of visual methods currently opening up new possibilities for field research, from graphic art to new media such as digital video and on-line technologies.

Contributors: Cristina Grasseni, Gemma Orobitg Canal, László Kürti, Ana Isabel Afonso, Iain R. Edgar, Paul Henley, Victoriano Camas Baena, Ana Martínez Pérez, Rafael Muñoz Sotelo, Manuel Ortiz Mateos, Manuel João Ramos, Olivia da Silva, Sarah Pink, Roderick Coover, Felicia Hughes-Freeland.

Editors: Sarah Pink lectures in the Department of Social Sciences at Loughborough University, UK. **László Kürti** teaches at the University of Miskolc in Hungary, and **Ana Isabel Afonso** lectures in the Department of Anthropology at Universidade Nova, Lisbon.

Working Images

Visual Research and Representation in Ethnography

Edited by
Sarah Pink, László Kürti and
Ana Isabel Afonso

Routledge
Taylor & Francis Group

LONDON AND NEW YORK

First published 2004 by Routledge
2 Park Square, Milton Park, Abingdon, Oxon, OX14 4RN

Simultaneously published in the USA and Canada
by Routledge
711 Third Avenue, New York, NY 10017, USA

Routledge is an imprint of the Taylor & Francis Group, an informa business

Typeset in Galliard by Graphicraft Limited, Hong Kong

British Library Cataloguing in Publication Data
A catalogue record for this book is available from the British Library

Library of Congress Cataloging in Publication Data
A catalog record for this book has been requested

ISBN 0-415-30641-8 (hbk)
ISBN 0-415-30654-X (pbk)

Contents

PART II
Representing visual knowledge

Figures

Colour plates

Contributors

Ana Isabel Afonso lectures in the Department of Anthropology, Universidade Nova de Lisboa, teaching Research Methods; Ethics and Anthropological Practice. Her main research interests are new technologies, social change and development, kinship and applied anthropology. She has done fieldwork in north-east Portugal and co-ordinates a project on Portuguese gypsies. Her recent publications include *Terra, Casa e Família* (forthcoming); co-edition of *Retóricas sem Fronteira* (2003) and *Visual Teaching, Virtual Learning* (2002).

Victoriano Camas Baena is a Psychotherapist at the Centre for Interpersonal Relations and a Social Researcher and has made a number of documentaries with *A Buen Común*.

Roderick Coover teaches at the School of the Art Institute of Chicago. His works include the interactive CD-ROM, *Cultures in Webs: Working in Hypermedia with the Documentary Image* (Eastgate.com) and the documentary, *Burgundy and the Language of Wine* (NaturalWords.org). His awards include a Whiting Post-Doctoral Fellowship in the Humanities and a USIA Hays-Fulbright Fellowship.

Iain R. Edgar lectures in Anthropology at Durham University, UK. He has written *Dreamwork, Anthropology and the Caring Professions: A Cultural Approach to Dreamwork* (1995), and *Guide to Imagework: Imagination-based Research Methods* (forthcoming).

Cristina Grasseni is researcher in Anthropology and Epistemology, Bergamo University, Italy. She has published on skilled practice and development in northern Italy, 'Skilled landscapes', in *Society and Space* (forthcoming), and produced the video *Those who don't work, don't make love* (GCVA 1998).

Paul Henley has been Director of the Granada Centre for Visual Anthropology, University of Manchester, since it was founded in 1987. He has published extensively on the anthropology of Amazonia and as a film-maker has worked both in South America and Europe.

Felicia Hughes-Freeland has researched and filmed performance in south-east Asia, and is also interested in art and old-fashioned darkroom photography. She works as Senior Lecturer in Anthropology at the University of Wales Swansea where she teaches anthropological theory, south-east Asian ethnography, and also trains her undergraduates in film-making.

László Kürti teaches at the University of Miskolc, in Hungary; his interests include visual anthropology and new media technology. He is the author of several books including *The Remote Borderland: Transylvania in the Hungarian Imagination* (2001) and *Youth and the State in Hungary: Capitalism, Communism and Class* (2002).

Ana Martínez Pérez is a social anthropologist. She lectures in Sociology at the Universidad Rey Juan Carlos, Madrid. She is a co-founder of the *Taller de Antropología Visual* (Visual Anthropology Workshop) and has been making documentaries with *A Buen Común* since 1997.

Rafael Muñoz Sotelo is a primary school teacher in Madrid and a Social Researcher. He has made several documentaries with *A Buen Común*.

Gemma Orobitg Canal is Lecturer in Social Anthropology at the University of Barcelona. She has done research among the Pumé Indians of Venezuela for the last ten years. Her previous publications are *Les Pumés et leurs rêves. Étude d'un groupe Indien des Llanos du Venezuela* (1998) and *Dreaming to Live. Memory, Oblivion and Experience among the Pumé Indians* (2000).

Manuel Ortiz Mateos is an anthropologist and a maker of films and videos. He is currently working in social intervention with gypsy communities.

Sarah Pink lectures in the Department of Social Sciences at Loughborough University. She has done fieldwork in Spain, Guinea Bissau and England on visual culture, the senses, gender and performance using visual images and technologies as part of research and representation. Her books include *Women and Bullfighting* (1997) and *Doing Visual Ethnography* (2001).

Manuel João Ramos (doctoral studies at the École des Hautes Études en Sciences Sociales, Paris; PhD Hons Instituto Superior de Ciências do Trabalho e Empresa, Lisbon) is Associate Professor of Anthropology at the ISCTE, Lisbon. His publications are mainly on Christian symbolism and visual anthropology, including his books *Ensaios de Mitologia Cristã* (1997) on the legendary Prester John, and *Histórias Etíopes – Diário de Viagem* (2000) on Northern Ethiopia.

Olivia da Silva is Head of Photography at the Instituto Politecnico do Porto and Curator of Photography at the Tram Museum, Porto. She started her career as a photojournalist working for the Portuguese national newspaper *O Publico*, and her exhibitions include *8/2* and *In the Net*.

Acknowledgements

Working Images has from the outset been a collaborative project as it began life as the *Working Images* Conference, an initiative developed between the Visual Anthropology Network and the Teaching Anthropology Network of the European Association of Social Anthropologists (EASA). We would like to thank a good number of individuals and organisations who have been involved in the different stages of its development and production: the EASA committee, at that time chaired by Gerd Bauman, for the association's backing as we developed the conference; Joaquim Pais de Brito, the Director of the Museu Etnologico in Lisbon for inviting us to hold the conference in the ideal environment of Lisbon's impressive ethnographic museum; the The Wenner Gren Foundation, the Fundação Calouste Gulbenkian, the Programa Operacional Ciência, Tecnologia, Inovação do Quadro Comunitário de Apoio III and the Fundação Luso-Americana para o Desenvolvimento for generously funding the conference; and PT Comunicações and Delta Cafés in Lisbon for supporting the conference. The *Working Images* Conference was co-organised by the editors of this volume and Clara Carvalho from ISCTE, Lisbon. It hosted over forty participants, including anthropologists, museum curators, film-makers, photographers and multimedia artists. This volume has a particular brief to explore the use of visual images, media and technologies in research and representation. Another set of papers from the conference has been published in a special issue of *Anthropology in Action* on visual teaching and virtual learning. We would like to thank Clara Carvalho especially, and all the other conference participants (particularly Stewart Coleman and Rogério Abreu for their help during the conference) who helped to create the event from which this *Working Images* book has emerged. Many thanks finally to John Postill who translated Chapter 8 and was responsible for English language checking, and to our Readers and all the staff at Routledge who have been involved in this project.

Chapter 1

Introduction

Situating visual research

Sarah Pink

Now, more than ever before, ethnographers are using visual and digital images and technologies to research and represent the cultures, lives and experiences of other people. Theoretical and technological innovations have made the visual both acceptable and accessible to anthropologists and this has created a contemporary context where new ethnographic media, methodologies and practices are emerging. *Working Images* explores these uses of the visual in ethnography. Through a series of theoretically informed recent case studies and fieldwork experiences its contributors describe how photography, video, drawing and hypermedia might be engaged in the processes through which ethnographic knowledge is created and represented.

A new context for visual anthropology

The turn of the twenty-first century was a key moment in the development of visual anthropology. Preceded by some important publications in the late 1990s (e.g. Banks and Morphy 1997, MacDougall 1998), between 2000 and 2001 a series of new books, articles and websites about visual anthropology and ethnography came into the public domain. Between them these texts have considered the history of visual anthropology (e.g. Ruby 2000, Grimshaw 2001, *Visual Anthropology Review* 17(2) 2001–2); suggested how visual methods of research and representation might play a fuller role in ethnography as a whole (Pink 2001, Banks 2001, Edgar forthcoming); urged us to engage with the potential of historical images to articulate submerged realities (Edwards 2001); and generally reiterated MacDougall's call for a closer integration of the visual in mainstream anthropology, as both a critical and reflexive voice and a means of communicating understandings that are 'accessible only by non-verbal means' (1997: 292). New works in visual anthropology (e.g. in Spain, Garcia Alonso *et al.* 1996, Grau 2002) and that represent ethnographic work visually using photography and drawing (e.g. in Portugal Silva 2000, Ramos 2000 respectively) are spreading across Europe, and moreover visual anthropologists are starting to realise that the British, French and North American traditions in ethnographic film-making that dominated the discipline in the twentieth century were simply the mainstream – not the only – contributions to visual anthropology at the time.[1] On-line visual anthropology now has significant presence with new websites such as the two Italian sites visualanthropology.net[2] and Reciproche Visioni,[3] and Working Images[4] the website of the Visual Anthropology Network of the European Association of Social Anthropologists. This, coupled with the rapid developments in visual and digital technologies that now facilitate visual research and representation, represents a new context for visual anthropology and ethnography. We are embracing new texts, technologies, approaches and perspectives. New academics are participating in the debates. With this flurry of publications we have a fresh profile for the visual on our bookshelves and on-line. Moreover it is not only within visual anthropology that visual methods of research and representation are inviting new possibilities. There is an increasing interdisciplinary interest in visual methods in visual cultural studies (Lister and Wells 2000), visual sociology (Pauwells 2000, Emmison and Smith 2000), cultural geography (Rose 2001), queer studies (Holliday 2000) and in multidisciplinary volumes (Van Leeuwen and Jewitt 2000). As the visual has begun to have a more established role in mainstream social science research and representation, researchers have begun to draw on existing literatures in visual anthropology and sociology to develop and inform their own fields. However, as Pauwells warns, the path of interdisciplinarity is 'not at all an easy road to take' because 'When crossing borders of disciplines the danger of "amateurism" is always lurking. This may manifest itself in a quick (and dirty) exchange or borrowing of ideas and techniques without grasping the full implications' (2000: 12–13). Indeed visual anthropology has been the victim of some inappropriate interdisciplinary critiques (see below).

There are two other pertinent features of this interdisciplinary interest in visual methods. First, it requires us to define how visual anthropology is different. Here, although other social scientists also use ethnographic methods, our focus is on ethnography as practice and specifically with visual ethnography that is informed by anthropological theory and embedded in anthropological research questions. The contributors to this volume share methods used by sociologists and other social scientists. For example practising variants of photo-elicitation (albeit in a more serendipitous form than sociologists do), asking informants to discuss existing photographs, using the visual as a documenting tool, as a form of interrogation, a 'way of knowing/seeing' and representation. However, the projects discussed in the book form part of work that is in one way or another specifically anthropological in its focus and are part of wider ethnographic projects. The second strand of our interdisciplinary theme inspires us to engage with other disciplines. In this book this engagement is represented in two ways. On the one hand some contributors' practice as visual anthropologists is developed with or draws from influences from other disciplines. For example, in Chapter 8 Camas *et al.* describe the work on an interdisciplinary unit made up of visual anthropologists and psychologists, and Edgar's image work also drawing from psychology has some parallels with therapeutic disciplines, in particular art therapy (see Hogan 2001). On the other hand some of its contributors (with the exception of Ramos who combines both) are not so much anthropologists, but artists who use ethnographic research and anthropological ideas to inform their practice (da Silva, Coover). As da Silva and Pink note in Chapter 10, Foster (1995) has suggested that such interdisciplinary uses of ethnography might be superficial and serve to validate the author/artist's own vision rather than the people represented. Nevertheless, careful and respectful interdisciplinary appropriations such as those presented here can offer as much to anthropology as they do to the disciplines that appropriate its methods and approaches.

The argument that visual anthropology should be much more than ethnographic film is not new. In the USA Jay Ruby and Sol Worth argued for an anthropology of visual communication that involved 'studying how pictures are put together to make statements about this world' (Worth 1997: 195). In *Rethinking Visual Anthropology* Morphy and Banks sought to 'deflect the centre of the discipline away from ethnographic film and photography, allowing them to be re-incorporated in a more positive way that is more cognizant with the broader anthropological project' making visual anthropology thus 'the anthropology of visual systems, or more broadly visual cultural forms' (1997: 5). The new context captured by this volume, with its emphasis on processes of visual research and representation, has achieved this integration. The contributors represent anthropologists and practising artists from around Europe and the United States who work with visual and digital media, anthropological theory and ethnographic methods. They include established visual anthropologists who have for many years been involved in the most 'traditional' form of visual anthropology, ethnographic film-making, analysis and training; anthropologists who have diversified from this to work with photography, video, hypermedia and drawing to research and represent their work; and visual artists who use anthropological theory and ethnographic methods to develop their photography, hypermedia and drawing.

Changing methods and practices in ethnography

In recent years new approaches to ethnographic research have emerged making reflexivity, collaboration, new approaches to ethics and new technologies necessary themes in any ethnographic methods text and especially in visual ethnography texts (Pink 2001a, Banks 2001). These developments offer an implicit critique of the approaches of earlier advocates of visual methods (e.g. Bateson and Mead 1942, Collier and Collier 1986) and invite new ways of working with people, words and images with an emphasis on the *processes* of research and representation.

New approaches to ethnography have established a closer relationship between research and representation, signified largely by the insistence on reflexivity inspired by the 'writing culture' debate (see Clifford and Marcus 1986, James *et al.* 1997). The emphasis on reflexivity has been the singular most important strand in recent visual anthropology literature and interdisciplinary visual methods texts. There have nevertheless been unnecessary and ungrounded attacks on visual anthropology for being an unreflexive and unethical discipline (e.g. Holliday 2000, Emmison and Smith 2000, see Pink 2001b). Rather than taking such critiques at face value, readers should consider how voices and practices from within anthropology have made reflexivity central to ethnographic film-making (see e.g. MacDougall 1998 and Grimshaw 2001: 121–48). Indeed Ruby has argued for a reflexive approach for over twenty years (see Ruby 1980, 1982). For Ruby reflexivity, through which the author reveals the assumptions that guided her or his work, is essential to an ethical approach in visual anthropological practice and is synonymous with doing 'proper' anthropology (2000: 167). Comparing ethnographic film and writing MacDougall distinguishes between 'deep' and 'explanatory' reflexivity. Deep reflexivity is possible when we use video (or film) as it represents the relationships that produced the video. In contrast explanatory reflexivity, which is more usual in ethnographic writing, takes the form of subsequent reflection upon these relationships (1998: 89). The contributors to this volume share these concerns to recognise and reveal the processes through which one's visual representations or written descriptions of visual research are created, thus emphasising the subjectivities of the anthropologist/film-maker/photographer/artist, of the informant/subject, and of the audience/viewer/reader of one's work.

Linked to this reflexivity advocated in visual anthropology are collaborative and participatory approaches to research and representation. These stand in stark contrast to purely observational approaches (such as that advocated by Emmison and Smith 2000). As Banks suggests 'All image production by social researchers in the field, indeed all first hand social research of any kind, must be collaborative to some extent' because 'the researcher's very presence amongst a group of people is the result of a series of social negotiations' (2001: 119). The contributors to this volume involve their informants/subjects to different degrees and in different ways with their research/visual practice, offering at least some consultation and at most full involvement in image production processes and recognising that such collaborations are a vehicle through which knowledge, understandings and visual representations are produced.

New media, new methods, new texts

New media invite new methods of visual research, new ways of presenting and viewing research, and new ways of creating reflexive texts. This itself assumes new configurations of the relationship between images and words in anthropological research and representation – a theme which runs throughout the volume. It is difficult to divide up the different methods covered in this book in relation to different media – film, video, photography, drawing, hypermedia, the intangible images of our imaginations and writing – most contributors combine two or more in their work in different ways and at different stages. Instead in this section I consider how the work discussed in *Working Images* represents a set of themes in contemporary visual anthropology: changing approaches to filmic (including video) and photographic representations of ethnography; the development of ethnographic hypermedia; art and drawing in ethnographic research and representation.

Changing approaches to anthropological film and video

In the present context a set of converging factors suggest (digital) video is the future of moving ethnographic images. (1) The romance between visual anthropology and British broadcast television, so vibrant in the 1970s and 1980s with Granada television's *Disappearing World* series and the BBC's *Under the Sun*, has completely broken down. This leaves visual anthropologists with fewer possibilities to obtain funding for big budget ethnographic documentaries. (2) Simultaneously visual anthropologists argue that freed from the limitations collaboration with these institutions imposed they can produce new films that respond more directly to the agendas of anthropology (see MacDougall 2001, Ruby 2000) and of their informants (see Camas *et al.*, this volume, Ch. 8) rather than television. An important aspect of this liberation is that it has been achieved by technological innovation: the advent of affordable digital video has allowed ethnographic film-makers to change their work practices and budget structures. (3) It is now recognised that film or video is not simply useful for representing ethnographic research but is a research method in itself. In the 1990s some anthropologists began to describe how they used video to these ends (e.g. Ferrandiz 1998), and more recent work on identity and practice reflects on this in more detail (see Pink 2001a, 2004; Grasseni, this volume, Ch. 2) showing how video has a place in projects seeking to explore questions (in this case about identity and practice) pertinent to mainstream anthropology. (4) Increasing links between visual anthropologists and industry mean that whereas previously funding came from the glamorous world of television, it is now more likely to come from corporate sponsors interested in visual ethnographies about their consumers. This encourages different types of video ethnography, in their turn constrained by funders' objectives, but also presents new possibilities for producing and representing video ethnography (see Pink, this volume, Ch. 11). This changing context raises the question of the future of observational ethnographic film, the style and medium that has dominated visual anthropology for the last 30 years. In Chapter 7 Henley insists that observational cinema continues to be appropriate to anthropological research and representation, but urges ethnographic film-makers to be innovative in their uses of it. This option calls for a 'renewal' of ethnographic film to fit the present context in ways that more directly address the concerns of and are more closely integrated with mainstream visual anthropology.

Ethnographic hypermedia and digital imaging

A second solution to this question of how to integrate visual representations into mainstream anthropology is the use of hypermedia. Anthropological hypermedia is rapidly developing in teaching and learning (see Pink, Kürti and Afonso 2002) and academic publishing. The ERA (Experience Rich Anthropology) website[5] offers a large range of written and visual resources, and other on-line, CD-ROM and DVD projects exist as research resources, presenting field notes, photographs and film clips, as reflexive texts and as materials other researchers might interrogate. See, for example, Biella's *Maasai Interactive* (Biella 1997); Pink's *The Bullfighter's Braid, Interweaving Lives, Gender at Home* and *Women's Worlds* (see Ch. 11); Coovers' *Burgundy and the Language of Wine* (see Ch. 12); Kürti's community digital photography archive in Hungary (Ch. 4). On-line journals have also prospered. Some use the interactivity of hypermedia to imitate the multilinear reading processes we practise when reading printed texts. For example, through hyperlinks to bibliographic references, and presenting papers in sections each of which is accessible from a menu page, as in *Sociological Research On-line*.[6] Some on-line journals include sound, and also still and moving images presented either within articles (e.g. *Sociological Research On-line*), as downloadable ethnographic videos and photographic exhibitions (e.g. *Av-Materiali*[7]), or as CD-ROM inserts to print journals (e.g. *Visual Sociology* [now *Visual Studies*]). Visual anthropologists suggest that new forms of publishing on CD or DVD represent (at least part of) the future of visual anthropology (Ruby 2001, MacDougall 2001, Henley, this volume) and sociologists (Dicks and Mason 2001) have begun to experiment with a series of ethnographic hypermedia projects. Nevertheless the use of hypermedia for visual anthropological and ethnographic representation is still hardly established outside the work of a small number of visual anthropologists and documentary artists.

With its potential to be multimedia, multilinear, multivocal, interactive and reflexive, hypermedia clearly does satisfy many of the demands currently put on not only visual ethnography but on ethnography in general (see above). In Chapters 4, 10, 11 and 12 the contributors to this volume describe some recent experiences of using digital imaging and hypermedia, both as part of the ethnographic process and for anthropological representation. Kürti (Chapter 4) writes about a collaborative digital photography archive project that has facilitated his research into the meanings of 'local' postcards that both represent and circulate within a village. Pink (Ch. 11) discusses hypermedia as a way of reflexively representing ethnographic materials and anthropological ideas. In Chapter 10 da Silva and Pink describe how the video, photographs and other research materials that da Silva (a photographer) collected during the visual ethnographic research that was to inform her photographic work were presented on CD-ROM in two of the intermediate stages of her work about fishing communities in England and Portugal. Similarly in Chapter 12 Coover (a documentary film-maker) describes how a digital CD project became part of his research process when undertaking photographic ethnographic research to inform his documentary film project about winemaking in France. Together these chapters begin to engage with the questions raised by Ruby, MacDougall and Henley by applying digital images and hypermedia in anthropological analysis and representation. They show how combining images and words in hypermedia can emphasise the interdependency of image and word for the production of anthropological knowledge and bring visual representation closer to the written mainstream in anthropology.

Art and drawing in ethnographic research and representation

There has been a long history of the use of different art forms (including painting and drawing) as means of both encountering and expressing oneself (e.g. in art therapy – see Hogan 2001) and for visual documentary and note taking in travel diaries. Certainly people are able through drawing to represent aspects of their experiences that cannot be recounted verbally, whether that has involved a journey into one's own self (see Edgar, Ch. 6), to another country and culture (see Ramos, Ch. 9), or to a supernatural level of one's own world (see Orobitg, Ch. 3). Although the anthropology of art is well established and drawings have long since figured substantially in anthropological research and monographs in the form of kinship diagrams and sketches of tools, and other artefacts, anthropologists have paid little attention to the other side of both these coins – the anthropological analysis of informants' sketches and exhibiting or publishing art in monographs (e.g. Ramos 2000) to represent anthropologists' experiences. *Working Images* takes these on board. Orobitg (Ch. 3) describes how through her informants' drawings of their other world, inhabited by spirits and gods, she learned how they 'saw' this world and how they structured their understanding of it. Edgar (Ch. 6) describes his technique of image work, whereby his informants' drawings or other artistic representations become a way of communicating about their own experiences. In both these examples the collaborative aspect of visual research is drawn out, as we see it is not simply a matter of anthropologists analysing their informants' drawings but one of learning through their images about how they feel, see and experience the world. In Chapters 5 and 9 respectively Afonso and Ramos discuss drawings produced by an artist/anthropologist in collaboration or consultation with informants. Afonso focuses on how such collaborations can represent experience and produce anthropological knowledge that is inaccessible verbally and photographically. Finally Ramos, an anthropologist and artist discusses his involvement with the people whose lives he researches vis-à-vis his fieldwork sketchbooks and exhibited work. Such work entails much more than the visual recording of earlier anthropological sketches of tools and the like. Rather, Ramos argues, it engages the researcher and informants in intercultural dialogue.

As a group these works signify a new route for visual anthropologists working reflexively as producers themselves and with other producers of artistic representations. Moreover they invite us to imagine a future strand of visual anthropology that incorporates not only drawing, but other forms of visual practice, including for example, sculpture and installations.

The chapters: representing the visual ethnographic process

Working Images is divided into two parts. Part I examines visual research methods in ethnography while Part II concentrates on visual ethnographic representations. Ethnographic projects are by nature diverse and it would be impossible to model 'the' ethnographic process as one might a scientific experiment. Instead, to guide the reader through the volume, I outline below how each chapter contributes to our understanding of the ways in which images might be embedded in the ethnographic process.

Part I focuses on visual methods in the field, covering the uses of video, photography and drawing in ethnographic research. In Chapter 2 Grasseni discusses video as a research method through the case study of her research about cattle and cattle farmers in Italy. In this innovative study she shows how by using video one may learn to see through what she calls 'skilled vision' – demonstrating how video might become a route to ethnographic knowledge that provides a deeper understanding of our informants' ways of seeing, knowing and understandings. Grasseni also develops the book's themes of reflexivity and working with informants. Chapters 3 and 4 focus on photography, although in different ways. In Chapter 3 Orobitg reflects on photography and drawing in ethnographic research, through her own experiences of research amongst the Pumé in Venezuela, making explicit the relationship between images and words and the visual and other aspects of her fieldwork. Whilst Orobitg and Grasseni focus on the production of images as a way of doing ethnography, in Chapter 4 Kürti discusses the meanings of found images, in this case a collection of Hungarian postcards that form part of a digital archive that he has developed collaboratively with local people. Like Orobitg, Kürti also emphasises the relationship between visual and verbal meanings, going 'beyond the frame' to examine the 'parallel worlds' evoked by these images. Chapters 5 and 6 shift the focus towards the two aspects of the use of drawing in ethnographic research (a theme also introduced by Orobitg in Chapter 3). First, in Chapter 5 Afonso discusses how by drawing informants' ideas and description anthropologists might collaborate with them to produce visual representations of their memories, activities or experiences, thus providing visual knowledge that could not be expressed verbally. Then, in Chapter 6, Edgar explains the method of imagework using case studies from his research. Imagework is a form of ethnography in which informants reflexively explore their own imaginations, and that is subsequently objectified visually in (for example) artwork, drama and mask making.

Part II focuses on four key areas of visual anthropological representation: photography, video, drawing and hypermedia. Chapters 7 and 8 concentrate on ethnographic film, each examining the relationship between visual ethnographic research and representation and offering different solutions to the crisis of representation in anthropology that has problematised observational ethnographic cinema. In Chapter 7 Henley proposes that what he calls 'post-observational cinema' might develop ethnographic films that are relevant to a wider anthropological audience (like Grasseni in Chapter 2 seeking to resolve problems of observational cinema). In Chapter 8 Camas *et al.* describe how in their work they have developed a collaborative model of ethnographic film-making that also departs from traditional ethnographic film styles to make films that have a collaborative, applied element and that use reflexive working practices. Chapter 9 links with some ideas developed in Chapters 5 and 6 to discuss the use of drawing in ethnographic research and representation. Drawing from his own experience and work as an anthropologist/artist Ramos presents a visual and written essay that explores the relationship between words and image in anthropology through a discussion of drawing in the production of anthropological knowledge and as part of intercultural communication. Chapter 10 is also a visual and written essay – in this case photographic. Here da Silva describes the role of visual ethnographic methods (photography and video) in the process through which her exhibition *In the Net* (a series of portraits of Portuguese and British fisherpeople) was produced, including the focus on the intersubjectivity between photographer and photographed that formed a basis of her practice. In this work words and images were combined in both the visual research process and through da Silva's use of tape-recorded interviews in the subsequent exhibition. Finally Chapters 11 and 12 explore the possibilities of hypermedia as ethnographic representation. Each chapter offers a different perspective. In Chapter 11 Pink writes as a visual anthropologist who works with hypermedia to produce multimedia representations of anthropological work. Describing a case study from her own video ethnography of gender and home, she explores questions of the relationship between image, word and sound in the production of reflexive ethnographic hypermedia representations. Like Grasseni, she links this to the use of video as a research method, and like Henley and Camas *et al.*, to the question of the future of ethnographic film. In Chapter 12 Coover writes as a multimedia artist who works with anthropological themes and ethnographic materials to produce digital representations of culture. Finally in Chapter 13 Hughes-Freeland sums up the key issues and themes raised in this book, to suggest their implications for contemporary and future visual research and representation.

A final thought

Returning briefly to Portugal where the 'Working Images' conference took place, in *The Stone Raft*, Jose Saramago, the Portuguese novelist, reflects on the writer's dilemma:

Writing is extremely difficult, it is an enormous responsibility, you need only think of the exhausting work involved in setting out events in chronological order, first this one, then that, or, if considered more convenient to achieve the right effect, today's event placed before yesterday's episode, and other no less risky acrobatics, the past treated as if it were new, the present as a continuous process without a present or ending, but, however hard writers might try, there is one feat they cannot achieve, that is to put into writing, in the same tense, two events that have occurred simultaneously. Some believe the difficulty can be solved by dividing the page into two columns, side by side, but this strategy is ingenuous, because the one was written first and the other afterwards, without forgetting that the reader will have to read this one first and then the other one, or vice versa.

(Saramago 1994 [1986]: 5)

Anthropologists should not stop writing. But perhaps some problems we face when we write linear texts with words as our only tool can be resolved by think-ing of anthropology and its representations as not solely verbal but also visual and not simply linear but multilinear.

This book has an accompanying website at http://www.easaonline.org/workingimagesbook.htm

Notes

1 For example in one of the panels of the *Working Images* conference we discussed the little known contribution of the Hungarian anthropological film-maker, Fejos, to visual anthropology.
2 http://www.visualanthropology.net/
3 http://web.tiscali.it/antropologiavisiva/
4 http://www.lboro.ac.uk/departments/ss/newwisite/newworkingimages.htm
5 http://era.anthropology.ac.uk/
6 http://www.socresonline.org.uk/
7 http://www.visualanthropology.net/av-materiali/colophon.htm

References

Banks, M. (2001) *Visual Methods in Social Research*, London: Sage.
Banks, M. and Morphy, H. (eds) (1997) *Rethinking Visual Anthropology*, New Haven and London: Yale University Press.
Bateson, G. and Mead, M. (1942) *Balinese Character: A Photographic Analysis*, New York: New York Academy of the Sciences.
Biella, P. (1997) 'Mama Kone's Possession: Scene From an Interactive Ethnography', in *Visual Anthropology Review* 12(2): 59–95.
Clifford, J. and Marcus, G. (eds) (1986) *Writing Culture: the Poetics and Politics of Ethnography*, Berkeley: University of California Press.
Collier, J. and Collier, M. (1986) *Visual Anthropology: Photography as a Research Method*, Albuquerque: University of New Mexico Press.

Da Silva, O. (2000) *In the Net*, Porto, Portugal: Rainho & Neves Lda. Exhibition catalogue.

Edgar, I. (forthcoming) *Guide to Imagework: An Introduction to Imagination-based Research Methods*, London: Routledge.

Edwards, E. (2001) *Raw Histories: Photographs, Anthropology and Museums*, Oxford: Berg.

Emmison, M. and Smith, P. (2000) *Researching the Visual*. London: Sage.

Ferrándiz, F. (1998) 'A trace of fingerprints: displacements and textures in the use of ethnographic video in Venezuelan spiritism', in *Visual Anthropology Review*, 13(2): 19–38.

Foster, H. (1995) 'The artist as ethnographer', in G. E. Marcus and F. R. Myers (eds), *The Traffic in Culture: Refiguring Art and Anthropology*, University of California Press.

Garcia Alonso, M., Martinez, A., Pitarch, P., Ranera, P. and Fores, J. (eds) (1996) *Anthropologia de los sentidos: la vista*, Madrid: Celeste Ediciones.

Grau Rebollo, J. (2002) *Antropología Audiovisual*, Barcelona: Ediciones Bellaterra.

Grimshaw, A. (2001) *The Ethnographer's Eye: Ways of Seeing in Anthropology*, Cambridge: Cambridge University Press.

Hogan, S. (2001) *Healing Arts: The History of Art Therapy*, London: Jessica Kingsley.

Holliday, R. (2000) 'We've been framed: visualising methodology', *The Sociological Review* 48(4): 503–22.

James, A., Hockey J., and Dawson, A. (1997) *After Writing Culture*, London, Routledge.

Lister, M. and Wells, L. (2000) 'Seeing beyond belief: Cultural studies as an approach to analysing the visual', in T. van Leeuwen and C. Jewitt (eds), *Handbook of Visual Analysis*, London: Sage.

MacDougall, D. (1997) 'The visual in anthropology', in M. Banks and H. Morphy (eds), *Rethinking Visual Anthropology* and New Haven, London: Yale University Press.

—— (1998) *Transcultural Cinema*, Princeton: Princeton University Press.

—— (2001) 'Renewing ethnographic film: Is digital video changing the genre?' *Anthropology Today* 17(3).

Mason, B. and Dicks, B. (2001) 'Going beyond the code: The production of hypermedia ethnography', *Social Science Computer Review* 9(4): 445–57.

Pauwells, L. (2000) 'Taking the Visual Turn in Research and Scholarly Communication', *Visual Sociology* 15: 7–14.

Pink, S. (2001a) *Doing Visual Ethnography: Images, Media and Representation in Research*, London: Sage.

—— (2001b) 'More visualising, more methodologies: on video, reflexivity and qualitative research', *The Sociological Review* 49(4): 586–99.

—— (2004) *Home Truths: Changing Gender in the Sensory Home*, Oxford: Berg.

Pink, S., Kürti, L., and Afonso, A. I. (eds) (2002) *Visual teaching, Virtual learning: Anthropology and Pedagogy in Europe*, a Special Issue of *Anthropology in Action*.

Ramos, J. (2000) *Histórias Etíopes: diário de viagem*, Lisbon: Assírio & Alvim.

Rose, G. (2001) *Visual Methodologies*, London: Sage.

Ruby, J. (1980) 'Exposing Yourself: Reflexivity, Anthropology and Film'. *Semiotica*, 3[1–2]: 153–79.

—— (1982) 'Ethnography as Trompe L'Oeil: Anthropology and Film', in J. Ruby (ed.) *A Crack In The Mirror*, University of Pennsylvania Press, Philadelphia.

—— (2000) *Picturing Culture: Explorations of Film and Anthropology*, Chicago: University of Chicago Press.

—— (2001) 'From ethnographic film to hypertext ethnography', unpublished commentary.

Saramago, J. (1994 [1986]) *The Stone Raft*, London: The Harvill Press.
van Leeuwen, T. and Jewitt, C. (2000) *Handbook of Visual Analysis*, London: Sage.
Visual Anthropology Review (2001–2) *The Origins of Visual Anthropology*, 17(2) Special Issue.
Worth, S. (1997) 'Margaret Mead and the shift from visual anthropology to the anthropology of visual communication', in Ruth Bunzell (ed.), AAAS, *Margaret Mead Festschrift*.

Part I

Visual fieldwork methods

Chapter 2

Video and ethnographic knowledge

Skilled vision in the practice of breeding

Cristina Grasseni

This chapter focuses on skilled vision, as both method and object of anthropological research, namely as an anthropological notion and an ethnographic object lying at the intersection between 'the use of visual material in anthropological research' and 'the study of visual systems and visible culture' (Morphy and Banks 1997: 1).[1] It recounts how the use of a video camera aided my attempt to gain an insight into the skilled vision of a community of cattle breeders, and reflects on how filming may help the researcher to think about how ways of seeing are framed by practices.

The case study I present here was part of a larger project combining the making of a film and ethnographic writing. Earlier on in this project I experimented with observational cinema and made an ethnographic video. In the course of this case study though, I did not commit myself to observational video-making, but rather kept a broader approach on skilled practice and the anthropology of vision, focusing on the relationship between the analysis of my informants' skilled vision, and my own exercise of looking through the lenses of a video camera.

There are a number of ways in which to rethink visual techniques for research, beyond the strictures and the limits of observational film-making as a heuristic technique.[2] On the one hand, observational documentary aims at re-creating everyday life experience through a shooting and editing style that gives the impression of rendering reality without analytical fragmentation. Often this is achieved by focusing on tacit knowledge and embodied skill in such a way as to recreate a situation in which 'the camera operator as witness, experiments and perceives the boundary between saying and doing . . . getting in touch with experience itself beyond the sayable' (Busoni 1996: 23). In an observational documentary, the aim is thus to call the audience itself to witness the rhythms of everyday activity, the significance of repetitive but skilled action and of what has been described as 'embodied technical knowledge' (Angioni 1984: 61).[3]

On the other hand, it has been claimed that 'cinematographic observation' is also appreciable in its own right – and not only for the objective of making a film – as 'filmic anthropology', being capable of 'rendering the flux of human activity, the gestural continuum, the dead gaps and the weak events of a whole process with its noises and restful silences' (de France 1981: 51). In other words, video recording can serve 'as a propedeutic element to any in-depth observation', as a tool for refining the ethnographer's attention, for monitoring and aiding the training of the eye. Also, recorded material can be revisited and accompanied by an analytical description and a systematic explanation of specific aspects of skilled vision.

Thus filmic anthropology would not just be about stressing the image-storing capacity of recording technologies, but rather about using them as facilitators of the ethnographer's access into a structured perceptual environment. The training of perception is intrinsic to the social structuring of practice, and is achieved by attuning oneself to the rhythms and sensitivities of a complex environment. The thesis of this piece is that an apprenticeship of the eye can further our ethnographic understanding of how practice and skills construct identities. Hence, participant observation here means sharing a process of sensory apprenticeship in order to appreciate and, to some extent, even appropriate the 'way of seeing' (Berger 1972) of the ethnographic subject.

The results of a specific training of the eye and the development of a skilled vision may be wider-ranging and further-reaching, in terms of the construction of identities, than recent anthropological critiques of visualism may indicate. An ecological reading of skilled vision, practice and identity as closely integrated allows one to appreciate certain 'ways of seeing' as important avenues for understanding values, interests and symbolic discourse. In other words, skilled vision may represent a paramount feature characterising a 'community of practice', whose shared skills engender sensibilities that are largely social, tacit and grounded in material contexts (see Grasseni 2004).[4] Skilled vision is invariably the result of training, that is, of an 'education of attention' (Gibson 1979; Ingold 2000). In suitable settings, then, camera-aided participant observation can enhance our ethnographic awareness of the largely unspoken processes of apprenticeship or of the education of attention.

The ethnographic core of this case study concerns the practice of breeding dairy cows in a mountainous region of northern Italy: Valtaleggio in Lombardy. Between 1997 and 1999 I spent some time with a family of dairy farmers who breed Alpine Brown cows, selling milk and cheese for a living. Technological change in the breeding practice and a drive towards artificial selection of the breed characterises the larger economic and social context of their profession. The tenet of my participant observation was that meaning and identity emerge through engagement in an environment which is characterised by the materiality of visual artefacts (Banks 2001: 73–8) that are socially, symbolically and aesthetically relevant to their practice – ranging from posters of prize-winning cows, to colourful magazines of the Breeders' Association, to on-line catalogues of cattle sales, to glossy repertoires of the genetic indexes of cattle fair champions, to the domestic photographs of a breeder with his grandchildren and favourite cows. Meaning is inherent in such shared practices, internal to a community of practitioners and 'objective' only in that it is an aspect of participating in a practice – with its aesthetics and moral order. Consequently, my observational technique included collecting some of the visual materials that accompany and frame a breeder's social understanding of animal beauty, such as photographs published in specialist magazines and websites.

Camerawork was undoubtedly an integral part of my field research and of the way I reflected upon the issues raised by fieldwork: did my recording mean somehow grasping a piece of reality? Why did my informants so often recur to visual materials and themselves use still and video cameras, for instance at cattle fairs? Beyond a simplistic counteraction of words vs. vision, I shall try to develop an argument about methodology starting from these questions. The video camera hence features here both as a catalyst of the ethnographer's attention and as a tool for self-distancing from familiar or generic ways of framing ethnographic objects.

I am proposing a parallel between the process of apprenticeship that a visual ethnographer has to undergo, and the process of education of attention that is required of anyone participating in a community of practice (Lowe and Wenger 1991), of professional breeders or of other skilled practitioners. With the help of a breed expert, I tried to discipline my vision, trying to develop an 'eye' through an apprenticeship into looking at cattle. The exercise of 'shadowing' (Sclavi 1989: 13) a cattle breed inspector involved the need to be aware of what to point the camera at, and made me aware of the skill of vision through the very act of representation. In other words my efforts to reproduce his skilled vision through my camera radically changed the way I saw cattle.

Also, taking field notes in the form of a video diary served the purpose of making my role of observer more transparent, and to structure the field for me: I gave away footage and edits in return for time, food, access etc. and I elicited feedback through footage or edits. This gave my hosts the chance to monitor, evaluate and disagree with my work. I should stress that material shot for one purpose – i.e. gathering data or just shadowing a breed expert – could not easily be 'recycled' for another – i.e. editing a film. Camerawork is not an unproblematic record of reality, and shooting for a film directs one's attention to objects, facts and events in a particular way and order. On the contrary, using a camera can help us especially to think about how others see the world, and about how the world is framed for us through the skilled practices that we have been trained into. As Claudine de France succinctly put it, 'the true objective of filmic anthropology should be the comparison of our vision with someone else's' (1981: 58).

Training vision

My interest in an ethnographic investigation of practice came from a conviction that identity is bound up with world-views, i.e. with the ways people see their world from within their 'forms of life' (Wittgenstein 1953, Grasseni 2003a). In my experience of field research, doing visual ethnography increasingly took

on the meaning of trying to access the skilled vision of the ethnographic subjects, in their going about the practices of their lived experience. The questions
directing me were: how do breeders look at cows? When they say that an
apprentice is blind, what do they mean? How much has vision got to share with
other modes of perception and with a whole sensory, discursive and cognitive
experience, in the context of developing a breeder's skill? In addition, I noticed
that a sense of belonging and propriety was conveyed by the social appreciation
of skilled vision, or capacity to 'see'. Charles Goodwin has used the phrase
'professional vision', for 'socially organised ways of seeing and understanding
events that are answerable to the distinctive interests of a particular social group'
(1994: 606). Visual methods of research and in particular an ethnography of
skilled vision help detecting the construction and reproduction of the skills and
imagery that structure the life-world of a community of practice.

I shall illustrate this with an ethnographic example. My first impact with fieldwork on a farm hinged around the problem of distinguishing my host's cows
from one another, and assessing whether they were considered to be 'good cows'
(or rather 'beautiful cows', in my host Guglielmo's opinion). It became important
for me to pick up Guglielmo's discourse about their herd, since he found reason
for pride and a sense of purpose in his and his family's success as breeders and
in the beauty of their herd. My hosts take great pride in their new stable, in the
size of their herd, in the fact that they are modernised and logistically organised,
well enough to carry out haymaking and *alpeggio* (high-pasture grazing) at the
same time. They pride themselves on the comparatively comfortable life they
enjoy on the high pastures – conversely, they look down on ex-farmers who
have sold their herds and have become employed in the city, relinquishing any
productive link to cattle and land. They claim that they have never forgotten
how to tend cows on the mountains and have stuck to tradition while everyone
else was abandoning the pastures, letting them be invaded by woods.

In the research and film proposal preceding fieldwork I had written that
'I would focus on people and not on their cows', as a reaction to the aestheticisation of alpine pastures into reservoirs of 'traditional lifestyles'.[5] I wished to avoid
showing grazing cows in Heidi-type settings, without insight into the actual life
of mountain dwellers. But I was wrong to assume that focusing on my hosts as
'people', on their opinions, their discourse and identity would mean leaving
aside their daily practice, which involves cows. This is how I came to focus on
the practice of breeding, in particular on the experience of developing an eye for
looking at cattle, trying to answer questions about what makes good 'form', and
how it is generated and reproduced in the breeding practice.

During fieldwork on the high pastures, my hosts' skill in looking at cattle
and my difficulty in picking it up alerted me to the relationship between skill,
identity, and place. When I asked Guglielmo or his grandchildren to explain
what distinguished one cow over another, I received confusing answers. The kids
said it was from the face, or from the udders. My host replied something like:
'can't you see this is an entirely different cow from that other?' In fact, it was

not difficult to see how cows are all different from each other. But picking up how they each differed required more 'skill'. What was required was different from discerning gradual variations of certain traits. In a sense, this was a case similar to Wittgenstein's 'family resemblance' (1953): each cow may share only some similarities with some others, which make them stand out as a group in certain contexts. Seeing the cows next to each other would create complex patterns of cross-referencing. The fact that cows on the pastures move around and are seen in different associations with each other enhanced the complexity of this network, defying the notion of a static list or system of classification.

Guglielmo was contemptuous of his current trainee from the local agricultural school, saying that he was 'blind'. He was unable to pick up the trade by watching the others' expertise. He could not learn how to make out every single cow from the herd and call them by their name. He would rather ask what he was supposed to do and how, whereas he was supposed to learn by mimesis rather than via instruction. On the contrary, Guglielmo's 7-year-old grandson Marco had an astonishingly trained eye. Marco and his sister Sara, aged 12, tried to explain to me how they tell one cow from another and tried to direct my attention to specific features of the animals' faces, gazes and attitudes, to details of their skin or differences in their profile. But somehow their lists of relevant features seemed irrelevant and missed out their 'real' observational skills.

The children played 'cow-spotting' as second nature – recognising each cow as they graze about in the pasture and calling them by their name. My miserable failures at their daily game were not due to my incapacity to detect the features that were pointed out to me, but to make the animals out in context, by their very posture and movements under different lights, at dawn or dusk and from different angles. Marco on the other hand knew every single cow, heifer, calf or steer in the herd, and he would recognise them 'from the way they look at you'. Also the breed inspector I subsequently toured with, who also owns a farm with his brother, claimed that he can see what is wrong with one of his animals before it becomes apparent to the vet's (or indeed to his brother's) eyes: 'I can tell from the way she looks at me . . .'.[6]

Such expressions testify to a shared experience of mutual understanding between breeders and cows, which goes beyond simple recognition. My hosts seem to have developed a capacity of mutual acknowledgement with their animals through look, 'that look between animal and man, which may have played a crucial role in the development of human society' – to put it in Berger's words – 'and with which, in any case, all men had always lived until less than a century ago' (Berger 1980: 4).

To be able to look at cattle means more than just using one's eyesight. It is similar to being able to move through a familiar landscape by noting its relevant features from any chosen viewpoint without getting lost. In other words, to be able to 'see' has become my hosts' shorthand for being integrated into the environment of one's practice and for having developed a thorough sensory relationship with one's cattle. Therefore I decided that the way to answer my questions was to try and re-enact, to a degree, the learning process of at least one aspect of their skilled vision: an apprenticeship into looking at cattle. I approached vets and agricultural advisers, shadowing their everyday routines.

The expert's look

The role of the progressive standardisation of selective cattle breeding became crucial for my apprenticeship. First I toured with a vet on his round of TB controls in minor farms of Valtaleggio. I also tagged along with one of my host's sons, who evaluates cattle herds as a breed expert in the nearby province of Brescia (in Lombardy). He then introduced me to the breed inspector in charge of evaluating cattle in Val Brembana. With him, I visited about forty farms in Val Brembana and Valtaleggio. I also accompanied a professional artificial inseminator to cattle fairs and on his visits to lowland farms, where industrial agribusiness is well established. Here I shall focus particularly on the breed inspector and his milk round of cattle checks in Val Brembana. Breed experts are mostly farmers, trained progressively into a hierarchy from experts (*esperto di razza*) to province expert, national expert (*esperti provinciali, nazionali*) and finally breed inspector (*ispettore di razza*). They visit farms that are registered with the Breeders' Association (APA) in order to evaluate genetically selected cattle, gathering data for the APA's genetic database.

When I started touring farms with a breed inspector, I found it very difficult to film the activity of evaluation that he called *punteggiare* (score giving). I tried to film the process of pragmatically assessing a cow's genetic worth, at the same time recording my own efforts to acquire some kind of skilled vision. I expected that my way of looking at cattle would change in the effort, but I did not know what to point the camera at, because I could not *see* what was going on. The fact that I could not get meaningful shots alerted me to the fact that I was not mastering the correct way of looking at cattle – or that my eye was not trained to discern anything meaningful in what I was shooting. The only way of learning was to come to share the breeder's vision and test my opinion against his.

The inspector's eyes were moving fast from one point of the cow's body to another, as he punched numbers into his calculator, quickly but not mechanically. He seemed to stop and get an overall view of the animal and compared her with others in the shed. He asked for the name of the bull who had fathered her, had a look at the calves born of the cow, sometimes comparing her with her mother or siblings in the same stable. All the time, he was moving around or leaning forward, to judge the udders from a better angle, occasionally feeling the udder ligament, or just anticipating a cow about to lay dung on his shoes . . .

It wasn't until the expert started to direct my attention to the traits he was evaluating that I began to make sense of it all, and I could film something more consistent than wandering shots. Directing my attention was different from just telling me what he was doing. As he said: 'If I were to describe the whole cow to you, you would not understand, so I'll describe her to you bit by bit.' As a result of his instructions, I started to look at the udders from underneath, lowering the camera to knee-height. I concentrated on the volume of the udder, trying to shoot from under the cow's tail to line up her teats. I also began to frame the cows mainly from behind, keeping the camera high above their back to show the line of the spine and the width of the shoulders. In this case, the camera functioned as the catalyst of my attention, tuning my eyes to the visual angles and the ways of framing the cow through the inspector's gaze.

Learning by mimesis did not necessarily mean learning without rules. The inspector was not acting neutrally, but positively directing my attention and disciplining my vision of the animal. The aim was for me to learn to see like he did, so that we could agree in our judgement of a cow. As Goodwin argues, 'the ability to see a meaningful event is not a transparent process', but rather 'all vision is perspectival and lodged within endogenous communities' (Goodwin 1994: 606).

A vast amount of theory and of practical assumptions about what is preferable in a cow is mediated by the skill of looking at them. Breed experts, and consequently dairy cattle breeders, 'frame' the animal's body and assign scores to individual 'linear' traits, which are believed to indicate the most important parameters towards the objective of selecting cattle of big dimension, solid constitution, early productive development, fertility and capability of high and constant yield. The traits considered in the morphological evaluation of selected cattle are distributed among structure (stature, strength, body depth, dairy form, top line, rump angle and thurl width), legs (rear leg set, hock quality, pastern and foot height) and mammary system (fore udder attachment, rear udder attachment, udder cleft, udder depth, teat placement and teat length).

By focusing on selected traits, breeding skill is in fact being translated in a specialised language and an acutely narrowed gaze that surveys and dissects the animal's body and lifetime in standard units.[7] The skilled vision of a breed expert is focused on these specific traits and is trained to assign each of them a numerical score, which will add up to the 'genetic' worth of the animal as a milk-producer and a reproducer. Nevertheless, if skill amounts to the capacity to see, learn and act appropriately, the social recognition of the breeders and the aesthetic appreciation of their cows go hand in hand. In other words, specialised knowledge creates world-views, and in the case of the practice of breed experts, these sediment in ideas of animal beauty, and much more.

Breeding aesthetics

A breeder's appreciation of good form so far seems to be reduced to looking at cows' udders and rears. But in fact it underlies a fundamentally *aesthetic* experience, by which I mean the way an activity of perception is organised and informed to tacit but shared standards for recognising beauty. Coming to share these standards may give some insight into some important aspects of identity-construction. The aesthetic appreciation of a cow's shape is not an abstracted ideal and has changed in the history of breeding: a seventeenth-century cow would not look like a twentieth-century dairy cow. And, compared with photos of cattle-fair champions in contemporary breeders' magazines, even a prizewinner of thirty years ago would certainly not pass the test of the 'ideal form'. In particular, through recent selection, cows' bodies have shifted from a respiratory to a digestive type. Whilst a respiratory type would be leaner with a wide torso and strong muscular capacity, a digestive type has a wider abdomen for enhanced digestive and milk-producing capacity.[8]

Breeders who accept the challenge of economic competition fully take on board the modern breed selection programme, objectives and methods. Such compromise with standardisation and the commodification of their skill may also entail, and be conveyed through, performative assumptions about what makes good form and about virtuous knowledge and skilled vision. Like-minded breeders are, more often than not, from the same locality but not living in each other's immediate neighbourhood (which instead tends to engender occasions for competition and friction, for instance at village cattle fairs). So, sharing the aesthetic and specialist enjoyment of a 'good view' of prize cattle is both a sign of mutual professional recognition and a sign of trust that engenders friendship and invites future occasions of reciprocal visits or joint attendance of national or regional events. Such mutual recognition is not abstracted but often accompanied by concrete demonstrations of trust, such as advising a friend about the choice of bull semen for inseminating his heifers, on the basis of one's experience with similar heifers in one's herd.

The capacity to develop an eye for cattle amongst breeders is appropriated and asserted through the scrutiny, exchange and evaluation of images of animal beauty. The continuous encounter with images displaying ideal standards (in specialised breeders' magazines, neighbours' herds, videos of cattle fairs, and photographs of prize animals) amounts to a process of visual training, aimed at detecting and pursuing those desirable traits in the scrutiny of one's own animals. The appreciation of good form – displayed for instance in colourful ads for bull semen – is an important skill integrated into a visual 'system' (Morphy and Banks 1997: 2), i.e. a distinct way of seeing, which marks the inclusion and participation in a community of practice.

Such disciplining of vision augments and complements an education of attention that starts from childhood: early training in cow-spotting, expertise on the family resemblance within one's herd, and the development of a gaze of reciprocal recognition in the shed, certainly complete and refine the adult breeder's skilled vision. Skilled vision is then configured as the capacity to 'resonate' (see Ingold 2000) within a continuously evolving but structured environment which is rife with stimulating and educating interactions.

Thus 'breeding aesthetics' is organised around the skilled vision developed in practice, but finds its externalised referents in the visual environment both in stylised diagrams and in photographic materials. For instance, taking and exchanging footage of cattle fairs is both a good professional exercise (for keeping up-to-date with the most recent peaks in the trend of dairy cattle breeding) and a genuine aesthetic enjoyment. 'Official' recordings of cattle fairs are often distributed as freebies by agricultural sponsors, or even sold by the fair organizers, whilst amateur recordings are exchanged as gifts between breeders or kept as souvenirs of one's cow's prestigious outcome at a highly ranked fair. The recording of cattle fairs on video is both commissioned to local professional photographers with video-making facilities, and carried out by some breeders in the audience, who then enjoy playing them back at home, often in the company of other breeders. Part of the materials and favours exchanged between good friends who acknowledge each other as good breeders, then, are VHS tapes or photographs of one's herd prize cattle, portrayed for the breeders' magazine or photographed with the owner when receiving the prize.

Hence, my investigation of breeders' skilled vision, after gathering and analysing footage shot by myself, continued by collecting videos made by farmers at cattle fairs. I analysed material shot by professional photographers and breeders with amateur video cameras, looking for clues to the way in which they look at cattle, as well as to what they consider cattle should look like in order to be worth filming. For this purpose and to this extent, the camera can be seen as a means that objectifies the breeder's skilled gaze. The filmed material makes apparent which parts of the animal are being mostly focused on and from which angle, in order to evaluate how each particular animal develops genetically relevant traits. For example, cattle-fair footage is typically devoted first to looking at the cow as a whole from different angles (but mainly from above and behind), then it decisively zooms in to get a close-up of the udders from below, indulging in swollen lactiferous veins and powerful ligaments.

A further ethnographic example will highlight how skilled vision is not a technique without social context. My tour of the stables of Val Brembana with the breed inspector culminated in the visit to my hosts' stable. By this time I already knew that they were renowned both in and outside the valley for having built their new, bigger stable – a novelty in the context of their valley: I had heard positive comments about it among trade union representatives; the breed inspector had been commenting about their entrepreneurial spirit, their ambition and their positive influence on the agricultural performance of the rest of the valley. What I did not expect is that I would share in the social appreciation of my hosts as skilled breeders when I entered their stable again, with new (if only slightly), trained eyes. I had seen and filmed that stable throughout its stages of construction; I had spent two summer seasons with the calves and steers that were now being evaluated after their first birth giving; but I simply had not been aware before of how *beautiful* the animals were.

Sharing a fundamentally aesthetic experience gave me a new insight into the social standing of my host family. Hence, my 'apprenticeship of the eye' with a breed expert furthered my understanding of local identity and its relationship to skills, since in their stable, in comparison with the tens of stables I had visited before, I could see the determination of this family to stay in place. To any other fellow breeder, that stable would tell more than just *breeding* skill. It testified to a well-connected network of information and distribution that could be relied upon to get high-ranking bull semen at the right time. It showed the choice and adaptation of standard industrial architecture to the modes of mountain farming and to its functional needs, placing artificially selected, bigger cows in a suitably spacious environment where they are free to move about, instead of keeping them in the constrictive conditions of traditional stationary and stuffy sheds. It hinted at the political connections and the good relations with bureaucrats that allowed them to get planning permission in time to apply for farming aid. . . . Incorporated in their herd was a display of the large network of people and competencies supporting their enterprise, weaving the 'traditional' skills of cattle rearing, milking and cheese-making together with the 'new' skills of trading in genetically evaluated cattle, milking in high-tech parlours and securing state aid.

Most of all, my eyes now told me the reason for their pride. Because I was literally, if only to a degree, 'sharing the view' of the breed inspector, I could testify to them being an example of excellence in the context of mountain farming in their area. How localised this appreciation can be, has been shown by their failure to win significant prizes at national and regional cattle fairs. Nevertheless, even if selective breeding favours regimented and standardised global contexts, the judging of breeding competitions is still bound to take into account local specificities. The personal reputation and social standing gained through local acknowledgement of their breeding skill was testified when my hosts decided not to bring their cattle to the local fair. The judge, informed of the comparatively high standard of their herd, visited their stable in private after evaluating the cattle at the fair. The visit turned into a spontaneous social occasion when about a dozen people, mostly farmers from outside the valley, tagged along to visit my hosts' new stable. Therefore my hosts gained even more prestige locally and could exchange views and advice with a professional breed expert, displaying their whole herd on their own ground.

Breeding aesthetics can assume the scope of a world-view and become embodied into a specific way of looking at the world. The breeder's gaze incorporates local meaning even though it is acquired and performed in accordance with global standards. An understanding of such gaze cannot be limited to what goes on inside the shed. A skilled jargon and a skilled gaze, which is also a social gaze, extends from the shed onto one's identity and one's social life. As Busoni stresses in her study of the oral testimony of retired naval carpenters in Livorno, 'by operating *a occhio* (by sight, namely without the aid of measuring tools), the carpenter's eyesight sums up the competence derived by experience, which involves the capacity for an aesthetic and normative judgement' (Busoni 1996: 54).

Figure 2.1 A cow is being displayed to the judge. I attempted to highlight the traits mostly looked at: angularity ('dry bones' are indicative of good 'dairy form'), legs, foot height, and most of all udder size and set. (I took these photographs (Figs 2.1–2.3) on the occasion of the cattle fair of Valtaleggio, at Sottochiesa, in October 1999.)

Figure 2.2 Judge and an APA technician inspect the paraded candidates. The point of view preferred by the judge is from behind, while the cows are lined up next to each other, in order to assess comparatively legs, udders, thurl width and dairy form.

Figure 2.3 My host with two fellow breeders evaluating my host's cattle on his ground, on the occasion of the visit of the cattle fair judge. Notice the attitude and posture shared by the three, looking toward a cow off frame.

Conclusion

The debate on the capacity of ethnographic film, whether observational or not, to yield an adequate, or even superior, ethnographic construction, is complex and still open (see for instance Ruby 2000, Morphy and Banks 1997, MacDougall 1997). Within the terms of such debate, visual ethnographers have to confront several issues: whether to consider themselves first and foremost as documentarists or anthropologists; whether visual ethnography is only good as a teaching tool and whether they should abide by the rules of cinematic narrative or experiment with an exclusively 'anthropological' form of representation. Here, I have not discussed the possibility of producing a visual monograph, i.e. an ethnographic *film*. I leave to others (also in this book) the task of negotiating a score for or against observational film. In order to do so, I should have discussed the non-obvious links between ethnographic film, the observation of mundanity, and voyeurism as it is summed up in some critiques of observational film (Ruby 2000: 250).

Some maintain that a necessary theoretical framework for the visualisation of culture in its embodiment in sociocultural behaviour is a communicative or performative – in a word, semiotic – model of culture, and draw from this the conviction that 'a passive camera used to create pure observational-style films does not reveal culture' (Ruby 2000: 241). Without being thoroughly convinced that observational style means passivity, I propose here a way to actively use the camera as both a testimony and a reminder and also as a catalyst of attention for those continuous processes of apprenticeship and of attuning that are required, on the one hand, of the apprentice and the newcomer, and on the other hand, of the anthropologist seeking access and understanding.

Jay Ruby wonders why anthropologists engaged in a rediscovery of 'sensory' ethnographies and of 'radical empiricism' have not 'looked to film as an alternative means' (2000: 260). I think the answer lies in the tension between the rediscovery of 'sensuous scholarship' and the critique of visualism that has branded virtually all exercise of intelligent vision on the part of the ethnographer, or the analysis of visual representations, as 'oculo-centric', 'Cartesian', or 'voyeuristic'. I argue for a rehabilitation of vision as a skilled sense and not only as a colonial tool. As pioneered by Bateson and Mead (1942), ethnographic understanding may be the result of an exercise in differential vision, of careful observation and of the recognition of relevant patterns in everyday activity (Grasseni 2004).

Doing visual ethnography can also mean to entertain an exercise in 'filmic anthropology' (de France 1981), which is not targeted towards the production of a visual monograph but tries to address creatively the possibility of an 'anthropology of vision'. I agree with Ruby that culture is embodied, enacted and learnt in practice, and that visualising practice contributes to understanding culture. I have focused here on how this visualising can be done through an engagement in processes of apprenticeship and an education of attention, and how awareness of these processes may be heightened, aided and mediated by a reflexive use of imaging technologies and an analysis of visual production. Granted that culture can be seen in displayed behaviour, this model implies a different model from the semiotic one, according to which 'the self becomes the sum of all the performances and audience memberships' (Ruby 2000: 254). Rather, an ecological model envisages an individual and collective self that is the result of a history of enskillment, which the ethnographer needs to recapitulate to some extent, in order to appreciate notions such as identity, belonging, sense of place.

Far from being a device of neutral observation, a means of recording transparent reality, the camera can be considered as a tool and an aid to heighten awareness, while serving as a testimony of the various processes of refinement, disciplining and attuning of the senses that accompany any process of becoming a member of a community of practice. Hence, however slow-paced or commonplace the activities studied or filmed, the focus is shifted to the sensory, cognitive and social apprenticeship that is required in order to grasp their meaning, beauty and relevance to the social context of the practitioners.

Since this also entails various stages of meaning-sharing, identity construction, and adjustment to a world-view, we can come to appreciate the many facets of this idea of skilled vision. In this sense, camera research can be transformative in a different sense than that envisaged by Rouch and advocated by Ruby (2000: 247), when he opposes it to the passivity of observation. On the contrary, observation of mundane practice can be transformative, i.e. may call forth a necessary transformation of the observer. In this sense, anthropology should indeed strive to 'see the world through the eyes of the native' – not because the images are transparent, nor because of a generic openness or empathy, but as a result of a process of enskillment of vision, aided by a reflexive use of technology. Whether such process and development can effectively be expressed in an ethnographic film, and whether this would amount to film realism or passive observation, I leave for discussion elsewhere. Here I limited myself to expose how the use of recording technologies can aid, not only teaching or reporting, but positively seeing, hence researching.

People do not encounter their surroundings in an unmediated way. I hope to have shown how by acquiring an ethnographic vision that is aided and disciplined by technology, for instance video, one may be alerted to the many forms of skilled vision. The ethnographic core of this essay has been devoted to highlighting how suitable anthropological focus on vision, and visual methods of research, can help to analyse the breeder's world-view. Professional breeders' magazines, professional and amateur videos shot at cattle fairs, and the dissecting exercise of 'giving scores' to cows according to their genetically selected traits, all testify to a skilled vision that incorporates a 'world-view' and applies it to local practices, contexts and relations. Skilled vision is constitutive of a farmer's expertise and reputation, according to her capacity to evaluate, envisage and breed 'good' cows.

I hope to have begun to highlight some of the links between aesthetics and skill in the ethnography of breeding, and how visual ethnography can be a useful means of exploring them. Looking through the lenses of a video camera forced me to focus on the representation and communication of a breeder's world-view in practical terms, and led me to analyse further visual representations produced locally. Trying to develop an eye for cattle, the camera catalysed my attention, objectifying the breeder's gaze, but I only began to 'see' when my attention was directed in a disciplined way. My tour with a breed inspector was thus an apprenticeship into looking at cattle, after which I could see how beautiful my hosts' herd was. My 'apprenticeship of the eye' furthered my understanding of local discourse: in particular, sharing an aesthetic code gave me insight into the social standing of my hosts.

There is increasing evidence, discussed also within the biological and neural sciences, that human visual perception is constructed and complex, namely it is part of a complex relationship of co-implication of organism and environment, a relationship that cannot be reduced to one of mimesis but rather of co-evolution (Varela, Thompson, Rosch 1991). Also in the light of this, the whole meaning of 'observation' should be re-examined, especially in the realm of the anthropology of vision. Such a re-examination should go beyond the mantra of the social construction of facts and should start analysing in depth the ecological dynamics by which communities of practitioners come to share a perception of what they deem as reality. Appreciating the cluster of visual artefacts, imaging technologies and aesthetic standards through which a skilled practitioner weaves practical judgements, aesthetic preferences and moral considerations about a fellow breeder's skill and capacity, means just this.

Notes

1 Many thanks to the participants of the *Working Images* workshop who gave incisive and sympathetic advice on my paper, and especially to the editors and reviewer of this volume for their interest and appreciation of my research. Naturally any faults are entirely and solely my responsibility.
2 For instance, Henley (Ch. 7), Camas *et al.* (Ch. 8) and Ruby (2000) elaborate on the limits of observational film-making.
3 Tacit and embodied knowledge is not the exclusive domain of pre-industrial or traditional settings – Charles Goodwin for instance alerts to the many factors of the 'professional vision' of archaeologists or forensic analysts (1994).
4 According to Lave and Wenger (1991: 98), 'a community of practice is a set of relations among persons, activity, and world, over time and in relation with other tangential and overlapping communities of practice. A community of practice is an intrinsic condition for the existence of knowledge [. . .] The social structure of this practice, its power relations, and its conditions for legitimacy define possibilities for learning.' For seminal works on the ethnographic analysis of practice see Chaiklin and Lave (1993) and, for a specific focus on vision, Goodwin and Ueno (2000).
5 For an analysis of the aestheticisation of the alpine environment in the publicity of alpine local products, see Grasseni (2003b).
6 Javier Taks' recent ethnographic survey of Uruguayan milkers also confirms that 'one important perceptual activity, at least in small parlours, is eye-to-eye contact. To be sure, from the time the cow enters the milking room until it leaves it, milkers "read", in the way a cow looks at them, the way it feels. For instance, local dairy farmers pointed out that a "sad look" [*una mirada triste*] means that something is wrong with a cow, and represents "advice" to look for other symptoms of sickness' (Taks 2000: 296).
7 For a critical analysis of the selective programme of the Brown breed and of the 'Linear system for evaluation of traits', see Grasseni (2003a).
8 For a historical reconstruction of the making of the Swiss Brown breed through the concerted effort of land improvement programmes, herdbooks and cattle fairs see Orland (2003). For a historical analysis of the establishment of a visual rhetoric of cattle breeds, see Quinn (1993).

References

Angioni, G. (1984) 'Tecnica e sapere tecnico nel lavoro preindustriale', *Ricerca folklorica* 9: 61–9.
Banks, M. (2001) *Visual Methods in Social Research*, London: Sage.
Bateson, G. and Mead, M. (1942) *Balinese Character. A photographic analysis*, New York: New York Academy of Sciences.

Berger, J. (1972) *Ways of Seeing*, London: BBC, Penguin.

—— (1980) 'Why look at animals?' in *About Looking*, New York: Pantheon Books, 3–30.

Busoni, M. (1996) *I ritmi della memoria. Conversazioni sul lavoro con i carpentieri navali a Limite sull'Arno*, Florence: Centro Editoriale Toscano.

Chaiklin, S. and Lave, J. (eds) (1993) *Understanding Practice*, Cambridge: Cambridge University Press.

De France, C. (1981) 'I fondamenti di un'antropologia filmica', *La Ricerca Folklorica* 3: 51–8.

Gibson, J. J. (1979) *The Ecological Approach to Visual Perception*, Boston: Houghton Mifflin.

Goodwin, C. (1994) 'Professional Vision', *American Anthropologist* 96(3): 606–33.

Goodwin, C. and Ueno, N. (eds) (2000) *Vision and Inscription in Practice*, special issue of *Mind, Culture and Activity* 7(1/2).

Grasseni, C. (2003a) *Lo sguardo della mano. Pratiche della località e antropologia della visione in una comunità montana lombarda*, Bergamo: Bergamo University Press/ Sestante.

—— (2003b) 'Packaging skills: calibrating Italian cheese to the global market', in S. Strasser (ed.), *Commodifying Everything: Consumption and Capitalist Enterprise*, New York: Routledge, 341–81.

—— (2004) 'Skilled Vision: An apprenticeship in breeding aesthetics', *Social Anthropology* 12(1): 1–15.

Ingold, T. (2000) *The Perception of the Environment. Essays on Livelihood, Dwelling and Skill*, London: Routledge.

Lave, J. and Wenger, E. (1991) *Situated Learning: Legitimate Peripheral Participation*, Cambridge: Cambridge University Press.

MacDougall, D. (1997) 'The visual in anthropology', in H. Morphy and M. Banks (eds), *Rethinking Visual Anthropology*, New Haven: Yale University Press, 276–95.

Morphy, H. and Banks, M. (1997) 'Introduction: rethinking visual anthropology', in H. Morphy and M. Banks (eds) *Rethinking visual anthropology*, New Haven: Yale University Press.

Orland, B. (2003) 'Turbo-Cows. About the production of a competitive animal in 19th and early 20th century', in S. Schrepfer and P. Scranton (eds) *Industrializing Organisms: Introducing Evolutionary History*, New Brunswick, N. J.: Rutgers University Press.

Quinn, M. S. (1993) 'Corpulent cattle and milk machines: nature, art and the ideal type', www.psyeta.org vol. 1 n. 2.

Ruby, J. (2000) *Picturing culture. Explorations of film and anthropology*, Chicago: The University of Chicago Press.

Sclavi, M. (1989) *A una spanna da terra. Indagine comparativa su una giornata di scuola negli Stati Uniti e in Italia e i fondamenti di una 'metodologia umoristica'*, Milano: Feltrinelli.

Taks, J. (2000) *Environment, technology and alienation. An anthropological study among dairy farmers in Southern Uruguay*, Ph.D. thesis, University of Manchester.

Varela, F., Thompson, E., Rosch, E. (1991) *The Embodied Mind. Cognitive Science and Human Experience*, Cambridge, Mass.: MIT Press.

Wittgenstein, L. (1953) *Philosophical investigations*, New York: Macmillan.

Chapter 3

Photography in the field

Word and image in ethnographic research

Gemma Orobitg Canal

> The *oté* [mythical beings] send the *tió* [intermediary spirits between men and *oté*] here to look after the ill people. They are around here and, although we cannot see them, they are looking after us.

These words by Jorge García, an adult Pumé man from the village of Riecito, refer to an essential element of Pumé indigenous culture, the constant and vital communication between the visible and the invisible world. Images, particularly images from dreams, are central to this communication. In this context where the most relevant cultural images exist only in spoken narrative, photography and drawing enabled me to understand the experiential and sensory relationships of Pumé culture.

This chapter reflects on the use of images in ethnographic data production. The pictures analysed here were taken between 1990 and 2000 as part of anthropological fieldwork among the Pumé Indians of Venezuela. The chapter is organised in five subsections. The first sets the indigenous research context and describes the Pumé's relationship to vision and image. The following four describe the dialectical relationship between visual images and spoken narratives during fieldwork through a focus on: the process of collaborative image production involving the anthropologist and her interlocutors (Pink 1996); the production of images by the Pumé themselves to explain their culture; and the production of spoken narratives from photo-elicitation (Banks 2001; Harper 1987, 2002).

Introduction

During the initial design of my fieldwork in the Pumé village of Riecito I did not consider using a camera. Rather it was a fortunate coincidence that led me first to experiment and then reflect methodologically on the value of visual technologies in ethnographic research and for anthropological analysis. By chance Belgian Television (RTBF) and the French German channel ARTE, inspired by documentary producers Catherine De Clippel and Jean-Paul Colleyn, became interested in financing a documentary about Venezuela (De Clippel and Colleyn 1993). I met the producers when they were preparing this documentary project. They asked me to characterise life in Riecito and other Pumé villages from the Riecito and Capanaparo river area to help design the script for filming at least a year later. They also told me that they needed some photographs and lent me an automatic camera with a zoom. Catherine De Clippel gave me some instructions about how to frame the photos, the use of the zoom and light. Therefore when I returned to Riecito my first mission was to take pictures to illustrate the film project for submission to the executive board of directors of ARTE's documentary programmes. I was also asked to provide the producers with some ideas for possible locations and main characters of the documentary.

These first photographs, originally taken for the documentary project, took on new significance for my research when I showed them to my Pumé interlocutors, and from then on photography became central to the development of my fieldwork in a number of ways. First, the photographs served as a notebook. Such uses of the visual as *memory, illustration and testimony* for ethnographic description are common in anthropology (Buxó 1999). For example Bronisław Malinowski (Malinowski 1964; Young 1998), Claude Lévi-Strauss (Lévi-Strauss 1955; 1994) and Margaret Mead (Bateson and Mead 1942; Sullivan 1999) all emphasise the relationship between *photography, memory and indexicality* in their writings on the use of photography in their fieldwork. Second, during fieldwork among the Pumé my photographic record also helped me as a *way of communication*. Viewing these photographs with the people who are represented in them offered a way of communicating that produced different stories to those of our verbal interactions. Finally, I used the visual to *reconstruct the imaginary* of the people I was working with by compiling and analysing the images they produced or the images they recognised themselves in. Paradoxically, photography is an ideal medium for reconstructing the imaginary sphere and the invisible processes of social realities we were researching.

Pumé culture as photographic context

The Pumé, also known in the ethnographic literature as Yaruro, are traditionally fishermen and hunter-gatherers practising a seasonal nomadism following the climatic conditions in the zone of the Llanos of south-western Venezuela. At the time of the last indigenous census of Venezuela (1992) there were 5,885 Pumé. The Pumé are a geographically peripheral population. Because of the several Creole agricultural or cattle-raising colonisations they have been progressively cornered since the nineteenth century towards the poorest, most underdeveloped regions and away from the city boundary zones. They are a politically forgotten group (except at election time) and economically dependent on government subsidies and NGO help. Their resource depletion resulting from their forced settlement and loss of territory is clearly visible. In Pumé everyday conversation, in their myths and, more generally, in their world construction references to their isolation and marginalisation are not simply recurrent but constant.

Over the years, as ethnologists have testified, the Pumé have given up believing in their survival from this land (Petrullo 1969; Le Besnerai 1962; Mitrani 1973, 1988). Nowadays, for them it is during the night, in the world of dreams, that important things happen. Daytime is nothing but tragedy, disappointment and waiting for the promises of the coming night. For, it is at night that the Pumé celebrate the *Tõhé* ceremony. From dusk to dawn they sing the *Tõhé*, they dream, they reach the blessed countries of gods and ancestors. Life seems insignificant without this never-ending movement between the human 'here' and the mythical 'over there' (Orobitg 1998).

The *Tõhé* begins at dusk and ends at dawn when the first sun's rays appear in the horizon. Men and women, youngsters and adults participate in the ceremony. Throughout the whole night, four to five times a week, they repeat the melodies improvised by the adult man who conducts the ceremony and by those to whom he gives a turn at chanting – all the adult men that participate in the ceremony. Through the *Tõhé* chant, they explain what they 'see', what they have dreamt and what they are dreaming. During the *Tõhé* men and mythical beings communicate with each other through singing, as they also do when they sleep or when they are ill. During the *Tõhé* sick people are cured and everyday life conflicts are solved. In the words of the Pumé, the *Tõhé*'s purpose is to help them to live, to survive.

In Pumé the word *da* (to see) is cognate of *daba* (to know). To know (*daba*) also means to access the experience of the dream world either through the *Tõhé* chant, illness or sleep. Such knowledge is necessary for the Pumé to explain the events of wakefulness. The most invisible is the most 'real' because Pumé relationships with this invisible world are necessary for the dynamics of social life (Orobitg 1998). This equation was fundamental in informing my use of drawings and photographs in fieldwork. Similarly, it determined my decision to use black-and-white film to take photographs of wakefulness and colour to visually represent the world of dreams.

Catherine De Clippel (the documentary producer) had suggested it was better to take black-and-white photographs. Black-and-white, she would explain later, creates an 'atmosphere', it reproduces better the 'new reality' which the photographer creates from the relation that she establishes with the reality she photographs. Whether or not we agree with her ideas about the meaning of black-and-white, her view constitutes a good point of departure for the debate about visual semiotics and the expressiveness of the photographic image in anthropology. Different meanings can be elicited from the use of black-and-white and colour within ethnographic photography. And, this is because of the crucial importance of the *fieldwork context* for deciding how to use visual tools in anthropological research (Banks 2001). It was specifically in the Pumé ethnographic context that the use of black and white for the *here* and colour for the *over there* should be understood.

The first photographs in the field:
from words to images

The first photographs I took were pictures of buildings and remains of rusty machines and vehicles covered in undergrowth. According to my interlocutors they were the only visible remains of the 'golden' time, from the foundation of the village and the indigenous assistance group (NAI) of Riecito in 1959. Mainly during the first months of my fieldwork the adult men in the village had talked to me about this particular period of their history for hours. I started to become interested due to the repetitiveness of their stories and, although I was most interested in aspects related to the representation of illnesses, my interlocutors gave me long descriptions of the foundation of Riecito. This was their favourite theme of conversation.

In particular at the beginning of my fieldwork, the Pumé insisted on describing what happened in November 1959. Francisco Prada, an anthropologist and government employee of the then recently created Dirección de Asuntos Indígenas (DAI: Board of Indigenous Affairs), arrived in the area to set up a project, as he describes in his reports, of 'planned acculturation'. Unlike the situation of violence and exploitation that indigenous people were then suffering at the hands of the Venezuelan Creole population, the stories of the arrival of Prada describe a 'golden' period. The Pumé worked in the agricultural and livestock project initiated by Prada, they received salaries so they could afford necessities, a school was set up, there was running water and electricity in the newly created Pumé village of Riecito, and an airplane landed every Saturday bringing medicines and provisions and carrying seriously ill people to the nearest city. Pumé narratives about this period represent it as an almost mythical time (Orobitg 1998). Whenever the Pumé talk about their history they use the time of Prada and the foundation of Riecito as a temporal reference point: 'this happened before Prada had founded the village' or 'this happened after Prada had left and the project failed through . . .'. In this area, on the border with Colombia, where influential figures in the country were involved in cattle smuggling, an official presence like the DAI was seen as a threat. According to the reports of the army and of the DAI in 1960 Prada was accused of being a communist agitator and had to flee from Riecito.

Roberto Lizarralde, one of the anthropologists who was in Riecito at the time of its foundation, had given me some negatives of photographs from that time. Given my Pumé interlocutors' narratives and those 1960 photographs representing the period I became fascinated by taking photographs of the present remains of a so frequently related past. Initially I took these photographs to illustrate the stories of the enchantment (the foundation of Riecito) and the disenchantment (the present situation in which the Pumé live). Initially one might regard them as photographs, which do not make sense without a written text of Pumé narrations (Mead 1995; Buxó 1999). Margaret Mead insisted on this dependence of images on words. According to Kirsten Hastrup, photography will never be as effective as written work for a detailed and emotional description of reality (Hastrup 1992). Certainly photographs reinforce spoken or written narratives. However they also lend words a new dimension; that is, photographs inspire new narrations.

Instanteity, strong focus on detail and fragmentation of reality are inherent characteristics of photographic images. By fixing the image photography allows us to observe more details than we would see in the moving image, which has the same characteristics as ordinary observation (Birdwhistell 1970: 149–51). Photography: (a) shows what the anthropologist/photographer wants to show in its framing, (b) allows us to see what had not been intended to be shown but which appears in the image accidentally, (c) calls attention to those aspects which are invisible to the ordinary eye (Piette, 1996: 150). This is what Kirsten Hastrup has conceptualised, albeit critically, as the effects of the photographic images and its uses in ethnographic research: the *show up effect, the blow up effect and the make up effect respectively* (Hastrup 1992: 11–13). These various contributions can be summarised by Roland Barthes' idea that the interest of photography lies precisely in the simultaneous manifestation of two elements. The *studium* is the general informative interest that a photographic image can have. While the *punctum* questions the *studium*, it is the detail or the supplement, which appears in the picture without the anthropologist/photographer's intention, it is the fruit of serendipity (Barthes 1980; Piettte 1996: 151). Other authors suggest that by fixing and fragmenting experience, photography can cover what seems uncoverable: the fragmentation of a reality which film narrations invariably present in an integrated form. In this sense photography represents a new narrative form (García Canclini 1997: 112; Edwards 1999). By examining the effect the photographs of the foundation of Riecito and of the present remains of that period had on the Pumé we can see how these different aspects of the photograph can become part of ethnographic research.

The Pumé accounts led me to take certain photographs (see above). However, the photographic corpus I gathered about the foundation of the village by Francisco Prada and of the present remains of that period aroused a series of narrations that invoked the creation of an imaginary sphere, where any situation and event was possible and whose logic was not questioned. Francisco Prada, an adult Pumé told, brought a doctor who came swimming through the river, who explained to them the Pumé conception of the person, healed all the Pumé and left as he had arrived, through the river. Prada would travel to Riecito, and from there to other Pumé communities, bringing cattle, electricity, food, mosquito nets, outboard engines, petrol, etc. He would invariably say – or at least this is the sentence they put into his mouth in all the stories: 'All this is for the Pumé, I brought it for the Pumé only.' I soon realised that the stories of Prada's time were part of a mythical or imaginary sphere. One same photograph rapidly evoked these stories that turned the anthropologist into a founder hero and the foundation into a myth of origin. It was precisely through these stories, which emerged and took shape as a corpus through the photograph, that I started to

Figure 3.1

discover the cognitive structure common to any story or image created by the Pumé. Every story and every Pumé image present two elements that are always related through a third element. I have termed this the ternary rhythm. This also occurs during the *Tõhé* ceremony when the *oté* contact the men through the intermediary beings, the *tió*, through another intermediary, the shaman. This ternary structure can be found both in the composition of stories and in the composition of Pumé drawings (which I discuss later in this chapter).

Nevertheless the stories from the first photographs were not only interesting because they revealed the ternary structure of Pumé stories, chant, and image composition. Rather, in the next section I describe how they also inspired and strengthened new narratives about reality.

From images to words

The historical photographs discussed above demonstrated the value of photographs in evoking narratives, as historical documents and for the anthropological study of the passage of time. As such we can see how photographs are involved in both constructing and representing reality. When ethnographic photographs are a result of collaboration and dialogue between the anthropologist and her interlocutors, rather than simply reconstructing the past, photographs tell us a lot about how the people we are working with see/understand reality (Buxó 1999: 6–8). This was the case when I returned to Riecito in February

2000 after six years of absence. Now the adult men and women's favourite theme of conversation with me was not the creation of Riecito but the great increase in the child population (even though, in these six years, one male or female child of under a year old had died in each home). 'Did you notice how well we did?' Cesar, an adult Pumé man asked me at the schoolyard where children between the ages of 5 and 14 were playing. 'There were only a few of us before, weren't there? . . . You wouldn't believe it now seeing so many children about,' a youngster told me as we stood opposite the daily care-house – where children from 1 to 6 years old eat every day. Led by these narratives, I took photographs of children playing at school, at the daily care-house and elsewhere.

The photographs I took in the early 1990s made much more sense when contextualised by those I took in 2000. My photographic report of Riecito, which now covers this period of ten years represents the passing of time from the Pumé of Riecito's point of view, through landscapes, buildings and people. This discourse on the passage of time contains above all a political and demanding discourse. The stories of the foundation of Riecito, and the population increase are related to the sense of protest and of cultural resistance that the Pumé gave to my ethnography. The images I produced with the Pumé's collaboration created an imaginative/narrative space. Here they reinforced and reshaped their discourse: first, about marginalisation and cultural resistance and how the Creole population and the socioeconomic policies of the Venezuelan government have marginalised them; and second, about their past, present, and future prospects, about their Utopia. In this sense, the images produced during fieldwork, and the relations that the Pumé themselves established with them, revealed what Anne Christine Taylor characterises as the indigenous expression

Figure 3.2

of temporality. Which is not a linear temporality, marked by a series of specific events, but a processual temporality, where the past is constantly made present in order to gain access to the deep sense of events and in particular, in the indigenous case, to express the painful process of interethnic relations that has marked their past and is still marking their present (Taylor 1997). Photographic images can simultaneously represent a singular version of time and space while challenging that very representation of time and space (Benjamin 1969; Edwards 1998). Therefore photography is a fascinating way to capture different cultural relations to temporality, as we have been able to see in the Pumé case. See also Edwards' analysis of place of photography in the Torres Straits expedition (Edwards 1998).

Images, words and the ethnographic experience

Both photographic content and the narratives photographs evoke offer anthropologists routes to knowledge that cannot be achieved by verbal communication. Using photographs in an interview bring anthropologists to understand reality in new ways and can act as an important prompt when the anthropologist does not know how to set out a question (Collier and Collier 1992). Nowadays using photographs in interviews is considered not solely a means of data collection, in the sense Collier and Collier proposed but as a means of producing data through negotiation and reflexivity (Banks 2001; Harper 1998; Pink 2001). Using photographs in interviews places the anthropologist in a proactive role, both in selecting the images to be used and the context in which they will be viewed – from the most arbitrary and coincidental situations to the most structured and planned ones (Banks 2001: 87). As Banks puts it (2001: 88): 'the basic principles of photo-elicitation rest upon a fairly transparent reading of the internal narrative of photographic content, issues of photographic multivocality and the complexity of the entanglement of photographic objects in human social relations means that photo-elicitation (and the more rarely used film-elicitation) is not always straightforward in practice.'

When I was organising my photographs I was surprised to notice that many of them represented how my arrival to a house to talk to one of their members always caused a conglomeration of other people in that place. These photographs show groups of mainly children and women sitting and observing. Portraits also represent similar ethnographic experiences as most were taken at the request of some family member or the protagonist of the photograph in the context of conversations or interviews. These photographs were valuable in my conversations with my Riecito interlocutors. Photographs with a strong indexical value (those which represented a clearly identifiable action) did not provoke many comments. In contrast these portraits had great iconographic value in this indigenous context, and thus invoked narratives about reality.

In his discussion of photo-elicitation Harper has shown how interviewing with photographs can produce much richer materials and responses that simply

Figure 3.3

asking questions (2002). My Pumé research is a case in point. I found that the comments on my photographs questioned the genealogical diagrams that I worked so hard on in my door-to-door survey. 'Look! That's the daughter of so and so,' said somebody looking at a picture. 'What? . . . wasn't she the daughter of that other person?' I asked. 'Yes she is, too,' they would answer me in some cases, 'but it is because she has two fathers, one who fathered her and another one who brought her up while she was in the mother's womb.' In another case the father himself (to my knowledge), looking at the photo said: 'that is my cousin's daughter' (classificatory brother). 'But isn't she your daughter?' I asked him, thinking about what they had told me when I had been researching my genealogical diagrams. 'It was a time when I was away . . .' These photographs evoked new narratives on genealogical relationship. They produced stories about inheritance and fluid transmission, that when I was devising genealogical diagrams my question had not invited.

Emotions and imaginaries

The most exciting moments of Pumé life to photograph were the monthly slaughter of the cow and the *Tōhé* ritual. They are the only moments where men, women and children from the whole village unite in joint activities. The silence which characterizes the daily routine of the Pumé community is broken for a few moments for the monthly slaughter of the cow, and throughout the whole night for the *Tōhé* ceremony. Laughter, conversations, interactions, children's games burst into the routine of everyday life. 'They look like other people,' I sometimes thought with surprise. I represented this impression/ sensation in my photographic sequences of the monthly slaughter of the cow. These photographs clearly show these interactions, the distribution of tasks among men and women, and the presence of children in those moments that are so special for everybody.

To photograph these moments of social interaction I framed the photographed reality differently. These images represent what in the rest of the photographic report appears fragmented: the gender and age relations. Whereas the majority of my Pumé photographs are long and close-up shots, to photograph these social interactions I intuitively opened up the lens, to take wide shots. I regretted not having taken more wide shots when photographing other events, like food and cigarette preparation and hammock and chair making. Such wide shots and their use can be seen in early visual anthropology projects (e.g. Malinowski, see Young 1998; or Bateson and Mead, see Sullivan 1999). Nevertheless my over-use of close-ups can be explained when this practice is seen as embedded fieldwork itself – fieldwork that from my conversations with the people from Riecito was gradually focusing on dreams, on the more individual and invisible dimension of reality that cannot be photographed.

The *Tõhé* ceremony is celebrated in complete darkness: 'The *oté* [mythical beings] don't like light,' the Pumé explained. As with no light it was impossible for me to photograph the *Tõhé* I made drawings of the ritual space and the distribution of gender and age groups in it and tape-recorded at least two hours of ceremonial chants. I added to this with photographic sequences of women preparing *karambá* (cigarettes) before the ceremony, men preparing the *yopo* (hallucinogenic substance inhaled by men during the ceremony) and maracas, the only musical instrument used during the *Tõhé*. Scenes of the ceremony and trips from the *pumethó* (vital essence) during dreamtime and the ritual chanting are engraved on the maracas. These visual representations of the invisible on the maracas were contextualised further by a series of drawings of the chants made by the 'chanters'.

These drawings created by the people themselves generated the story of the imaginary (Goldschmidt and Edgerton 1961; Spindler and Goldschmidt 1952). Rather than being a planned method, the production of these drawings itself was catalysed through my experiences and discussions with the Pumé; it emerged from this particular fieldwork context. I had been dreaming, and in my Pumé interlocutor's interpretations my dreams reproduced this mythical Pumé world that they had described to me through their stories of dreams and chants for eight months.

One night, lying on a hammock during the *Tõhé* ceremony, I had a strange dream. I was walking along a runway like the one in Riecito. When I reached the end of the runway I jumped over a cliff and found myself in a city. I suddenly realised that I couldn't hear myself when I was speaking; I met people, I talked to them, but I wasn't sure they could hear me. I came back to the *Tõhé*, and kept on walking looking for someone to heal me; I took the lift that led me

Figure 3.4

Figure 3.5

beneath the surface into a room with screens, where some Chinese doctors in white lab coats told me that although my illness was serious they could heal me. Suddenly I woke up and it was the end of the *Tōhé*. At first I was amazed at what I had just dreamt; however, this dream became really significant when the Pume interpreted it. 'This is a good dream, a very good dream. The saints [*oté*, in Pumé language] know that you know us here, and they want you to know what it is like over there as well', Cesar told me. Could the images in my dream reproduce such a singular domain of Pumé culture? My Pumé interlocutors suggested it was possible.

I was bewildered: their interpretation of my dream increased the confusion that the stories about the trips of the *pumenthó* (vital essence) during dreamtime and chanting time had caused me. The dream lands did not seem to have defined geographical limits and the beings who inhabited them had neither a precise location in this space nor stable and clearly defined personalities. 'I don't understand very well,' I told Cesar, who according to everyone in Riecito knows those lands best, 'could you draw it for me?' It was a rainy day and like every morning Cesar had come to visit me very early. Although he had never drawn on paper before he agreed to try to draw the *oté* lands. I put four sheets together making him a bigger surface to draw on and collected the coloured pencils I lent the many children who came to my house at night, for them to draw while I was finishing my field diary. Cesar spent almost all day making a sequence of four drawings of the same size. While he was drawing, but especially after he had finished he explained their meaning to me. The drawings represented the same narratives of trips and interactions in the lands of the *oté* that Cesar had told me about during those months. But, it didn't end there. Cesar decided to ask some young 'chanters' whom he had been teaching to draw the 'lands of the *oté*' so he could evaluate their learning. We arranged to meet the following two days during which drawing was the central activity of my fieldwork. A series of portrait photographs represent these ethnographic experiences. Cesar was more or less happy with the drawings. Mainly they helped him to scold those who, according to him, had not learnt about the '*oté* lands', the *oté* themselves and the *Tōhé* very well.

This Pumé mythical geography is represented as a superimposition of strata. If we use the men's lands as a point of reference, the mythical lands are located above, beneath and over the line of the horizon. The mythical lands from above and beneath represent a kind of distant mythical periphery. The ancient creators who rarely communicate with the Pumé and thus have little influence on daily life inhabit these remote lands. In contrast the horizon lands and the beings who dwell in them are in constant communication with the Pumé and are important in the organization of social life. The *Tōhé* and, more generally, the dream allow communication with the *oté* who live in the horizon line. The *oté* are constantly renewed, they are the protagonists of dreams and are most evident in Pumé drawings. Ethnographies of the Pumé from the 1930s show movement of *oté* from the horizon to the periphery as they are replaced, as

Anthony Leeds put it, by 'new generations of gods' who 'understand' better the changes taking place in Pumé society (Leeds 1960).

However, the significance of the drawings did not end there. Some months later I thought I had lost the fieldwork records in which I had written Cesar's explanation of his first drawing. I went to Cesar's house with the drawing to ask him to explain it to me again. I remembered a few things but was afraid that something important might escape my memory. To my surprise Cesar told me a story that was completely different from the one he had told me initially. The same happened when I asked the others about the meaning of their drawings again. The drawings reveal this dynamic character of the Pumé image and imaginary. The new stories about the drawings described the new contexts that were currently being learnt through the *Tõhé*, or perhaps some previous reference to the narrator's relation with the mythical world. That is, different stories of dreams. The drawings, from the Pumé's point of view, were not signs but referents from which to denote narratives about relations, essential in this indigenous culture, between the Pumé and the *oté*. The drawings, and the diversity of relations that they evoked, indicated once again, the central role of experience and individual creativity in the construction of social dynamics.

Moreover, the drawings confirmed that I should not worry about the apparent 'disorder' and 'inconsistency' of the stories about the imaginary dimension of Pumé culture. What was really interesting was to discover the underlying order beneath this apparent chaos (Todorov 1962). Visual methods are especially suited to exploring cognitive processes (Collier and Collier 1992: 118). In the Pumé case I wanted to explore cultural guidelines underlying Pumé individual

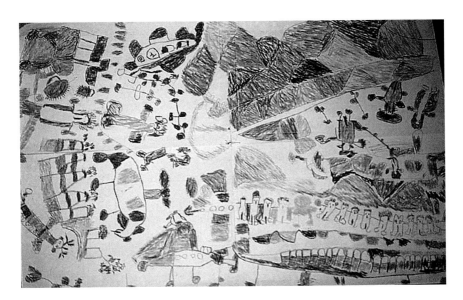

Figure 3.6

creativity and I identified a Pumé cultural structure that applied to new individual creative processes. The drawings corroborate visually the narrative structure of Pumé oral stories: the ternary structure I described above, which implies that any narrative or image is organized around two elements to be related and a third one which links them. On the basis of this structure (which can be clearly seen in Figure 3.6) a variety of itineraries and dream-world experiences, that produce constantly updated stories about the individual and the society, are expressed (Orobitg 2002).

Conclusions

In an indigenous context where dreaming is crucial for the construction of social life, photography and drawing have produced ethnographic understandings that deepened my knowledge of Pumé reality. Throughout fieldwork, Pumé narratives led to my producing images in collaboration with indigenous people. These ethnographic photographs and drawings indicated not only the cognitive structure underlying all Pumé cultural creativity, but moreover these images generated an ideal context for the production of new narratives about the past and present.

The Pumé example indicates the complementary and dialectical relations between image and the text, between the visual and the oral. The ethnographic narrative I presented above demonstrates the expressivity inherent in the image as a representation. It is precisely on the basis of this expressive quality that we have begun to think about the specificities of a 'new anthropological language' produced from analysing the visual.

Note

This text owes much to the Pumé of Riecito who for many years have welcomed me and they are still teaching me their world view. I am also very thankful to Sarah Pink, László Kürti, Ana Isabel Afonso and Carles Salazar for their careful reading of this text and their lucid comments.

References

Banks, M. (2001) *Visual Methods in Social Research*, London: Sage.

Barthes, R. (1980) *La chambre claire: note sur la photographie*, Paris, Cahiers du cinéma.

Bateson, G. and Mead, M. (1942) *Balinese Character: A Photographic Analysis*, New York: New York Academy of Sciences.

Benjamin, W. (1969) *Illuminations*, New York: Schocken Books.

Birdwhistell, R. L. (1970) *Kinesics and Context: Essays on Body Motion Communication*, Philadelphia: University of Pennsylvania Press.

Bourdieu, P. (ed.) (1989) [1965] *La fotografía un arte intermedio*, México: Nueva Imagen.

Buxó, M. J. (1999) '. . . que mil palabras', in *De la investigación audiovisual. Fotografía, cine, vídeo, televisión*, Barcelona: Proyecto A Ediciones; 1–22.

Collier, J. Jr and Collier, M. (1992) [1967] *Visual Anthropology. Photography as a Research Method*, Albuquerque: University of New Mexico Press.

De Clippel, C. and Colleyn, J.-P. (1993) *Les Pumé et leurs rêves*, Paris, Bruxels : ACME Films, RTB, ARTE-La Sept, 16 mm, 59′.

Dubois, P. (1994) [1983] *El acto fotográfico*, Barcelona: Paidós.

Edwards, E. (1998) 'Performing Science: Still Photography and the Torres Strait Expedition', in A. Herle and S. Rouse (eds), *Cambridge and the Torres Strait: Centenary Essays on the 1898 Anthropological Expedition*, Cambridge, Cambridge University Press, 106–35.

—— (1999) 'Beyond the boundary: a consideration of the expressive in photography and anthropology', in H. Morphy and M. Banks (eds), *Rethinking Visual Anthropology*, New Haven: Yale University Press, 53–79.

García Canclini, N. (1997) 'Viajes e imaginarios urbanos', in *Imaginarios urbanos*, México: Eudeba; 109–49.

García Canclini, N., Castellanos, A. and Rosas Mantecón, A. (1996) *La ciudad de los viajeros. Travesías e imaginarios urbanos: México, 1940–2000*, México: Universidad Autónoma Metropolitana/Grijalbo.

Goldschmidt, W. and Edgerton, E. (1961) 'A Picture Technique for the Study of Values', *American Anthropologist* 63(1): 26–47.

Harper, D. (1987) 'The visual ethnographic narratives', *Visual Anthropology* 1: 1–19.

—— (1998) 'An Argument for Visual Sociology', in J. Prosser (ed.), *Image-based Research. A Sourcebook for Qualitative Researchers*, London, Falmer Press, 24–41.

—— (2002) 'Talking about pictures: a case for photo elicitation', *Visual Studies* 17: 13–26.

Hastrup, K. (1992) 'Anthropological visions: some notes on visual and textual authority' in P. Crawford and D. Turton (eds), *Film as Ethnography*, Manchester: Manchester University Press.

Le Besnerais, H. (1951) 'Quelques aspects de la religion des Indiens Yaruro', *Société Suisse des Américanistes*, Bull. 2, Geneve, Musée et Institut d'Ethnographie de la ville de Geneve.

Leeds, A. (1960) 'The ideology of the Yaruro indians in relation to socio-economic organization', *Antropológica* 9.

Lévi-Strauss, C. (1955) *Tristes Tropiques*, Paris: Plon (Terre Humaine).

—— (1994) *Saudades do Brasil*, Paris: Plon.

MacDougall, D. (1999) [1997] 'The visual in Anthropology', in Marcus Banks and Howard Morphy, *Rethinking Visual Anthropology*, New Haven, London: Yale University Press; 276–95.

Malinowski, B. (1964) [1922] *Argonauts of Western Pacific: An Account of Native Enterprise and Adventure in the Archipelagos of Melanesia New Guinea*, London: Routledge and Kegan Paul.

Mead, M. (1995) 'Visual anthropology in a discipline of word', in Paul Hockings (ed.), *Principles of Visual Anthropology*, Berlin and New York: Mouton de Gruyter, 3–10.

Mitrani, P. (1973) 'Contribution à l'étude des formes religieuses et culturelles chez les Yaruro de l'Apure', *Antropológica*, 35, Caracas.

—— (1988) 'Los Pumé' in Jacques Lizot (ed.) *Los Aborígenes de Venezuela*, vol. 3, Caracas: Fundación La Salle/Monte Ávila ed.

Orobitg Canal, G. (1998) *Les Pumé et leurs rêves. Étude d'un groupe indien des Plaines du Venezuela*, Paris: Éditions des Archives Contemporains.

—— (2001) *Word and Image in Ethnographic Research*, VHS-Pal, 20'. On-line. E-mail: gorobitg@uoc.edu.

—— (2002) 'Sonar para vivir. Memoria, olvido y experiencia entre los indígenas Pumé', in R. Piqué and M. Ventura (eds) *América Latin. Historia y Sociedad*, Barcelona: ICCI.

Petrullo, V. (1969) [1939] *Los Yaruro del río Capanaparo, Venezuela*, Caracas: Instituto de Antropologñia e Historia. Facultad de Humanidades y Educación, Universidad Central del Venezuela.

Piette, A. (1996) 'Focalisation sur le détail particulier', *Ethnographie de l'action*, Paris: Métaillé; 144–86.

Pink, S. (1996) 'Excursiones socio-visuales en el mundo del toreo', in A. Martinez Pérez *et al. Antropología de los Sentido. La Vista*, Madrid, Celeste Ediciones, 125–38.

—— (2001) *Doing Visual Ethnography. Images, Media and Representation in Research*, London: Sage.

Rose, G. (2001) *Visual Methodologies. An Introduction to the Interpretation of Visual Materials*, London: Sage.

Spindler, G. and Goldschmidt, W. (1952) 'Experimental design in the study of cultural change', *Southwestern Journal of Anthropology* 21: 68–83.

Sullivan, G. (1999) *Margaret Mead, Gregory Bateson and Highland Bali. Fieldwork Photographs of Bayung Gedé, 1936–1939*, Chicago: The University of Chicago Press.

Taylor, A. C. (1997). 'L'oubli des morts et la mémoire des meurtres. Experiences de l'histoire chez les Jivaro', *Terrain* (March): 83–96.

Todorov, T. (1982) *La conquête de l'Amérique. La question de l'autre*, Paris: Seuil (Essais).

Young, M. (1998) *Malinowski's Kiriwina. Fieldwork Photography 1915–1918*, Chicago: The University of Chicago Press.

Chapter 4

Picture perfect

Community and commemoration in postcards

László Kürti

Introduction: photography, postcards and history

For one reason or another, anthropologists carefully select and send postcards when away from home. Similarly, anthropologists just like anyone else also send postcards when they are at 'home' to those who are not with them. For many these picture postcards represent the combination of self and other, traversing between various locations, and a visual possibility of searching for identities lost or questioned. As consumers most individuals are little concerned with actual finances and benefits to the local economy and society; we tend to buy and send postcards feeling satisfied that these miniature images, and the few hastily written words, reconnect us through the, often highly stylised, forms of visual and textual narratives. Undoubtedly, postcards may provide a sense of reality about where we are, how far we have travelled and the changing social contexts that our life is anchored to at the moment. Local postcards, those produced by the locals themselves termed as such here for the lack of better term, are a special category combining locality and historicity with visuality. They are special because they amalgamate geography and territory with cultural identity often with the use of miniature maps drawn directly on the postcard. Viewed this way postcards more often than not are connected to a specific group, territory and identity. Framed by both time and space, they are definitely novel forms of representations of late modernity closely resembling what Michel Foucault has called heterotropias, a variety of parallel worlds that live side-by-side with us in the midst. 'The space,' writes Foucault, 'in which we live, which draws us out of ourselves, in which the erosion of our lives, our time and our history occurs, the space that claws and gnaws at us' (Foucault 1986: 23). Thus one of the primordial functions of postcards is to draw both the producer and the consumer into the visualised history as memory, a notion fitting well with Augé's suggestion that 'our relation to reality is mediatized' (1999: 65). Since their invention, postcards certainly have assisted in the popular mediatisation of our lives with the use of heterotropias.

In this chapter I would like to investigate the use, function and meanings of twentieth-century postcards from Lajosmizse, a small town south-east of Budapest. This inquiry is also necessary in order to reinterpret photography as we witness an upsurge of interest in DVD, CD-ROM, Internet and digital video being utilised by professionals and students alike in the classroom, in the field and in everyday life. In order to balance the overwhelmingly filmic presence, a somewhat undue stress on the 'moving image' in contrast to photography and other more traditional visual forms, I continue my earlier preoccupation with media and especially photography (Kürti 1999, 1998).[1] Here I wish to create a bridge between moving images and their more stationary visual predecessors such as photographs, a concern raised earlier by Willis as well (1995). In this chapter I interrogate postcards, which I hold to be miniature image-sequences connected with much larger and earlier image sequences. By utilising postcards, I rely on the insight provided by David MacDougall who, when comparing similarities and differences between written and visual texts, argues that 'images and written texts not only tell us things differently, they tell us different things' (1998: 257). However, I argue that the two have more in common than recently has been acknowledged and that we should seek out symbiotic convergences between them.

Despite their seeming banality and simplicity, postcards are not easy to decipher (Edwards 1997, 2001; Street 1992).[2] While most analyses focus on 'western' photographs of the native 'others', rightfully stressing their romantic and exploitative nature, here I wish to consider why some kinds of postcards cannot be easily foisted into this exploitative and overtly romanticised category. Therefore I privilege them as unique cultural texts and images for the following reasons:

1   Since most are taken by professionals we need to consider intentionality and purpose together with the contexts and ideology within which they are produced and used.
2   Most postcards are made for individual use but in the consumption process they may successfully subvert the private–public dichotomy.
3   Photographs framed as postcards are highly stylised narratives of events, locations and personalities carrying multiple and diverse meanings and messages.
4   Postcards, even the single-shot picture card, are composed of an intertextual collage of heterotropias, multiple worlds that coexist with us in the midst of them.

Undoubtedly the manifest function of postcards is about connectedness of territory and our relation to it (Edwards 1996, 1997; Lübbren and Crouch 2002). Postcards sent home are often unsettling markers of status: travelling to a place where few ventured or where perhaps previously no one even could. However, not all postcards are touristy, for some ostensibly detail a community and its people as they wish to present themselves.[3] Most postcards may be testimonies of achievement and statements of execution of what Pierre Bourdieu has called the 'objective relations, obscurely felt, between the class as such and other classes' (1990: 9). The relationship between the seen and the unseen, acknowledged and the muted, is what I find to be the fascinating element in postcards, needing careful scrutiny. Tourism, (Kahn 2000) fairs and exhibitions – like the Universal Exhibition in Paris in 1889 (Geary and Webb 1998; Staff 1966)[4] – and iconic sites and cities (Schor 1992) all have their well-deserved places in the mass production of picture postcards in Europe. Viewing the past century of the postcard industry reveals that postcards have been extremely tightly woven visual and written narratives informing us about the passage of time and the changes in the contours of space surrounding us. They entail invaluable, often interconnected metastories, by consciously homogenising ideas and cultural patterns into special images. Thus, compressing space and time, postcards purposefully essentialise and sanitise ideas into miniature representations of multiple worlds.

When viewed in a longer time frame, postcards reveal vivid individual and collective transformations and heterotropic framed relations. They are, I argue, more than debates about historical authenticity, ethnographic present and the authoritative voice of the photographer, as many have argued so recently (Pink 2001). Most arguments discuss why and how pictures are used *in addition* to visual texts and how and why they challenge and alter textual representation (Edwards 1992).[5] Here I suggest we view postcards as multiplications of narratives composed by multitudes of voices that speak both textually and visually. In fact, they are multi-layered and many-faced appropriations of words, symbols and messages masked, as they often are, by primary functions and purposeful contents.

The first postcards were mailed in 1869 but not without some initial opposition, as most critics objected to the 'openness' of letters supposed to embody privacy and individuality.[6] During the 1870s, postcards were commissioned by August Schwartz in Germany with patriotic messages reflecting on the major preoccupation, the Franco-Prussian war. It was not long before postcards began to multiply by the millions so much so that by the early decades of the twentieth century people used them for all kinds of occasions. The first postcards in Austro-Hungary were printed mostly by Austrian and German companies, and only in 1896, with the millennial celebrations underway, did Hungarian businesses begin to produce their own postcards with patriotic and nationalistic themes and slogans. The 1896 postcard series celebrated the one-thousandth anniversary of the foundation of the Hungarian kingdom with thirty-two graphics as well as lithographs based on historical depictions of buildings and sites in Budapest. This propaganda project sealed the fate of national postcard production to come. Most of the later postcards, especially those of World War I (*Kriegs Karte*), depicted military themes thereby contributing to a special form of ideologically manipulated militarised postcards.[7] In 1904 the postal service allowed the division of the card into a picture side and the reverse for the address as well as the actual letter. It was during the first decade of the twentieth century that the picture was itself divided to allow space for more images thereby projecting a more dynamic interplay of sites and buildings. This is also the time when we witness the more personalised (individual and family) postcards, the 'memory-cards' (*emléklap*). As travelling became either necessary or part of the consumerist culture we witness the way in which text and image disengage from each other and slowly evolve into the grid-like collage carrying extremely diverse, often contradictory messages.[8] As soon as it was invented, however, ideology colonised the image creating the propaganda postcard faithfully following alterations in the political contours of society and the local community.[9]

Photographs as postcards in the revisualisation of Hungarian memory and past

Collecting and publishing old photographs is, of course, not novel, nor is it a particularly (East) European phenomenon: communities in Europe, North America, and Asia possess them too, enhancing and recreating memory with the aid of visual histories. In Hungary one of the first collections, 'Budapest Anno', was published in 1981 but the real publishing boom started in the early 1990s, a time Hungary was proudly declaring herself a multi-party, western-style democratic republic. Why such a frenzy of interest in identity as preserved in visual memories? To answer we must look at the Hungarian state and society as they have reinvented themselves after the collapse of the Soviet bloc in 1989. By publishing old photographs and especially vintage postcards most communities have engaged in shedding their communist past by resorting to their earlier, non-communist heritage. In this remake, old photographs and postcards are valuable, and nobody can question their raison d'être, yet such representations are by no means self-explanatory and without glaring hiatuses.[10]

Some of the most recent collections wonderfully capture this rush to recreate the past in order to remake current identities with the use of photos and postcards: 'Picture postcards of Kiskunhalas, 1898–2000' (Szakál 2000), 'Photographs of Törökszentmiklós' (Galsi 2001), the picture book on Bátya (Fehér 2002), and the collections of postcards from Salgótarján, an industrial city in northern Hungary (Szvircsek 2002) and that of Kőbánya (Ungváry 2002) are also illustrative of the problems generally connected with such visualised histories. Questions are unending: about the framing of the time period, the extreme reliance on the Catholic heritage,[11] the voice of the photographers making these pictures for different purposes from those they are subsequently used for,[12] sanitising history by carefully skirting issues of poverty, hunger, conflict and inter-ethnic problems,[13] and, finally, the authorisation and legitimation of photographic histories either by scholars or local politicians.

Recreating local history: the Lajosmizse Digital Photo Archive

In the early 1990s I returned to the place I was born, Lajosmizse, a town about 65 kilometres south-east of Budapest. Through some unfortunate family circumstances, involving separations, parental hostilities, and custody battles, I only heard about this place occasionally from my mother.[14] My decision to return and to live in this country setting is detailed elsewhere (Kürti 2000) and what really concerns us here is that this 'homecoming' (Kürti 1996) has resulted in my becoming more and more involved with the community, its past, present and people, a few of whom, as it turned out, are my relatives. In 1999, with a few concerned individuals we created a Historical and Cultural Association (HCA), a loosely formed institution to research our town, long labelled by both locals and outsiders alike as 'a settlement without serious history'.[15] This, as it turned out, was true to some extent. In reality, what this masked was the fact that there was no written history.

The first project, that met the approval of the town's council and its agile mayor, was an archival photo project: to collect, analyse and archive family photographs. Thus, the local Digital Photo Archive (DPA) was born. In collecting old photographs for the DPA in Lajosmizse we were somewhat surprised for the family albums provided interesting ideas and categories for analysis. At first there were many, seemingly diverse and unconnected collections of both professional studio pictures and numerous family albums of amateur quality. Slowly the town started to emerge in its true colours. As more and more photographs were offered and scanned into our DPA, the more the town's past began to emerge as unique and colourful. However, with the increasing number of pictures new questions and problems also arose: who are the ones in the picture? what were their names? what was the occasion depicted? In addition, the DPA soon started to take on a life of its own as locals started to analyse and interrogate pictures they were seeing for the first time. With the many thousands of pictures available I have also been increasingly asking myself the question: 'What happened to these people after the picture was taken?' This way the multifarious past has been emerging and urging me to consider more data not available. Through the available photographs and postcards, the past has begun taking shape in two dimensions: the moment the picture was taken, and the post-photographic event that the pictures clandestinely suggested.

Among the family albums a special group of photographs emerged: the family postcards that concerned privileged individuals and family celebrations. These were postcards with family members on them. At first glance, they all seemed too banal and stereotypical to warrant serious attention. However, when the postcards were grouped together some remarkable similarities as well as differences, sometimes with contradictory and disturbing information, surfaced. Thus, the two large groups that immediately became obvious are the individualised or personal postcards and the collective or community ones.

With the first postcard produced in 1896 and the last ones in 2002, altogether about eighty community postcards have been collected, and roughly the same number of family postcards.[16] In the first category there are many studio portraits and family shots that were printed and mailed as postcards. Between 1914 and 1950 many studio and location shots were printed on a paper that could be easily turned into a postcard.[17] When the family wished, more and more copies could be printed and used as postcards. Despite the seeming duality between the family-individual ones and the collective ones, both may be viewed as marking rites of passage: in one case, how an individual or a family experienced changes, in the other the way the community underwent transformation or recreated itself under political pressure. However, status change is a preoccupation for both kinds of postcards for they celebrate a reconfirmation of identities at a particular moment in time. Both kinds of postcards present a standard, agreed system of hierarchy: in family postcards outstanding members of a family are represented often within a context deemed special. For community postcards there is a selection of places, structures and events that local leaders wished to show to the outside world.

What is rather obvious is that there is a simple thematic grouping assisting us to view postcards in an analytical way rather than through a simple chronology:

1 War and military service are an important category for young men who took their pictures when they were drafted into the army.

2 Community postcards are those that show how the settlement undergoes changes with new buildings created, schools, churches and kindergartens constructed.

3 Elevations of class status are clearly visible in both family and community postcards. Often craftsmen and shopkeepers decided to have their pictures taken in front of their stores. As will be clear below, these doorway pictures are not simply about local industriousness but involve the whole community and its history.

4 Two important collective work groups – grape harvest and wheat threshing – were recorded overwhelmingly on early postcards, labour processes that are no longer seen.[18]

5 Family postcards represent rites and celebrations involving birth, marriage, baptismal feasts but never death and funerals.

6 Another thematic group prevalent in the DPA of Lajosmizse has to do with civic and religious associations visually representing their activities often at major holidays and national celebrations.

Framing history: postcards in Lajosmizse

Most of the postcards collected in Lajosmizse were produced locally but seem to have the mark of the outside world on them. Aside from those made by individual families and for special intimate occasions, most of the community postcards seem rather remote, and appear to have an air of static distance. The ones I have selected for this visual trajectory all share elements of the heterotropic image complex discussed in the beginning. A telling example is a postcard from 1907 (Figure 4.1) on which image and text coexist side by side, enhancing rather than opposing one another. We do not know who wrote it or sent it for the information is impossible to decipher. There are a few people in the foreground of the small black and white photo but we are not offered any clues as to

Figure 4.1 An archaic type of postcard with a small picture and text on the same side. The picture depicts a today unrecognisable part of the main street. The handwritten text reads: 'Greetings from Lajosmizse. How are you doing at home? Sunday I can join you. This time we could not go because we were busy. I greet all the in-laws and you as well. 1907. VI. 18'.

who they might be. The message written borders on banality reinforcing earlier arguments about why postcards work. The introduction begins *in medias res* by greeting the relatives, then it continues with a statement about the actual reason why the postcard was written (homecoming at a later date), and finally it comes to an abrupt end with the usual goodbye formula.

The coexistence of the written text and the image reveals the symbiotic interpenetration of the two kinds of narrative that do not project difference and opposition but, on the contrary, naturally complement each other. Thus, in this sense, David MacDougall's argument about differences in images and written texts (1988: 257) may be countered by stressing the commonality and unity of the two narrative styles. In its most general sense, the 'Greetings from Lajosmizse' actually implies the reading 'I, or we, send our greetings from here to you who cannot be present, cannot be with us at the moment.' Through the past one-hundred years of postcard mediatisation of our lives, all such 'greetings from' formulae may be read into the picture even if the actual sentences are not present. Or vice versa, when the text is glaringly written on the postcard the picture itself may be relegated to an almost secondary status because it is the greeting – conveying the idea that the people involved actually think of each other sensing both a presence and absence – that matters the most. This way most postcards are about the commonality of experiences and the knowledge of being together.

Similar to individual reminiscences, postcards, too, are collective and institutional remembrances of times past. One of the most general types of postcard for a community incorporates the commemoration of its development and constant alterations taking place within its confines. Major buildings (post office, mayor's office or town hall, traders' and craftsmen's association, farmers' association, schools, railroad station, fire stations), and public spaces (main square, the local market) are standard tropes in postcards. Individuals associated with these selected civic, political, religious and economic institutions are often incorporated in the postcards as emblematic of the institutions and what they represent. This latter type of postcard seems more personalised yet ideologically the individual and the institutions do represent each another.

Figure 4.2 is a three-picture mosaic postcard from the turn of the nineteenth and twentieth centuries depicting the local flour mill, the Budai Mill, the house and store of the same family, and the restaurant of István Bende (1870–1957). These institutions created by the two prestigious families (Bende and Budai) were surely the most important economic and social centres in Lajosmizse during that time. When the postcard was reprinted in the Lajosmizse picture book (Kürti 2002b) most residents viewed it with awe and disbelief and immediately commented on what had and had not changed. The fact is, however, that neither the original mill nor the owner's house is standing any more, even though for many

Budai malom

Lajosmizse

Budai ház

Bende-vendéglo

Figure 4.2 Grid-like postcard of the Budai Mill and Budai Store, and the Bende Restaurant, c. 1910.

citizens the present mill still bears the original Budai name. The Bende restaurant had disappeared as well: the building today houses a general hardware store.

This three-picture, grid-like postcard, and the two family stories it entails, is very much part of the emergence of the local entrepreneurial spirit during the capitalist phase. It shows how a formerly agricultural settlement was able slowly to transform itself with the help of prestigious families. This postcard also includes the later histories of these families and their businesses as recalled by current residents. Both families suffered twice as the result of nationalisation: first in 1919 and then in 1948. Both were also centres of economic and community life: the Budai Mills provided jobs, flour and baked goods to denizens and generated electric power for the town; the Bende restaurant was a gathering place for the up-and-coming petite bourgeoisie.

A gaze at this postcard, and the sheer mention of the two families' names, immediately recreates for locals a complex web of stories and events in the past. Despite the fact that the house of the Budai family does not exist – it was taken down in the 1970s when a housing complex was built in its place – the current apartment building is continually referred to by the same name as the Budai house. Similarly, many locals jovially recall the numerous political rallies, civic association gatherings and dinner-dances that took place at Mr Bende's inn. When looking at the postcard older and middle-aged residents also recall that after the Stalinist takeover, Mr Bende was blacklisted as a bourgeois proprietor and was forced to take a menial job as a salesman: 'Until his retirement and in his own store', as many remark, with their fingers pointing. These hidden family stories, too, are what the postcard carries to residents who knew Mr Bende and who lived through these troubling times, and to younger generations who heard the stories from their parents. By refusing to relate to the building's current function as a hardware store locals view it as it really was in the past. Since the façade continues to reveal aspects of its earlier self the store is still referred to locally as the 'former Bende restaurant'. This way local memory rejects currency and favours historicity and in so doing assists in moulding a collective remembrance with visuality to counter forty years of Stalinist and state socialist past. In all this collective visual recollection vintage photographs and postcards serve to legitimate such locally grounded views of history.

As we can see from the postcard (Figure 4.2), in any community certain family businesses are elevated to prominence. In retrospect, there is no real explanation why some craftsmen, traders and sellers are included and others left out except local politics. A specific individualised postcard of a shopkeeper I wish to utilise here depicts József Popper, a proprietor of a prosperous but small family general store on the main street (Figure 4.3). There is no general 'greeting' formula any longer, but interestingly, and somewhat surprisingly, it introduces the new idea that the postcard is a 'fragment', 'detail', or 'part' (Részlet) from something much larger.

A visual excerpt per se, this kind of postcard presents a larger picture and actually serves as a detail suggesting a scene that could exist only in the memory

Figure 4.3 Fragment of the main street and general store of József Popper, 1920.

or in the historical imagination. Lefebvre has written that 'Images fragment, they are themselves fragments, cutting things up and rearranging them, decoupage and montage, the art of image-making' (1991: 97). Without question we must accept that since the photographic image is mostly a fragmented composition, either conscious or subconscious, we need to pay more attention to it, especially when the artist–commissioner ostensibly points to such framing. Such postcards contain additional information: they carry small but important aspects of the larger picture, the important 'contents outside the frame, to history or memory or cultural experience' (Edwards 1997: 67). They provide a glimpse of main streets that once were which cannot be seen in their totality but could be imagined as they once really were through fragments. With several similar 'fragmented' or 'excerpted' postcards one could create the illusion of walking down any main street and meeting the proud shopkeepers and owners standing in the door-ways: the butcher, cooper, barber, wheelwright, innkeeper, blacksmith and the many shopkeepers and traders all appear in front of our very eyes simply asking for recognition as industrious merchants and craftsmen of their community. We may view them as they were and as they wished to represent themselves visually: as members of their families, as progressing through life stages, and even as having other interests besides their work.

The postcard in Figure 4.3 shows exactly this idea with a depiction of a general store on the main street with the proud owner, József Popper (1871–1944) standing in the doorway. It took some research, however, to be able to read the

Popper Store on the main street as a genuine narrative compressed in a postcard image. The shopkeeper was born in Monor and opened his store in Lajosmizse in 1893. In fact his shop was one of the first general stores in the community whose proprietor was also Jewish. This postcard is the only available testimony that presently is available in our archives (HCA) that preserves the memory of local Jewish shopkeepers in their shops. In addition to his religious background, he was a World War I veteran and active in the local civic and religious (Catholic!) association for which he received a medal of honour. Like many of his fellow countrymen he, too, believed in the nationalistic ideology of the Austro-Hungarian monarchy, an ideology that is well represented in postcards of the time. Despite all his efforts to be a member of the conservative local establishment he was taken together with his relatives to Auschwitz where they all perished. But this is not the end of the narrative that locals are able to recount when viewing this old postcard. Immediately the family relations are envisioned; for instance the fate of the son, István Popper (1906–45), who perished together with other Jewish men somewhere in western Hungary during forced military labour (*munkaszolgálat*). In addition to his tragic fate, locals also recall that his wife, a Roman Catholic by birth, and small daughter managed to survive the war in Lajosmizse. All this family tragedy is thus engraved into this postcard both as history and collective memory. To those not familiar with this tragic family narrative this postcard represents a section of the main street, 'only' a fragmented almost idyllic compression with a store owner standing in the doorway. Yet texts and images on postcards, as Sidney Kasfir argues cogently when discussing postcards of the Samburu, 'exist as fragments of something else – they are metonymic references to a larger cultural experience that is being remembered and objectified' (1997: 68). Incidentally, viewing this postcard, locals speak of a complex web of politics and social relations in history that are implicitly embedded in the postcard.

As seen from the implied narratives in the previous postcards, major political and military events always influence the way in which local postcard production progresses. The World War I postcards produced between 1914 and 1918 are the most numerous, and stereotypical themes of individual and family portraits were produced both to commemorate the farewell, the family remaining at home, and the possible celebratory event of homecoming. Special among these postcards are soldiers in military hospitals surrounded by wounded fellows and even nurses, a category of war postcards on which women appear as professionals and not as family members. A few postcards depict military cemeteries reminding both civilians and soldiers alike of the reality of war.

Interesting are the propaganda postcards and the somewhat idiosyncratic cards produced by the soldiers themselves in the frontline actually in the trenches. The propaganda postcards ostensibly identify themes promulgated by the state (governments) and bureaucratic organisations to offer shorthand visual justification for the regime's involvement in the war. These range from boasting military victory over the hated and despised enemy, to the military and technological might, victorious battles and outstanding war leaders and officers. A few even strengthen loyalty to and legitimacy for the house of the Habsburgs by framing images more in line with the immediate concerns of the soldiers themselves. These more personalised propaganda postcards were clearly commissioned to boost morale and fighting spirits among soldiers. These all had a sentence printed on them, such as 'Welcome home' or 'Waiting for you' depicting a soldier (often wounded) returning to his wife and children.

Unique among the wartime postcards are those that soldiers created themselves and sent from the frontline to their loved ones at home. These postcards are by no means without irony, and funny moments creating touching visual testimonies of emotions, humanness and survival against all odds. Such postcards and photographs, in general give us 'the illusion that we know everything while failing to dispel the feeling that we are helpless to do anything about what we know' (Augé 1999: 66). In opposition to state propaganda postcards, many of these more individualised postcards were produced by the soldiers who, consciously or not, wanted to create funny and humorous set-ups.[19] Countering the devastations of the war and in order to lessen the closeness of death, they purposefully depicted playful and often questionable themes and scenery. The officers' ward, the cantina, the platoon leadership, the camaraderie of the soldiers and the officers, the individualised war technology (my bunker, my machine gun, my platoon and my cannon) are but a few samples of the vast range of postcards sent home from World War I. The postcard in Figure 4.4 was sent in the fall 1916 from the Polish–Russian frontline by a corporal (standing).[20] Irony and humour, as well as utter surprise, is what this postcard creates in the viewer for its theme is not one would associate with the Galician frontline. Depicting a group of soldiers smilingly enjoying a card game and reading a newspaper in an orchard is a scene not much to do with war or death except what the uniforms and the written text reinforce.[21]

It is difficult to gauge whether, and to what extent, soldiers managed to create such an ironic and wholly unmilitary moment during trench warfare or whether such framing was quite stereotypical elsewhere as well. As Paul Fussell remarks with reference to irony and memory: 'By applying to the past a paradigm of ironic action, a rememberer is enabled to locate, draw forth, and finally shape into significance an event or a moment which otherwise would merge without meaning into the general undifferentiated stream' (1977: 30). 'Irony-assisted recall', as Fussell refers to this memory-enhancing device, is what these postcards of old events are all about. Like most artistic products of the war, including all aspects of popular culture (songs, pictures, films, rumours, stories), these images were creating visual examples to make sense of the senselessness, to bridge the gap between what was possible and what seemed impossible but still occurred, and to console those who were there as well as those who saw war from far away. This way irony in postcards serves to locate the image out of history, at least out of a hopeless historical experience. Such postcards may assist thoughts that the war is not really a war any more, and being far away from

Figure 4.4 Soldiers play cards and read newspapers in World War I, 1916. Volhynia, Galician–Russian frontline, 10 September 1916. The handwritten caption reads, 'I marked myself so you can recognise me. Remember me. From Wolhynia by Sándor Gorócz.'

home may be considered less remote through the more familiarised experience. It may also be possible that these privately produced eccentric images had not so much to do with what Hüppauf (1995: 108) calls the 'disintegration of the culturally conditioned self' the soldiers experienced in the trenches but exactly the opposite: the need for the reintegration of that self with life and humanity as well as the wish to survive.

But postcards may also be a vehicle to utilise photographs ingeniously to break up the monolithic view of the past by implying a more dynamic vision of the present. To achieve this, local history and architecture are juxtaposed to show the contemporaneousness of past events. Buildings, stores and public space are seen as depositories of the ancestral actions and traditions. In the Lajosmizse postcards these diverse images of previous actions and events coalesce to from integral wholes. It is true that most postcards from the interwar period reveal a Lajosmizse that is nationalistic and conservatively Catholic. The importance of rightist and Catholic zealotry is readily evident in a postcard produced in the early 1930s (Figure 4.5). This is the typical five-shot, grid-like postcard discussed above with the school in the middle, the railroad station on the bottom, and the local traders' and craftsmen's association building (built in 1928). The framing is important for the grid is closed on both sides by the Roman Catholic Church (built in 1896), and the soldiers' monument. This latter monument

Figure 4.5 A grid-like, five-picture postcard showing the local grade school, railroad station, Catholic church, the craftsmen's association building (top middle) and the heroes' statuette, *c.* 1930s.

has been centrally located in the main square, once also the area for the weekly market. It was not only a World War I monument, but a commemorative statue for the extreme irredentist claim promoted by the Horthy government to reconquer territories lost after the War. The statue was made more symbolic by the national flag (*Országzászló*) and the *turul* (a mythical falcon or eagle of Hungarian prehistory).

The significance of this statue is not only what it stood for but, in the minds of many, what kinds of conflicts and problems it represented throughout its troubled history. Looking at the postcard elderly citizens constantly recall the many state celebrations that were held in front of the statue, rituals that often involved the raising of the national flag and singing the anthem. In fact, being the most orderly and flowery part of the central square, many married couples and young people had their pictures taken in front of this statue. The whole surrounding as well as the postcard has been continually referred to as simply the '*turul* space'. Thus, the *turul* picture represents a particular style and moment during the inter-war period in Lajosmizse and recreates fond moments for many. Moreover, citizens continue to argue what really happened to their eagle monument, whether it was really blown up by soldiers of the victorious Red Army, or as some still claim, some daring youth took it down and hid it somewhere. Locals continue to call the area simply the 'place of the national eagle monument'. The presence of the statue has been so deeply ingrained in them that after 1990 a new national eagle monument was erected. These stories form integral parts of the local political folklore and are recalled whenever and wherever postcards surface with the original eagle monument on them.

Postcard production in Lajosmizse immediately changed with the sudden political and economic transformation of the society and country in general after 1947. Looking at a whole series of post-World War II postcards we may easily observe a dynamic local history in line with the changing tapestry of the national political landscape. After 1948, when Stalinism was established throughout Hungary postcards were also the means to promote state interests and Stalinist doctrine, an ideology that after 1963 slowly turned into what was known generally as 'goulash' or 'window socialism'. How does this tremendous political economic tremor make it into the visual narratives on postcards? One immediate sign was the replacement of the national eagle monument with a monumental red star so all the political rallies now could be held in a politically correct space. In tandem with this ideological gambit, the formerly so powerful Catholic Church associated with the rightist ideology began to occupy less prominence. Figure 4.6 is an apt illustration of this political transformation. The postcard is still divided equally into a four-picture mosaic: the old school is still

Üdvözlet Lajosmizséről

Figure 4.6 The dawning of state socialism as reflected in this four-picture, grid-like postcard depicting the local farmers' co-operative (lower left), headquarters of the Workers' Party (lower right, the same as the craftsmen's association building on top middle, Figure 4.5), the grade school (top left), and the co-operative's milk storage facility, c. 1949.

present, the lower left is the Farmers' Co-operative building, the upper right shows its milk collecting facility, and the lower right is the headquarters of the Hungarian Workers' Party. This latter also appears in the previous postcard but still as the craftsmen' association building that was nationalised in 1948 and then turned over to the communist party, the MDP (*Magyar Dolgozók Pártja*, Hungarian Workers' Party). The histories of these buildings, their erection, use and subsequent function, as well as the social and political conflicts they generated, are what locals see in, in fact read into, these postcards.

This postcard reveals the way in which leaders wanted to break with the past by carefully rearranging the grid-like framing. Instead of using straight vertical and horizontal lines the frames for each picture are tilted. The key point here is not whether postcards are authentic representations of social reality; they certainly can be at crucial moments but, contrarily they may also be extreme forms of virtual inauthentications of the world. The real issue is that postcards, similar to other forms of popular media (books, magazines, television, and films), are also part of the social world that produces them and as a natural outcome are influenced by the debates, conflicts and negotiations that characterise local existence in general. What makes postcards of this kind especially suitable for analysis is the fact that they were purposefully produced by elites to publicise and highlight progress and success. There are other socialist postcards of major construction works, nationalised peasant co-operatives, new school buildings occupied by joyful pioneers, and state leaders visiting newly opened factories. With such themes postcards are visual testimonies that the community's way of life is in line with the prescribed mainstream for the country as a whole. I see this as a significant departure because these kinds of postcards, and even the very first ones (such as the one with the Budai Mill and the Bende Restaurant) are similarly fine examples, are wholly antithetical to those produced largely by the tourist industry for non-local consumers. Adventurers seek sights and events they hold to be part of the 'traditional' and 'authentic' local flavour and gather souvenirs, embroidery, pottery, photos and postcards that coherently capture their expectations and serve as metonymic devices for later nostalgia. Hazel Tucker rightly suggests with reference to Turkish living-museum tourism but which also has a relevance to what I am discussing here, that 'tourists seek to photograph the "authentic", and preferably no signs of modernity should be present' (1997: 119). The local postcards of Lajosmizse introduced here, and I am afraid there are also many of this kind elsewhere, reveal exactly the opposite: a proud declaration that things have changed. The underlying message is that this is the natural as well as the expected way. With this in mind, we can grasp not only why buildings were revamped and new ones built according to socialist realism – or how postcard collections of industrial towns such as Kőbánya (Ungváry 2002) and Salgótarján (Szvircsek 2002) discussed above function – but also how they may symbolise signs of economic progress and political development.[22]

Postcard production in Lajosmizse did not stop with the end of socialism but, on the contrary, it multiplied manifold after 1990. In line with the total make-over of politics, democratisation of political life and reprivatisation of the economy, local elites have been feverishly engaged in revitalising and reinvigorating their town's political culture, landscape and iconography. Most communist street names have disappeared, new statues and buildings were commissioned and the main square also received a face lift. Dozens of postcards were produced between 1990 and 2002 documenting these alterations faithfully. In many ways, however, especially in their forms and contents, the new, 'democratic' postcards are reproductions of earlier ideas mentioned above: new buildings constructed, redesigned public spaces, and religious (Christian) monuments erected.

The Historical and Cultural Association (HCA) assisted in the recreation of this new profile and there were two reasons for this. First, to provide funds for the association and the second, more exciting, had to do with the expectation of members that the new postcards should be different from what 'outsiders' produced earlier on a commission basis. Certainly at the begining traditional postcard stereotypes were utilised, but with a twist: old public buildings and some of their newer versions were shown together. The non-communist identity was significant and this was provided by the town's coat of arms that was placed on most of the new postcards. In addition, the name of our community as well as the date of production had to be printed on each postcard. Several new private buildings were also included on the postcards prompting some to argue that instead of depicting the usual church/school/recreational centre/fire station, the postcard should show actual examples of how successfully people live and love their history. The postcard in Figure 4.7 depicts exactly this wish by vertical divisions into three equal frames projecting three inter-related concerns: on the left we see the medieval ruin of the former Cumanian village, the renewed eagle monument in the central square, and on the right, a wooden sculpture representing a herdsman. This last picture also combines not only the former pastoral nomads who settled this area in the thirteenth century, but more importantly the currently so fashionable village tourism. In a sense there is an implicit understanding that by redoing earlier stereotypical images a more faithful and tangible medium has been created for those travelling to our settlement.

Other ideas that members of the HCA included were the roadside crosses symbolising the overwhelming Catholic heritage of the town; places featuring the currently fashionable farm tourism; and the attempt to utilise some vintage photographs as postcards. While these may be not wholly novel departures in postcard production elsewhere, for the citizens of Lajosmizse this was a beginning. Most people involved in the production process believed that the actual examples for the imaginary 'picturesque past' (Willis 1995: 78) would be brought to the present and, vice versa, they will inarguably depict how the present can and should build on past experiences and achievements. I admit that several disturbing and probing questions remain: did we construct a hyper-real space of history in real space and time for others to see, touch and experience? Put

Figure 4.7 One of the new postcards produced by the Historical and Cultural Association, 2001.

in another way: have we manipulated customers and viewers to join us in this heterotropia? Would these be considered native photographic exercises, or applied anthropology par excellence? Or, did we attempt to project ourselves into a fake historical identity? Some individual members of the local town council raised serious objections about the way in which the new postcards included too much and in some instances too little. What they referred to is the fact that the postcards did not have the usual four or five shots in a grid-like fashion. In one postcard, for instance, we had only three pictures divided equally in a vertical grid. Several postcards also featured a fifteenth-century ruin just outside the town. For some strange reason, this ruin of the first Cumanian settlers never found its way to previous postcards. As some critics claimed the ruin was not a perfect picture for inclusion in a postcard. Therefore the decision was taken to try to photograph the ruin to make it more acceptable, to make it more 'picture perfect'. With all new postcards the decision was also taken to print the name of the town together with the town's coat-of-arms, information wholly missing on earlier postcards.[23] Interestingly, other critics claim that the new postcards, while different from the earlier ones and quite colourful, do not include some of the best images known widely on earlier postcards. Clearly, these previous images were so deeply ingrained in the popular mentality that critics immediately reacted to their absence. Their basic argument was that images that worked so well in the past – and thus outsiders immediately recognised the community via these few shots – should not be relegated to the archives but reused whenever possible. Old myths die hard, but old postcards have their afterlife too.

Conclusions: postcard images

One important consideration I would like to stress is that when viewed in chronological detail there is an instant realisation of difference, alterity and often contradictoriness in the vernacular photographic tradition. Far from being simply examples of 'western photography', these depictions highlight the visionary qualities of a fragmented ideology within a community itself far from homogeneous and united.[24] These postcards of a single settlement chronicle the diverse practices, cultural and political commitments that have generalised the past century. They reveal that the visual representation of a community is always suspect to being a momentary snap-shot-like description manipulated both by the makers and the users. Postcards, no matter how innocent they may seem at first, are never without questionable political sides as they are often produced to project an image that is the dominant view of a few individuals: like a stolen sequence from a moving image frozen at an arbitrary moment in time. In this sense there is not much difference between the photograph and the motion picture – especially when it is slowed down or viewed separately frame by frame in a repeated successive fashion as we are allowed to do with the new technologies, especially the computerised programmes and DVDs. This is what, for example, Maltby and Bowles suggest with regard to movies but which also reinforces the point I am attempting to stress here: 'movies . . . operate like postcards to furnish us with a selective and distorted sense of having seen the view for ourselves' (1994: 99). Recent email-attached digital postcards feature moving images and have sounds, and distortions may appear within and without the image itself.

This analysis of Lajosmizse postcards stresses the idea that postcards in general repeat earlier visual experiences by creating a possible with future experiences. Viewed chronologically from the beginning – first postcards of the main street, the school, churches or the town hall of a newly incorporated settlement – we realise that representations are slowly transformed as some buildings receive a facelift and some even disappear, altering the local landscape altogether. A series of postcards of the same structures reveals not only the changing time and landscape but what certain type of films project: a feeling of the ephemeral nature of reality and knowledge. That postcards function as snapshots or as visual examples of a fragmented reality is witnessed by those that actually specify that they are 'fragments' or 'excerpts' of something much larger. These broken and carefully cut-away images create reference points for main streets, stores, buildings and community expressions that are inchoate but nevertheless a unique frame-by-frame view similar to a slow-motion film.

Such postcards, embedded in time and locality, could be viewed as fragments of and for the irony-assistance connectedness to the reality/fiction boundary Fussell has suggested. They are fascinating miniatures of historical frames that hide more than they reveal. The gaze is directed towards these hidden aspects, the contents outside the frame. Indeed this is what the viewer as well as the researcher needs to elicit through careful observation and analysis: the hidden fragments and ironic sense of reality that postcards mask. A shopkeeper standing in his store's doorway, with 'fragment' written on it, warns us to be extremely careful for something much larger, a more complex history is buried deep and lurking there. Without other postcards from the same street we would not understand what the 'fragment' stands for and what historical time/space that fragment is referring to. Without details of the shopkeeper's life and his family ethnography, we would not possess what took place before or after the photograph was taken: that the shopkeeper was a distinguished citizen of many faces, a World War I veteran who happened to be Jewish, and that he met his death in the gas chambers in Auschwitz. To be sure, this is implied history but through the postcards we can extend our research into local history anew. Without the postcards and the many thousand vintage photos in the Digital Photo Archives most of the implied history would have remained muted forever.

Vintage local postcards assist us to understand how their narratives are different from those of the tourist industry discussed by Elizabeth Edwards. She argues that postcards 'fulfil Baudrillard's concept of "simulation" which threatens the difference between true and false in that they mask the absence of a basic reality; that is, in the tourist fantasy of unchanging "other worlds" of "primitive" society that stands diametrically opposed to the modern world' (1997: 61). Postcards do possess an amazing resilience and time flexibility especially nowadays in the digital globalised world as they are sent increasingly as attachment to emails. Old photos are scanned into the computer and with various software they may reappear completely anew with different form and context. With digital cameras pictures are now immediately transferred into computers and may be edited at will or used as electric (email) postcards for diverse purposes. However, this new digital postcard production is not exactly what the pre-digital postcards were all about. As I started out my chapter I mused that postcards are never really what they seem to be at first, now I am much more convinced that to view postcards is never a simple task. It is not a job without its dangers and pitfalls. Yet, and this is what I would like to reiterate, despite their seemingly primary visual forms, analyses of postcards do not support the disciplinary and theoretical separation between the written and the visual, the moving and the more stationary images. To make sense of them analyses of both images and texts, whether traditional or more current, need to be seen in relation to one another. They are both anchored to local cultural practices that are themselves fragments of globally meaningful human concerns and history.

Notes

1 Even though Grimshaw investigates the notion 'vision' she only discusses ethnographic films (2001).

2 I want to stress here, however, that postcards have rarely been used as a unit of analysis *per se*. Some, for instance, argue for the convergence of photography and postcard: 'The point is that a postcard is the means of transmission of a commercially produced and thus commercially targeted form of travel photography' (Edwards 1997: 77). I, however, want to argue here that postcards are a very special form of non-commercial photography that may or may not have something to do with travel photography.

3 I do not want to discuss here the specifics concerning the tourist industry that have been dealt with elsewhere recently (Abram, Waldren and Macleod, 1997, Boissevain 1996, Phillips and Steiner 1999).

4 The pioneering use of postcard photography, however, was connected to the World's Columbian Exposition in 1893 in Chicago (Brown, 1994).

5 Take for example the various uses and analyses of photographs by Bateson and Mead and their *Balinese Character* published in 1942 where image and text is separated; Goffman's 'Gender display', published in 1976; Stanley Brandes' study of the uses of photographs in Spain – but which is also emblematic in other anthropological works in which the real identities of places and informants are masked (Brandes 1997); or the way the anthropologists Lutz and Collins (1993) deal with the largely exploitative use of photographs in *National Geographic* magazine.

6 It was the Viennese Emmanual Herrman who argued that people in general tend to write briefly and on rather banal subjects in a matter of fact voice which would not in any case in fringe upon individual rights of secrecy. His argument was heard and the state decided to allow these open letters to be sent via the post office. Before this historic argument letters had to be closed and in many cases sealed.

7 Because of their sheer number, the World War I military postcards are a fascinating category needing a special treatment on its own. Aside from the plain postcard with a photograph, there are those that are miniatures of paintings and drawings, as well as those that were executed by the soldiers themselves. This latter category is perhaps the most interesting: the postcard is manufactured out of hard paper on which several small photographs were placed, often those that were made by the senders themselves. Naturally, all postcards sent from the frontlines had to pass military censorship. For a treatment on war photography, but not postcards, see Hüpauff (1995).

8 In order to counter this numerical dominance somewhat, we decided to play a small trick: one postcard was created by placing miniature (circa stamp-size) versions of all the other postcards we produced. This way one postcard is composed of twenty small postcards; in a way, a postcard representing postcards and vice versa.

9 In my book on Hungarian youth culture, *Youth and the state in Hungary*, I have printed a postcard from the workers' district of Budapest, Csepel (2002a: 197). This postcard amply illustrates the interconnectedness of postcard images and politics of the time. The district, well-known for its 'red' epithet during the twentieth century, represents itself as a stronghold of radical and communist working-class movement: the five-image mosaic type of postcard depicts one religious statue, one statue of Lenin, and three state socialist buildings constructed in the drab socialist realist style.

10 There are a host of Hungarian settlements which have utilised old postcards to reinvent their lost, earlier selves. Among them are: Mezőtúr, Kiskunhalas, Pécs, Sopron, Szombathely, Nagykáta, Pannonhalma, Baja, Karcag, Szeged, Siófok, Dunaújváros, Székesfehérvár, Kisújszállás, and Győr. The two books on Kőbánya (Ungváry 2002) and Salgótarján (Szvircsek 2002) are especially unique because both are highly industrialised centres and far from 'picture perfect'. The photographic history of Kecskemét (Székelyné 1998) is also alone in attempting to capitalise on the histories of nearby settlements instead of solely that of the town.

11 To be fair, I must mention that in the collection of Lajosmizse (Kürti 2002b) there is no picture of either the Jewish synagogue or the local rabbi, Mór Löwy. Despite the four years of intense search and the more than 10,000 photographs in the local history's archive not a single picture of either the building or the rabbi – who was for more than forty years the small Jewish community's religious leader – has turned up.

12 A few isolated studies have come to light: see e.g. Berta (2002) on the history of photographers in the town of Szolnok.

13 In contrast to these I only call attention to the photography of Kálmán Kata (1937) as a unique attempt to capture the poor with extreme close-ups of her subjects. Her photographic journey is also unique among Hungarian photographers because twenty years later she revisited her informants and models and took their pictures again (see, Kálmán 1955).

14 I have detailed this in my autobiographical ethnography see Kürti (2000).

15 The Lajosmizse Historical and Cultural Association (*Lajosmizsei Helytörténeti és Kulturális Egyesület*) was an institution that I helped to bring to fruition in 1999 with the idea that no such organisation existed and that previous such attempts by locals failed. The association was then legally registered in 2000. It follows the general legal requirements: a small initial fund, at least ten members, few officials, and a legal document describing its activities. The number of such civic legal organisations in Hungary is staggering. Many, however, are inactive as they only exist on paper. What makes the Lajosmizse a viable venture is its stubbornness in proving that this town of 11,000 residents has a much longer history than was previously projected. More on this history and my involvement with and return to the town see Kürti (2002b, 2000).

16 The reason for this hesitancy concerning the exact number of postcards has to do with definition. If there is a photograph portraying a family of six sent to a relative away from home would that be considered a postcard proper? If yes, then the actual number of postcards may well be in the hundreds. For the sake of simplicity, I have decided to use only those 'postcards' that were considered postcard by the family in question and whether they printed more than just a single copy sending them to different places and people. At least on one occasion we could ascertain that the young soldier ordered more than a dozen pictures of himself and actually sent them home to family members and relatives as well as friends.

17 One particular group of photographs, those produced by itinerant cameramen, could not be utilised as postcards. The reason for this had to do with the technology. Almost without a single exception these photographs were printed on a paper labelled Visit Portrait. Since these photographers worked in a makeshift travelling studio they did not use the best and the highest quality papers often photographing their subjects during market or fairs and giving them the final product within a few hours or a day the most.

18 Both forms of harvest were community-centred family occasions until the 1950s when land collectivisation took place forcing all producers to join state farms with their land, animals and equipment. These work-bees were special events that were recorded by the camera. In the Lajosmizse DPA, there are numerous photographs taken between 1900 and 1955 of grape and wheat harvesting. Analysing them needs a separate study on its own. For some of these pictures see Kürti (2002b).

19 One category of World War I propaganda postcards not directly of the Kriegs Karte type were produced by the weekly, *Érdekes Újság* (The Interesting Journal). This series was based on a photography competition in which soldiers were requested to send in their own amateur shots from which the journal editors selected the best ones for postcards. The winners received cash prizes.

20 These postcards were sent by Sándor Gorócz to his fiancée in Lajosmizse. He survived the ravages of war and eventually married her, see Kürti (2002b).

21 On the back of the postcard the text reads: 'My dear Theresa, I am sending you this latest postcard picture. What do you say? I ended up with a real gambling company, didn't I? But since I am not one of the gamblers you can forgive me, right? Greetings, GS.' The voice and the abbreviations, as well as the reference to the 'latest picture' suggest that these kinds of humorous postcards, with question-and-answer texts, were quite common. Four postcards, all written in 1916, are in the possession of the Lajosmizse Historical Archive.

22 One of the truly funny examples is the postcards that have, in addition to texts and images, maps drawn on them in order to give a sense that this community really exists and may be found easily by following the map.

23 In addition, all new postcards produced had to have on the back the name of the association and a date they were printed. Anyone collecting and attempting to analyse old postcards will encounter the problem that most of them never mention who produced them and when.

24 Most authors on photography continue to stress the westernness and eurocentricity of photographic practice (cf. for example, Pinney and Peterson, 2003) but there is only a cursory discussion of what these terms actually entail and very little mention of those photographs that subvert these ideological categories.

References

Abram, S., Waldren, J. and Macleod D. V. L. (eds) (1997) *Tourists and Tourism: Identifying with People and Places*, Oxford and New York: Berg.

Augé, M. (1999) *An Anthropology for Contemporaneous Worlds*, trans. A. Jacobs, Stanford: Stanford University Press.

Bateson, G. and Mead, M. (1942) *Balinese Character: A Photographic Analysis*, New York: NY Academy of Sciences, Special pubs. no. 2.

Berta, F. (2002). *A fényképészipar 150 éve Szolnokon* (A 150 years history of photography in Szolnok), Szolnok: Jász-Nagykun Szolnok Megyei Múzeum.

Boissevain, J. (ed.) (1996) *Coping with Tourists: European Reactions to Mass Tourism*, Providence and Oxford: Berghahn.

Bourdieu, P. (1990) *Photography: A Middle-Brow Art*, Stanford: Stanford University Press.

Brandes, S. (1997) 'Photographic imagery in Spanish ethnography', *Visual Anthropology Review* 13(1): 1–13.

Brown, J. K. (1994) *Contesting Images: Photography and the World's Columbian Exposition*, Tucson: The University of Arizona Press.

Edwards, E. (1996) 'Postcards – greetings from another world', in T. Selwyn (ed.), *The Tourist Image*, London: John Wiley.

—— (1997) 'Beyond the boundary: a consideration of the expressive in photography and anthropology', in M. Banks and H. Morphy (eds), *Rethinking Visual Anthropology*, New Haven: Yale University Press.

—— (2001) *Raw histories: Photographs, Anthropology and Museums*, London: Berg.

Edwards, E. (ed.) (1992) *Anthropology and Photography, 1860–1920*, New Haven: Yale University Press.

Fehér, Z. (2002) *Fekete faluban fehér torony látszik. Bátyai képeskönyv* (Black village, white tower. Pictures of Bátya), Bátya: Községi Önkormányzat.

Foucault, M. (1986) 'Of other spaces', *Diacritics* (Spring): 22–7.

Fussell, P. (1977) *The Great War and Modern Memory*, Oxford: Oxford University Press.

Galsi, Z. (2001) *Törökszentmiklósi képes lapok* (Photographs of the old Törökszentmiklós), Törökszentmiklós: Magyar Millennium.

Goffman, E. (1976) 'Gender display', *Studies in the Anthropology of Visual Communication* 3(2): 69–154.

Greary, C. and Webb, V-L. (eds) (1998) *Delivering Views: Distant cultures in early postcards*, Washington DC: Smithsonian Institution Press.

Grimshaw, A. (2001) *The Ethnographer's Eye: Ways of Seeing in Modern Anthropology*, Cambridge: Cambridge University Press.

Hüppauf, B. (1995). 'The photographic representation of war', in L. Devereaux and R. Hillman (eds), *Fields of Vision: Essays in Film Studies, Visual Anthropology and Photography* (Berkeley: University of California Press), 94–126.

Kahn, M. (2000) 'Tahiti intertwined: Ancestral land, tourist postcard, and nuclear test site', *American Anthropologist* 102(1): 7–26.

Kálmán, K. (1937). *Tiborc*. Bevezető: Móricz Zsigmond és Boldizsár Iván. Budapest: Cserépfalvi.

—— (1955) *Tiborc új arca*. Móricz Zsigmond, Móricz Virág és Boldizsár Iván írásai. Budapest: Művelt Nép.

Kasfir, S. L. (1999) 'Samburu souvenirs: Representations of a land in amber', in R. B. Phillips and C. B. Steiner (eds), *Unpacking Culture: Art and Commodity in Colonial and Postcolonial Worlds*, Berkeley: University of California Press, 67–86.

Kürti, L. (2002a) *Youth and the State in Hungary: Capitalism, Communism and Class*, London: Pluto.

—— (2002b) *Történelem és emlékezet. Lajosmizse fényképek, 1896–1946* (History and memory. Photographs of Lajosmizse, 1896–1946), Lajosmizse: Helytörténeti és Kulturális Egyesület.

—— (2000) 'The socialist circus: secrets, lies, and autobiographical family narratives', in R. Breckner, D. Kalekin-Fishman and I. Miethe (eds), *Biographies and the Division of Europe: Experience, Action, and Change on the 'Eastern Side'*, Opladen: Leske – Budrich, 283–302.

—— (1999) 'Cameras and other gadgets: reflections on fieldwork experiences in socialist and post-socialist Hungarian communities', *Social Anthropology* 7(2): 169–87.

—— (1998) 'A halál és a fotográfus' (Death and the photographer), *Néprajzi Értesítő* 79: 167–85.

—— (1996) 'Homecoming: affairs of anthropologists in and of Eastern Europe', *Anthropology Today* 12(3): 11–15.

Lefebvre, H. (1991) *The Production of Space*, Oxford: Blackwell.

Lutz, C. and Collins, J. (1993) *Reading National Geographic*, Chicago: University of Chicago Press.

Lübbren, N. and Crouch, D. (eds) (2002) *Visual Culture and Tourism*, London: Berg.

MacDougall, D. (1998) *Transcultural Cinema*, Princeton: Princeton University Press.

Maltby, R. and Bowles, K. (1994) 'Hollywood: the economics of utopia', in J. Mitchell and R. Maidment (eds), *The United States in the Twentieth Century: Culture*, London: Hodder and Stoughton.

Phillips, R. B. and Steiner, C. B. (eds) (1999) *Unpacking Culture: Art and Commodity in Colonial and Postcolonial Worlds*, Berkeley: University of California Press.

Pink, S. (2001) *Doing Visual Ethnography: Images, Media and Representation in Research*, London: Sage.

Pinney, C. and Peterson, N. (eds) (2003). *Photography's Other Histories*, Durham, NC: Duke University Press.

Romsics, I. (1999) *Kalocsa anno: Kalocsai fotográfiák* (Kalocsa photographs), Kalocsa: Múzeumbarátok Köre.

Schor, N. (1992) 'Cartes Postales: Representing Paris 1900', *Critical Inquiry* 18: 188–245.

Staff, F. (1966) *The Picture Postcard and its Origins*, New York: Praeger.

Street, B. (1992) 'British popular anthropology: Exhibiting and photographing the other', in E. Edwards (ed.), *Anthropology and Photography, 1860–1920*, New Haven and London: Yale University Press and The Royal Anthropological Institute.

Szakál, A. (2000) *Üdvözlet Kiskunhalasról. Kiskunhalasi képeslapok, 1898–2000* (Greetings from Kiskunhalas. Old postcards from Kiskunhalas, 1898–2000). Kiskunhalas: Thorma János Múzeum.

Székelyné Kőrösi, I. (1998) *Kecskemét Anno: Képek a régi Kecskemétről* (Kecskemét as it used to be). Kecskemét: Katona József Múzeum.

Szvircsek, F. (2002) *Salgótarjáni képeskönyv. Salgótarján régi képeslapokon* (A picture book of Salgótarján. The city on old postcards). Salgótarján: Nógrádi Múzeum Történeti Baráti Kör.

Tucker, H. (1997) 'The ideal village: interactions through tourism in Central Anatolia', in S. Abram, J. Waldren, and D. V. L. Macleod (eds), *Tourists and tourism*, Oxford and New York: Berg, 107–28.

Ungváry, J. (2002) *Üdvözlet Kőbányáról. Régi kőbányai képeslapok* (Greetings from Kőbánya – Old Kőbánya postcards). Budapest: Vexillum Kiadó.

Willis, A. (1995) 'Photography and film: figures in/of history', in L. Devereaux and R. Hillman (eds), *Fields of Vision: Essays in Film Studies, Visual Anthropology, and Photography*, Berkeley: University of California Press, 77–93.

Chapter 5

New graphics for old stories

Representation of local memories through drawings

Ana Isabel Afonso
Illustrations Manuel João Ramos

Words and drawings

This paper reflects on the possibilities of articulating drawing with text, as an expressive joint form of representation in anthropology – a topic that has been viewed unevenly by different national anthropological traditions.

There is a long-term tradition of anthropologists working with artists to produce museum displays, as emphasised by (amongst others) Bouquet (2001) and Price (1989). However empirical case-studies that directly address the possibilities of using drawings in anthropological research are rare, both in regard to the nature of drawings themselves (i.e. as acts and products), and in the way they may be combined with text. Rather, recent publications under the general theme of visual anthropology (Grimshaw 2001; Ruby 2000; El Guindi 1998; Banks and Morphy 1997) have been largely concentrated either on film or on photography, as privileged forms of visual representation.

Nevertheless, some exceptions to this trend can be found, which, albeit scarce, represent the potential of the use of drawings and paintings to elicit and analyse anthropological data. A good example is the work of Hildred Geertz (1994) based on the Balinese paintings and sketches that Mead and Bateson intuitively requested and collected from local peasants during their stay in Bali (1936–8). It is interesting to note that although this was intended as a study of the painters of one of the villages where Mead and Bateson conducted fieldwork, during the process of acquiring the pictures important data on local life and culture was also produced:

> Bateson and a Balinese assistant, I Madé Kalér, made over two hundred pages of notes on the pictures bought, recording each painter's comments and stories in his own words. In addition, Mead and Bateson designed a lengthy questionnaire that was used by Kalér to interview twenty-three of the main artists. They asked about their economic life, education, experience with foreigners, how they learned to make pictures, and how they usually marketed them.
>
> (Geertz 1994: 121)

More recent anthropological studies by Prinz (2001) and Stewart (1990) show a similar attraction for native drawings, namely children's drawings, collected or analysed in the course of fieldwork to supplement verbal information on different cultural domains. In other cases, drawings have been commissioned from reputed artists and used in educational projects for their aesthetic appeal in combination with texts, in order to communicate a message – for example in a campaign against hunger, promoted by the *Comité français pour la solidarité internationale* (Cothias *et al.* 2000). There are also exceptional situations where the anthropologist is especially talented and combines his artistic skills with ethnographic writing. For example, in his work on New Guinea, Nicolas Garnier (2000) adopts a travel diary style, vividly supported with his watercolours and ink-pen drawings. Stanford Carpenter's cartoon strips on Africa and Deena Newman's (1998) attempt to present the central part of her article on 'Ethnographic Rumors in Addis Ababa' in the peculiar form of a story conveyed through sequences of images and words, are further examples of this innovative medium of anthropological expression.

Another illuminating approach to the use of paintings and drawings in anthropological research was the retrospective exhibition (1975–2001) held at the Völkerkunde Museum of Zurich about the work of the Australian artist and architect Robert Powell, who lived and worked in the Himalayas for many years. The edited catalogue – *Robert Powell Himalayan Drawings* (Oppitz 2001) – offers an excellent examination of Powell's work, which include watercolours, ink and pencil drawings documenting different forms of vernacular architecture and different local customs and beliefs as reflected in material objects (Oppitz 2001: 7). The contributors to the volume, ranging from specialists in art and architecture to social anthropology and ethnography, have collaborated with the artist and discuss the potential of this form of visual documentation in anthropological research, either on its own or in conjunction with other visual media, providing stimulating insights in the domain of visual anthropology.

As regards smaller and peripheral countries like Portugal, where outside intellectual influence has traditionally been more or less bipolar (Anglo-Saxon versus Franco-German), 'graphic anthropology' – a special branch of visual anthropology – is still in its infancy (despite the promise this kind of illustration holds) since the first modern anthropological works (e.g. Dias 1953; Redinha 1956). The use of ethnographic drawing in Portuguese anthropology is linked to the historical figure of Fernando Galhano, a talented artist who integrated a pioneering mixed team of anthropologists, historians, musicologists, artists, archivists and photographers, led by the anthropologist Jorge Dias – the founder of the first ethnological research centre in Portugal (*Centro de Estudos de Etnologia Peninsular*). This centre was created in Oporto in 1947. From its inception to its later integration in the Museu Nacional de Etnologia (Lisbon) in the mid-1960s, the staff developed extensive fieldwork projects on material cultural, ranging from different traditional technologies to vernacular architecture, musical instruments, agricultural activities and agricultural implements (Veiga de Oliveira *et al.* 1977). This programme was based on the concept of 'urgent anthropology', which aimed at covering the country's popular culture and traditions, deemed at risk of disappearing under conditions of rapid social change. The project gave rise to a profusion of ethnographic records on different supports (audio, film, photography) and also to a vast collection of drawings authored by Fernando Galhano, whose activity was linked to the museum's projects and collections until the 1970s (Dias and Galhano 1968; Galhano 1968, 1971, 1973). A selection of his drawings was exhibited at the Museu Nacional de Etnologia and the published catalogues attest to the profusion and quality of his work (Cinatti 1987; Museu de Etnologia 1985).

Galhano's line of graphic documentation was carried through by Manuela Costa, previously a restoration technician at the Museum, who was taught and trained by Fernando Galhano, and later participated in collaborative works (Pereira 1990, 1997). Unfortunately, after her sudden retirement in 2001, the museum ceased to promote the art of ethnographic drawing, and indeed that of museographic photography, and instead turned to film/video as the dominant form of ethnographic representation. The same trend accompanied the expansion of undergraduate anthropology across Portuguese universities after the 1974 Revolution. To a certain extent, this has helped increase a generational gap between an old ethnographic–folkloristic discourse and a newer, more academically oriented, anthropological discourse. Common to both trends has been the same gusto for importing fashionable research models and adding very little home-grown reflection. After the Revolution, new orientations in teaching and research were adopted and extensively replicated, reflecting a rapid assimilation of fashionable paradigms and methodologies and a rather uncritical rejection of previous ones.

With regard to the inclusion of graphic elements in anthropological texts as a result of the use of drawing as a research method, the situation can be summarised as follows. A decline in the preference for scientific drawing in different domains (biology, archaeology, ethnology, vernacular architecture) was evident from the mid-1970s, when universities and research institutes underwent overall restructuring. Modernisation was seen as a rupture with the past and blind renewal seemed to have dominated the scientific world. During the 1990s a new generation of Portuguese anthropologists enthusiastically sought to pursue projects in Visual Anthropology. Photography and film became the privileged media, and drawing as an accepted or valued element of representation was clearly pushed aside as a 'handicrafty' and unfashionable device. In fact, published works appearing during last decade rarely integrate ethnographic drawing and most debates on the use of visual media in Portuguese anthropology focus exclusively on the uses of the video camera.

Recently, Manuel João Ramos (see Chapter 9 this book), who combines anthropological research and an artistic career, has been trying to rehabilitate the old tradition of ethnographic drawing, while visibly looking to the genres of comic strips and travel illustration as inspiration for his graphic approach to data collecting and presentation. In his illustrated travel–ethnographic account of his stay in Northern Ethiopia (Ramos 2000), images intertwine with field notes in a matter-of-fact way, enabling the reader–viewer to create the imaginary context upon which he is able to situate and interpret the series of transcripts of oral histories, that indicate the presence of the 'natives' voice'.

An aspect he underlines in the introduction of his book is that his drawings are a catalyst for observation, a path to reflexivity and a key to promote social interaction with local informants:

> When I travel alone, I cherish the feeling that time can be joyfully wasted. The act of drawing is a self-referential form of spending time. On the other hand, making drawings is a rather benign way of observing social behaviour: both local people and fellow travellers tend to react to my drawings in mixed ways where curiosity, availability and suspicion overlap. By drawing I provoke modes of interaction that humanise me in other people's eyes.
>
> (Ramos 2000: 9, my translation)

I have worked in collaboration with Manuel João Ramos in an experimental project where his graphic work was used to elicit information in the area of social change. He started by making a series of ink pen drawings, in a style that was rather different from his usual drawings. He intentionally chose a 'realistic' trait, an obvious pastiche of earlier ethnographic drawings, which was clearly recognised as such by the informants.

Below, I will refer to the conditions and results of this project, and will try to emphasise its potential as a collaborative device. This collaborative dimension is to be regarded in two ways – as a result of interaction with informants and also as a teamwork process conducted with the artist, who made the drawings that rendered possible this approach. Although I have the responsibility for this written version of our work, it is strongly anchored on complementary tasks and conspicuous conversations that gave rise to the reflections here presented.

From illustration to elicitation

When I was revising the first drafts of my Ph.D. thesis on urbanisation in a rural village of north-eastern Portugal, I asked Manuel João Ramos to make some drawings to illustrate particular features of old objects and past activities in the village that were lacking visual documentation. My first demands where quite specific – I commissioned him to draw from old photographs I had borrowed from family albums or to incorporate additional information into official village maps, to give an idea of the village's spatial dynamics.

With hindsight, what attracted me most was undoubtedly the aesthetic power of ethnographic drawings vis-à-vis other forms of visual representation (such as 'bad' photographs or official maps). In other words, I was aware of its *illustrative* richness. But when I confronted informants with the first sketches and tried to depict the ethnographic details that Manuel João required to make his meticulous ink pen drawings, we felt that this simple process was going beyond mere illustration.

In fact, when the first sketches, based on my early field notes, were presented to the informants, as a first proposal of iconographic interpretation of their own discourses, we could see that through this simple confrontation it was possible not only to annotate several comments about the contents of this type of representation but also to promote new arrangements, more detailed, of the informants' memories.

Given the profusion of ethnographic details that emerged from such simple confrontation of the informants with the first sketches, we tried to extend the enquiry in a systematic way. After analysing the registered comments, new drawings were made. These incorporated the successive annotations, corrections and interpretations added by the different informants to the sketches.

The execution of the drawings soon made clear that the overall process could be used as a powerful methodological tool in anthropological research. Thus, in a very straightforward way, it allowed us to deepen informants' involvement (as sources, checkers and authenticators) and also served as a probe to trigger and explore their social memories, transcending the limits of lineal textual representation.

Although this approach requires further testing, two brief examples offer a practical illustration of the possibilities of methodological convergence between iconographic and textual representation in the course of ethnographic research.

Re-creating social memories

The geographical context from which the two examples were drawn is the village of Sendim (500 km from Lisbon), in the frontier region of Miranda do Douro, three kilometres west of the river Douro, in the section where it divides Portugal and Spain. The village has a population of about 2,000 inhabitants and had undergone rapid change during the past fifty years.

The first phase of ethnographic research, conducted at various times between 1993 and 1995, followed conventional methods, such as participant observation; archival research; collection of census data; life-histories and interviews. Nevertheless, a preliminary analysis of these materials (especially the series of interviews conducted with several elderly members of the village) showed that the informants' memories were very fluid and susceptible to considerable reinvention, which resulted in fragmentary accounts that rendered ethnographic description and interpretation rather difficult.

It seemed that some socially meaningful testimonies remained hidden in the informants' minds, beyond the reach of conventional interviewing. The recurrence of some issues then suggested the possibility of attempting to do pictographic recompositions, exploring informants' mental images of some of the past activities especially referred to during the interviews.

As early photographic images were very scarce and limited in their subjects (mainly individual and family portraits), we thought this could be achieved through ethnographic drawing, supported by further oral enquiry and also by photographs taken of the places and objects depicted from successive transcribed materials.

As a starting point, we took one of the topics privileged by our informants and concentrated on villagers' nostalgic memories of intense social links bonding together several villages in the region – a situation that was frequently contrasted with the present-day isolationism experienced by many communities in the Portuguese hinterland. In social terms, neighbouring Spanish villages were also considered part of the region and the frontier interchange was an important dimension of the social life of people from both sides of the natural and administrative frontier.

However, until the 1960s, crossing the border was a hazardous and sometimes fatal endeavour – particularly in winter with the dangerous rapids. There were no ferryboats, no crossing points, trade was forbidden, and travel to Spain was restricted. Nevertheless, as far as the older informants could remember, movements to and fro of people and smuggling across the border were customary and frequent. The use of imaginative techniques, far from the control of the frontier guards, was widespread in order to overcome the natural and administrative barriers.

As previously mentioned, we could not find any visual documentation about these actions, and our knowledge about them came primarily from old stories of smuggling in the region that were wrapped in a veil of secrecy and adventure.

Although profuse, present individual memories were revealed to be fragmentary and sometimes contradictory, owing partly to the old age of the informants and partly to the cessation of these activities. There were different versions of how the regularly turbulent river Douro was crossed, or of devices used to illegally shuttle goods over it. We decided to start with a provisional illustration drawn from one extract of the written field notes:

> I can remember those times quite well, when we had to swim to cross the river. We did so in those old petrol tin boxes, the 30-litre ones, and were like a cube. Those boxes were empty and we closed them very well, to prevent the entrance of water and air. They were used like a buoy (to float).

Based on this type of description a first series of sketches was attempted, after collecting particular ethnographic details (materials used, measurements of some objects, the way people attached the box), which were necessary to make a drawing that proposed a representation as close as possible to informants' mental images (Figure 5.1).

Confronted with this re-creation made by the anthropologist–illustrator, our interlocutor became very impressed with our interest in his 'old-man histories' and I was able to capture his attention in a way that I had not managed to attain before. He went on with explanations, and some time later other villagers gather

Figure 5.1 Crossing the river using a petrol cube as buoy.

Figure 5.2 Helping to cross the river with a rope.

around us, watching the drawings and commenting on them. They remembered how they had also crossed, on what occasions they used to go to those Spanish villages, as well as criticizing the picture, suggesting corrections and giving ethnographic information with great enthusiasm. They focused, for instance on particular details:

> The ones who knew how to swim, swam, we had to help the others. But there is something that is not correct. I remember that most of them didn't go like that, because they were afraid. We had to protect them with a rope around the body and one of us who could swim pushed him. (Figure 5.2)

Figure 5.3 Crossing the river in pairs.

Once again, the presentation of this second drawing attracted a great audience, especially of elderly people I had interviewed before. They followed very attentively my progressions with the work in hand and several times volunteered to go with me to the places where they could cross the river. On other occasions they also brought me special objects used in different crossing engines, of which I took photographs. It is interesting to note that with the exhibit of my photographs I gained a reputation as a museum collector, while showing Manuel João drawings seemed to produce the effect of jogging their memories, and each time something else came to their minds that inspired new sketches:

Oh, yes, it was like that . . . and other times in spite of pushing, we also pulled. We passed in pairs. One could swim and swam at the front. The other was tied to the petrol tin and was pulled with a rope. (Figure 5.3)

Thus, by offering the informants the possibility of actively participating in creating and modifying sketches, I could see that we were involving them in further constructing their discourses and reinterpreting their memories, which contributed to give coherence to fragmentary accounts and allowed the successive incorporation of new details into the narrative. This is another example of informants' feedback to previous sketches:

I still remember the cliff at *Guinda*. Nowadays it is under water but before it was a rock that entered the river, in a special place where the margins were very close. From there we passed the ropes to the other side. We linked one margin to the other with the ropes, like a pulley. That is how we crossed the river.

The way this engine worked was not evident to me and thinking about the details Manuel João would need to make another drawing I continued with the interviewing, asking selective questions to learn how it actually worked, when it was used, who passed through the ropes, and so on. The next sequence of testimonies and sketches gives an idea of the interactive process which resulted in successive provisional sketches, each of which attempted to reflect information added incrementally by local interlocutors.

> With the ropes, we threw a thread to the other side. We chose a good place, with high rocks on each riverbank so that this thread wouldn't drop into the water, mainly when the river's waters rose. So, first we threw the thread (we always brought a coverlet to put on the ground so that the threads wouldn't get tangled), and when it reached good hands, we laced it to a rope. (Figure 5.4)

Figure 5.4 Throwing a thread to the other side.

Figure 5.5 Crossing with the rope engine.

We crossed by means of the ropes especially when the winter came and the water was too cold. We used a yoke hoop (*trasga*) to cross safely. We put the hands there, fixed with a second rope around the legs, and we crossed the river along the main rope. It was not far, from one bank to the other, say, some 30 metres. (Figure 5.5)

We also used this engine to smuggle commercial goods. We prepared a packet which followed the course of this rope engine with a simple manipulation of the convenient angle of inclination. Like that, it could easily reach the other bank, escaping the control of the frontier guards (Figure 5.6).

Systems of crossing the river were not the only topics that were evoked during our long conversations and walks around the village, following ancient contraband routes. But our collaboration around this subject became so intense, that a myriad of ethnographic details smoothly emerged, helping to consolidate my knowledge on different dimensions of everyday life that guided future analysis and interpretations.

Figure 5.6 Smuggling commercial goods.

The recurrent valuation of frontier interchange, for instance, led me to understand that one of the main orientations of social change within the village, operating at community level, was precisely the strong interaction between neighbouring villages (where Spanish villages could be seen as an extreme example of inclusion) as contrasted with the current atomism of the village. This constituted one central line of research that was further developed and sustained by contrasted images (verbal and pictorial) in the final version of my thesis.

The attempt at re-creating, through illustrations, recurrent memories of local people contributed not only to 'documenting' oral history in a way that other visual media could not, but it also allowed considereration of the symbolic context that frames this recurrence, providing lines of interpretation for otherwise bizarre descriptions of pages of fragmentary written records.

Depicting social meaning from particular objects

Following a similar procedure, another series of drawings were made by Manuel João to illustrate my chapter on the changes that occurred at domestic group level, considered during the same period under observation. From the analysis of my first field notes, two main lines of research had begun to emerge – the transformation of women's roles and the rupture between the work and domestic spheres.

When compared with ethnographic present, the main changes in household functions tend to affect women's roles in particular, whose traditional place within the domestic group seems to have become much less visible or socially recognized. This situation could also be supported by demographic trends, which show a steeper rise in young women migrants compared with young men.

Local middle-aged women had experienced those changes very intensively. Their life histories were filled with nostalgic childhood memories, evoked through descriptions of vivid situations where the strong intertwining between agricultural work and family life was a recurrent theme.

In an old handicraftsman's workshop, one of his wooden carvings hanging on the wall had caught my attention. It was a rectangular wooden tray entitled 'village life before machines'. On it, a range of traditional local occupations were sculptured. One of the pictures represented a woman with her children on her back while she was ploughing the fields. The carver seemed to have captured a powerful image of situations described by informants, where the intertwining of work and family was explicitly depicted.

I enthusiastically decided to take a photograph but was disappointed. Besides it not being a very good photograph, it contained 'too much' and the ambience that had so impressed me was lost.

The visual impact of an alternative pen drawing could be, I thought, much more expressive and appropriate. I brought the photograph with me and, based on it, Manuel João made a drawing where he depicted only the elements necessary to make explicit our interpretations of informants' discourses, this time supported by the local carver's own figurative representations (Figure 5.7).

Once again this suggestive drawing constituted a starting point for evoking villagers' childhood memories, and other details were brought into our

Figure 5.7 Woman ploughing a field with children on her back.

Figure 5.8 Baby safely sat down in a furrow covered by a coverlet.

conversations. 'Those old times were hard work times!' commented one of the women on seeing the picture. 'And most of the time we all went to the fields. If children were still young we carried them on our backs, just like that. But as they began to walk we would sit them down in a furrow with a coverlet under them while we ploughed one furrow after another' (Figure 5.8).

Our interpretations (made more explicit through visual images) suggested that we were approaching relevant dimensions of oral history, which in return informants corroborated by adding ethnographic information about different situations, but where the implicit subject of the pictorial proposals continued to be central.

To give a practical illustration of this interactive process – a process that guided research from written materials to pictorial re-creations and back again, each time casting new light on particular events or objects – I will concentrate on one of my favourite drawings, that constitutes an important visual complement of main arguments developed in that part of my thesis where changes in the domestic group were discussed.

This peculiar drawing, representing a woman rocking her baby's cradle with the foot while she was hand-spinning, suggests, very explicitly, that the strong interconnection between family and work domains operated not only outdoors but also within household space, where women's tasks underline similar strong complementarities (Figure 5.9). That drawing was followed by focused sketches

Figure 5.9 Woman hand-spinning and rocking her children.

of some of its constituent elements, each of which carried its own particular ethnographic details that were brought to light by informants at the simple confrontation with the image.

The first sketch represents a spindle (local name and measurements included), a distaff and a close-up of the distaff's head. According to local people, a chick-pea was often placed inside the distaff's head. It rocked with the movement of the distaff as the women were hand-spinning. Echoing informants' memories, this functionality of the object, which could not be 'seen' in the last drawing, became a central support to the interpretation of the previous picture (Figure 5.10).

The second sketch, derived also from the initial picture, shows detailed information about another important element – this time it was the old cradle that captured our eye. When I was gathering the details that Manuel João needed to make his drawing (measurements, fixing system, type of wood), people would bring me old cradles and talk about their childhood memories, when agriculture was the main economic activity in the village.

During one of these conversations, they explained how old cradles were frequently made by the future father, who recycled useless wooden wheels of traditional agricultural carts. This interesting explanation – that once again suggests the continuity of work and family even in the slightest details of particular

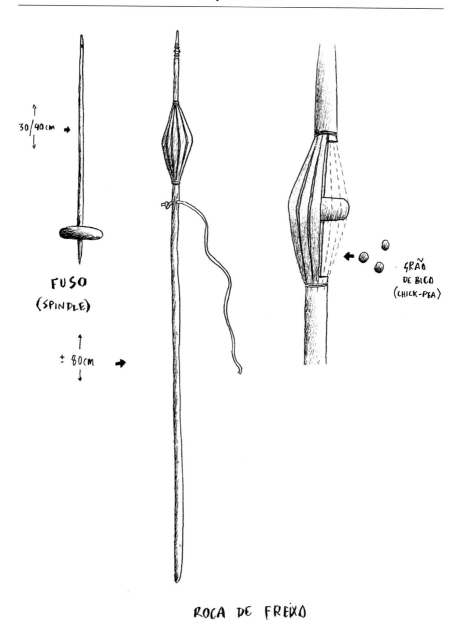

FUSO
(SPINDLE)

30/40 cm

± 80 cm

ROCA DE FREIXO
(DISTAFF, ASH-TREE)

GRÃO
DE BICO
(CHICK-PEA)

Figure 5.10 Detail of spindle and distaff.

Figure 5.11 Using recycled wooden wheels to make a cradle.

objects – inspired the next drawing that completes this sequence (Figure 5.11). This way of proceeding allowed not only to enlarge the narrative by rendering explicit, through visual representations, the implicit meaning of verbal records, but it also gave us the possibility of discovering features of material culture, which could be depicted and interrogated through a continuous crossover between words and images.

Drawings and other visual methods

This process of visually reconstructing local memories allowed us to achieve privileged relations with selected informants. In turn, this led to a more systematic and accurate processing of their memories and discourses to explore certain dimensions of social change.

Pictorial representation served as a mnemonic device, ensuring a comprehensive coverage of the context in which particular events and objects acquired cultural significance, helping to render 'visible' implicit meanings abstracted from the interviews. By offering local interlocutors the possibility of actively participating in creating, modifying and suggesting corrections to the sketches, it involved them in further constructing their discourses and reinterpreting their memories.

Thus, in methodological terms, the aesthetic and representational power of this approach became a valuable complement of lineal verbal expression at different stages of research, from the initial data collection to the final writing. On the other hand, the teamwork conducted by researcher and artist also seemed to enrich the traditional oral enquiry through a highly systematic interactive process of selective interviewing and photographing, developed in order to generate the many details that enabled us to represent pictorially the informants' descriptions.

When compared with other visual media (photography, film or video), the advantages of using drawings in anthropological representation and analysis have been very expressively summarised by the editor of *Robert Powell Himalayan Drawings*:

> Drawings, moreover, can be detached from the natural conditions in which their motifs are bound; they can isolate, single out, decontextualise; they can transport their subjects into different surroundings; they can take imaginary viewpoints. This makes drawings capable of conceptual idealisation and abstraction; of visually presenting symbolical significance; of depicting reality beyond realism; of transcending.
>
> (Oppitz 2002: 122)

Our research experiences demonstrate the communicative power of drawings when interacting with local informants and their ability to open paths to reflexivity – an issue which has been addressed in relation to photography and video in different social contexts. The problem of whether to use particular visual media (or combination of media), as Pink points out, is in fact a question of *appropriateness*: 'This includes considering how visual methods, images and technologies will be interpreted by individuals in the cultures where research will be done, in addition to assessing how well visual methods suit the aims of specific projects' (2001: 31). Thus, all possible methods of visual recording must be scrutinised and their adequacy put to the test.

It could be argued that as regards the use of drawings in anthropology, unless one has that special skill, it is easier to find a good camera (or indeed, a good cameraman) than a good illustrator. But it would be regrettable if this difficulty led us to ignore the potential offered by the plasticity of drawing, when new technologies open up so many interesting opportunities for convergence between words and images to construct and represent anthropological knowledge.

References

Banks, M. and Morphy, H. (1997) *Rethinking Visual Anthropology*, New Haven and London: Yale University Press.

Bouquet, M. (ed.) (2001) *Academic Anthropology and the Museum. Back to the Future*, New York and Oxford: Berghahn Books.

Cinatti, R. (Illustrations by F. Galhano) (1987) *Motivos Artísticos Timorenses e sua integração*, Lisboa: IICT/Museu de Etnologia.

Cothias, P., Le Corre, Y. and Loisel, R. (2000) *Mali Mélo*, Paris: Glénat.

Dias, J. (Illustrations by F. Galhano) (1953) *Rio de Onor: Comunitarismo Agro-Pastoril*, Oporto: Instituto Alta Cultura.

Dias, J. and Galhano, F. (illustrations) (1968) *Atlas Etnológico de Portugal Continental*, Lisbon: CEEP / Instituto Alta Cultura.

El Guindi, F. (1998) 'From Pictorializing to Visual Anthropology', in H. R. Bernard (ed.), *Handbook of Methods in Cultural Anthropology*, Oxford: Altamira Press.

Galhano, F. (1968) *Objectos e Alfaias Decoradas do Museu de Etnologia do Ultramar*, Lisboa: JIU/Centro de Estudos Antropologia Cultural.

—— (1971) *Esculturas e objectos decorados da Guiné Portuguesa no Museu de Etnologia do Ultramar*, Lisboa: JIU/Centro de Estudos Antropologia Cultural.

—— (1973) *O Carro de Bois em Portugal*, Lisboa: Instituto Alta Cultura.

Garnier, N. (2000) *Carnets de Paponasie*, Paris: Hazan.

Geertz, H. (1994) *Images of Power. Balinese Paintings Made for Gregory Bateson and Margaret Mead*, Honolulu: University of Hawaii Press.

Grimshaw, A. (2001) *The Ethnographer's Eye. Ways of Seeing in Modern Anthropology*, Cambridge: Cambridge University Press.

Museu de Etnologia (1985) *Desenho Etnográfico de Fernando Galhano* (Exhibition Catalogue), Lisbon: I.I.C.T./ Museu de Etnologia (vol. I Portugal; vol. II Africa).

Newman, D. (1998) 'Prophecies, Police Reports, Cartoons and Other Ethnographic Rumors in Addis Ababa', *ETNOFOOR*, XI (2): 83–110.

Oppitz, M. (ed.) (2001) *Robert Powell Himalayan Drawings*, Zürich: Volkerkundemuseum der Universität Zürich.

Pereira, B. (Illustrations by F. Galhano and M. Costa) (1990) *Sistemas de Serração de Madeiras*, Lisboa: INIC / Centro de Estudos de Antropologia.

—— (Illustrations by M. Costa *et al.*) (1997) *Tecnologia tradicional do azeite em Portugal*, Idanha-a-Nova: Centro Cultural Raiano.

Pink, S. (2001) *Doing Visual Anthropology: Images, Media and Representation in Research*, London: Sage.

Price, S. (1989) *Primitive Art in Civilized Places*, Chicago: University of Chicago Press.

Prinz, A. (2001) 'Mihidi's Drawings on Azande Witchcraft', paper presented at the Joint Meeting of Teaching Anthropology and Visual Anthropology EASA Networks on Working Images, Lisbon, September.

Ramos, M. J. (2000) *Histórias Etíopes*, Lisbon: Assírio e Alvim.

Redinha, J. (1956) 'Máscaras de Madeira da Lunda e Alto Zambeze', in *Subsídios para a História, Arqueologia e Etnografia dos Povos da Lunda*, Lisboa: Publicações Culturais da Diamang.

Ruby, J. (2000) *Picturing Culture: Explorations of Film and Anthropology*, Chicago: University of Chicago Press.

Stewart, J. (1990) *Malunde: The Street Children of Hillbrow*, Johannesburg: Witwatersrand University Press.

Veiga de Oliveira, E., Galhano, F. and Pereira, B. (1977; 2nd edn 1995) *Alfaia Agrícola Portuguesa*, Lisboa: Publicações Dom Quixote.

Chapter 6

Imagework in ethnographic research

Iain R. Edgar

In this chapter[1] I introduce the idea of imagination-based research methodologies and imagework. So far, such methods, initially derived from experiential groupwork, have been little, if at all, used as research methodologies. I articulate a potential taxonomy of differerent fields of imagework, ranging through introductory imagework, memory imagework, spontaneous imagework and dream imagework. I propose that the use of imagework methods can generate more holistic (in the sense of combining rational with affective and intuitive aspects of self) expressions of self-identities and implicit world-views than other current research methodologies. I illustrate my argument with examples.

I set this discussion and analysis of imagework within the context of the rapidly developing field of visual anthropology and advocate that imagework and its objectified forms (such as artwork, drama and mask-making) become part of visual anthropology in future. Interestingly, many of the main concerns in the field of visual anthropology are replicated in the field of imagework. Similar issues of social context, collaboration, representation, reflexivity, subjectivity, validity and replicability apply to the outer performance and representation of imagework. I consider the ethical and practice dimensions of imagework.

So far social science research has barely begun to utilise these powerful strategies that were developed originally for personal and group change but which are potentially applicable to qualitative research. This chapter will first locate these methods within the qualitative research domain and propose a novel view of their value. Even the second edition of the *Handbook of Qualitative Research* (Denzin and Lincoln 2000) makes almost no mention of these methods. The chapter on 'personal experience methods' in the 1994 edition of the *Handbook* refers only to journals, diaries, annals, storytelling and so forth (Clandinin and Connelly 1994). Nor do these methods seem to appear in even advanced focus group methods (Fern 2001). Only Stuhlmiller and Thorsen (1997) separately report on their use of a related method of using imagework that they call 'narrative picturing' (140–9). Recently some use of imagework and dreaming have emerged in the transpersonal research methods field of psychology (Braud and Anderson 1998). Transpersonal psychology, as Anderson writes, 'seeks to delve deeply into the most profound and inexplicable aspects of human experiences, including mystical and unitive experiences, experiences of transformation, extraordinary insight, meditative awareness, altered states of consciousness, and self-actualisation' (1998: 69). Anderson calls this approach 'intuitive enquiry' and advocates the acknowledged use of 'various altered states of consciousness, active dreaming and dream incubation, mystical vision and audition, intentional imaging, kinaesthetic and somatic awareness, and states of consciousness more typically associated with the artistic process than with science, in all phases of the enquiry' (1998: 76). Whilst imagework may be seen as a potential research method in transpersonal psychology, my exploration of it as a research methodology has shown that its value is potentially located across the broad qualitative research field. The hypothesis underpinning my approach is that experiential research methods, such as imagework, can elicit and evoke implicit knowledge and self-identities of respondents in a way that other methods cannot.

What is imagework and how does it work?

Imagework has variously been called 'active imagination,' 'visualisation' and 'guided fantasy.' Imagework is also a powerful therapeutic method, as described by Glouberman (1989) and Achterberg (1985). Imagework has developed from the active imagination technique of Jung and the theory and practice of psychosynthesis developed by Assagioli (1965). Jung's (1959: 42) concept of the 'collective unconscious' underpins imagework. This concept represented Jung's perception that the human psyche contained impersonal and archaic contents that manifested themselves in the myths, dreams and images of humans. Jung's idea that all humans contained a common and universal storehouse of psychic contents, which he called 'archetypes,' is the core model of the unconscious that enables imagework practitioners (see Glouberman 1989: 25) to consider the spontaneous image as being potentially a creative and emergent aspect of the self. More recently, transpersonal psychotherapy has integrated the work of Assagioli and Jung to form an imaginatively based approach to therapy. Rowan's definition of active imagination suggests that

> in active imagination we fix upon a particular point, mood, picture or event, and then allow a fantasy to develop in which certain images become concrete or even personified. Thereafter the images have a life of their own and develop according to their own logic.
>
> (1993: 51)

The imagework method is an active process in which the person 'actively imagining' lets go of the mind's normal train of thoughts and images and goes with a sequence of imagery that arises spontaneously from the unconscious. It is the quality of spontaneity and unexpectedness that are the hallmarks of this process. Imagework has creative potential because, as Clandinin writes,

In this view, images are seen as the mediator between the unconscious and conscious levels of being. What is known at the unconscious level finds expression in a person's thought and actions through a person's images. Images are thus seen as the source of inspiration, ideas, insight and meaning.

(1986: 17)

'The imaginal world' (or the 'websites of our mind')

The practice of imagework, in its visionary, contemplative and meditational forms is integral to the mystical paths of all the great religions (Happold 1963). Imaginative contemplation has been central to mystical and monastic practice in Christianity through the ages (see de Mello 1984) and visualisation has been a core component, for example, of religious practice in Tantric (see Yeshe 1987) and Tibetan Buddhism (see Tulku 1999).

Yet, interestingly, it is in the Sufi tradition within Islam (Corbin 1966: 406) that the concept of the 'imaginal world' is most developed to define a discernible world between that of sensibility and intelligibility. This 'imaginal world' is defined as a world of autonomous forms and images which is apprehended directly by the imaginative consciousness and was held to validate suprasensible perception. This concept of the 'imaginal world' reappears in Jung's (1959: 49) concept of the 'active imagination', Assagioli's (1965: 144) theory of psychosynthesis and visualisation techniques, and Rowan's (1993: 51) presentation of transpersonal psychology. Indeed Jung famously wrote of 'the crucial insight that there are things in the psyche which I do not produce, but which produce themselves and have their own life' (1977: 207). Suffice it here to recognise the possible apparent genesis of the concept of the 'imaginal world' in the Islamic theory of the visionary dream. Price-Williams (1987: 246–61) subsumes both the capacity to dream and 'actively to imagine' within the concept of the mythopoetic function in humans. The mythopoetic function, a term introduced by Ellenberger (1970: 314), is essentially a formulation of the creative capacity of the imagination to generate spontaneous imagery that is open to interpretation. Price-Williams speaks of how in a waking dream, 'the imaginative world is experienced as autonomous . . . the imager does not have the sense that he is making up these productions, but feels that he is getting involved in an already created process' (1987: 248).

Another theoretical formulation of the phenomenology and ontology of the 'world of images' derives from the study of both traditional and new-age shamanism. There is of course a vast anthropological literature on specific shamanic traditions (see Eliade 1964) and deep-seated controversaries as to the boundaries between traditional and new-age shamanism, and between shamanism and other forms of ecstatic technique such as trance, possession and mediumship. Detailed examination of these controversaries is well beyond the scope of this chapter on imagework as a qualitative research methodology. However, shamanic world-views do present another way of viewing, along with the Sufi concept of the 'imaginal', what the westerner would generally describe as the 'unconscious', whether that be the 'personal unconscious' of Freud or the 'collective unconscious' of Jung. Smith (1997) has tried to integrate the theory and practice of Jungian psychoanalysis with the traditions of shamanic practice. The shamanic world-view is that of the unconscious being a 'world of spirits' within which the shaman consciously, albeit in ecstatic form, interacts with his/her tutelary 'power animals' and guiding spirits. Typically, the shaman seeks wisdom for the community/people through guidance from these autonomous imaginative forms. However, whatever the historical antecedents to imagework, I will now introduce the practice of imagework in the qualitative research domain.

Imaginary Fields

There are several different kinds or fields of imagework. Imagework can be as simple as asking respondents individually or in a group to imagine an image in response to a question, such as 'how do you picture a certain situation?', as I shall illustrate shortly. I shall call this first field *introductory imagework*. Another, second field of imagework, involves guiding respondents into their memory of earlier events, such as their childhood socialisation. I call this second field *memory imagework*. A third field of imagework involves the use of the Jungian active imagination technique, which facilitates a spontaneous journey into the imagination. I define this field as *spontaneous imagework*.

Imagework and dreamwork are very closely related and in certain ways they overlap in that both refer to the mind's spontaneous production of imagery that people may consider is 'good to think with'. This fourth field of imagework I shall refer to as *dream imagework*. However dreamwork is not the focus of this paper but will be covered substantially in my forthcoming book (Edgar: 2004).

The analytic processing of imagework into data can have up to four stages: first, the descriptive stage wherein respondents 'tell their story'; second, analysis by participants of the personal meaning of their experience of symbols used; third, analysis of the models used to inform their imagery; fourth, the comparative stage when respondents compare their imagework with that of others in the group. Each of these stages needs facilitation and can be promoted through the amplification of the imagework into art and drama etc.

In using an experiential method such as imagework, it is also important to realise that while in itself imagework is a largely nonverbal activity it produces a verbal communication that incorporates the respondents' interpretations. Therefore, a respondent explaining the results of their imagework will typically relate a verbal account of their experience to the group, including the researcher. The results of imagework become a verbal communication capable of transcription and so becoming a 'field text' (Clandinin and Connelly 1994) for the researcher.

Imagework and visual anthropology

Vision has been both a central concern for anthropology and a marginal activity. Grimshaw (2001: 9), a visual anthropologist, suggests that we 'see' anthropology as a 'project of the visual imagination'. Anthropology is concerned with the ethnographer 'seeing' for him/herself and then more usually translating the seen into the written text. Moreover, a central concern for anthropology has been the arena of vision in indigenous society, whether that be the 'vision' of the shaman, the seer, the ecstatic, the possessed or the medium (Palmisano 2000), or the collective vision, embedded in mythogenesis (myth-making). Visual anthropology, however, has traditionally been seen as a somewhat marginal and problematical junior companion to the centrality of the observing and then writing anthropologist. There has been a 'suspicion of images' (Banks 2001: 9). However, visual anthropology is experiencing something of a renaissance with the increasing importance and availability of video and the internet in particular. Several recent texts (Pink 2001; Banks 2001; Grimshaw 2001; Rose 2001) have further theorised this developing field. Morphy and Banks (1997: 5) speak of visual anthropology's field of interest being, 'the anthropology of visual systems, or more broadly, visible cultural forms'. I suggest in this chapter that the field of inner visualisation, whether that of day or night dream, especially when objectified into artwork or other representational forms, become a particular focus or subfield, of this area of anthropology. Moreover, I suggest that anthropology's traditional immersion in the world-views of indigenous peoples can have facilitated its practitioners into 'seeing' western epistemological and psychological theories as being as much 'emic' constructions as those of the peoples they have studied. For example, when Rose (2001: 103) writes of a psychoanalytical perspective in visual anthropology and introduces this with a definition solely with reference to Freudian and Lacanian views of the unconscious, then this bias leads to closure with respect to understanding the potential riches and ways of 'seeing' the psyche.

Interestingly, many of the main concerns in the field of visual anthropology are replicated in the field of imagework and its related outputs: art, drama, dance, mask-making, etc. Similar issues of representation, reflexivity, subjectivity, validity and replicability apply to the outer performance of imagework. My contention is that imagework and its 'artistic' outcomes can be usefully compared in one way to the photo-elicitation method, well known in the visual anthropology field. In the photo-elicitation method respondents are interviewed through the medium of relevant photos, either produced by the respondent or the anthropologist (Banks 2001: 87–99; Pink 2001: 68). Collier, an early pioneer of the photo-elicitation method considered that this method opened up 'emotional revelations' and 'psychological explosions and powerful statements of values' (Collier 1967: 62), otherwise possibly unobtainable. The photo-elicitation method has been critiqued by, for example, Pink (2001: 68) as originally being conceived as providing 'social facts' that were drawn out of or evoked through this method. More recently such evoked narratives of respondents have been seen as a response to the ethnographers' representations (Pink 2001: 68). If, often old, photographic images can evoke intense and powerful emotions for respondents, concerning, for instance, deceased kin (Riches and Dawson 1998: 24) or the ageing aspect of the life-course (Okely 1994: 50), then how much more evocative will be the here and now production of images by respondents, who then interrogate, or ask questions, of their own life experience? Okely has argued that introducing photographs into the interviews with French rural elders, conjured up a depth of felt information inaccessible to the standard interview, 'A mere tape recording of her speaking in a formalised interview could not have conjured up the greater sense of her past which we mutually created with the aid of visual images' (1994: 50–1).

I argue in this chapter that the differing fields of imagework can be an even more evocative research methodology than the photo-elicitation method for example. Moreover, perhaps uniquely in the visual anthropology field, imagework practice does not start with the production of external imagery, rather imagework begins with attending to the flow of the mind's inner imagery in a number of different ways (i.e. via memory or sponataneously generated imagery). Thereafter this inner imagery can be manifested in a number of external visual forms, such as artwork.

Introductory imagework

The first example of the use of imagework is of the introductory kind. This 'introductory imagework' is designed to facilitate a group (or individual) in sharing and analysing how participants are feeling about a certain situation. Such a method can be used as a part of interviewing or in group-based interviews and in focus groups. The technique simply consists of asking respondents to imagine an image that reflects the situation being considered. It is as easy as that! In a recent example, the situation was a two-session study of personal and professional identity change among students on a vocational master's programme in social work at a UK university.

What was immediately striking about the student feedback was, first, that all of the twenty students were able to relate an image that they had pictured and, second, how 'discontented' their images were. Students particularly described 'seeing' pictures of train scenarios such as 'being in a siding', 'being derailed', 'in a tunnel' and 'I thought I was on a modern train but it's not!' Apart from the surprising amount of train imagery, other notable imagery presented was feeling 'in a fog', 'up against a brick wall' and 'climbing up a mountain without enough footholds'. I later realised that students had previously been attending a staff–student meeting about the course and that individual and group morale at that point was low.

However, the whole point about imagework is to facilitate the movement from 'seen' inner image to articulated theme through a process of 'reading' the imagery much as one might 'read' a picture in an art gallery; and indeed, further 'readings' can be obtained by asking the respondents to make a simple external picture of their imagery and then displaying their results on the wall for further individual and group discussion. Each respondent then speaks to their picture in turn before the researcher/facilitator possibly develops a group-based analysis of pertinent themes based on comparing the individual narratives that have emerged. Further amplification of meaning from such imagery can be made by doing a sculpt, which in the above case would have consisted of inviting the group to first design and create a train station, railway line and so forth using chairs, tables and so on as props; then each person would have been asked to position themselves in a pose that represented their feeling state about their position on the course (i.e. 'being stuck in a tunnel' or 'derailed'). This can be jolly, is not difficult to facilitate (see Jennings 1986 for details), and as people talk from their positions and poses in the sculpt, new kinds of insight and implicit knowledge can be revealed. It also enhances group cohesion and identity, and that in itself can facilitate richer kinds of discussion, disclosure and group analysis.

So we can articulate a research process that starts with imagework and then can move on into artwork, sculpting and possibly drama. Yet at whatever point the 'experiential' process stops, public analysis by each respondent needs to begin. Themes need to be drawn out and 'read' from the imagery, and as respondents talk about their imagery, they engage the intuitive and affective dimensions of the self in a way unlikely to be achieved solely through a cognitive engagement with an interviewer/researcher. Using the binary opposition model of the brain (Markham 1989), imagework connects many people to the right-hand side of their brain, the centre for creative, intuitive and lateral thinking, while the left-hand side brain hemisphere is known to control cognitive and intellectual processes. So imagework is particularly powerful as a tool for accessing the unarticulated embodied views of individuals and groups in the research process.

What imagework and related 'experiential' research methods can achieve is the articulation of respondents' as yet dimly perceived aspects of self and world. So, for instance, in the postgraduate Master's programme evaluation presented above, students speaking of their imagework, articulated through this process their feelings about the nature, content and structure of the course, and their individual and group progress on it; further, they accessed their original hopes and fears for 'the course' and how their imagery reflected their intuited and existential predicament concerning 'the course' in their life in the 'here and now'. Not only did it reflect their immediate felt concern but through further experiential techniques, such as the use of art and sculpting, the process gave respondents the opportunity of 'working with' and changing their existential predicaments. When I asked respondents at the end of the session whose 'images' had changed during the course of the session, three respondents replied affirmatively: the one who had 'thought she was on a modern train but wasn't' felt she was now on an 'express train'; another felt there was less 'fog' around her; and another felt there were more 'footholds' on the mountain.

So imagework and its amplification (artwork, sculpting and drama, updating/amplifying respondents' imagery) can both evoke significant insights into psychosocial situations and even change personal and group orientations, so becoming applicable in action-research settings. For instance, in this last example, respondents had almost no idea that fellow respondents/students felt so similarly about the course experience. Using imagework, even at this simple and introductory level, can evoke rich amounts of personal and group insight and facilitate enhanced self-disclosure and group analysis. Moreover, I find groups can be easily encouraged to develop their own meta-analysis of the imagery presented; asking respondents to 'identify common themes and significant differences' usually provides very useful analysis as respondents, if reasonably facilitated, are 'warmed up' by their personal and group encounter with the affective and intuitive aspects of themselves, something still relatively rarely encountered in contemporary western lifestyles.

Memory imagework

The second field of the imagework method that I want to introduce is the memory imagework method. Memory imagework can be used as part of an oral history approach. The method consists of leading participants through their early biographical memories as a way of picturing forgotten or little-considered aspects of their childhood awareness. Remembering and (re)picturing one's first experiences of a child of another race and/or gender to oneself can be powerful triggers for recollecting the earliest experience of culturally formed and/or stereotypical thinking. A pilot session, conducted with a group of twelve anthropologists as experimental subjects, involved, after a suitable relaxation exercise, a guided journey forwards in imaginative time starting with the participants' early memories/pictures of home, school and play experiences. Following the exercise discussion and analysis took place as to how early concepts of race, gender, ability and other differences were constructed. Participants' awareness came through the recollecting of others' bodily characteristics and social customs, such as table manners and joking behaviours, and their implications for the formation of self-concept and peer group formation.

There is probably almost no limit to the range of possible memory, and also imaginary, situations that can be 'dreamt up'. For example, recently, I have been developing and using an exercise in which respondents first imagine their original 'family' household (as long as this represents a 'comfortable' place for them; if not, I advise them to think of another well-known household from their childhood for this exercise) and have them, as an imaginative exercise, walk around this remembered house and the actual task is for them to look for a specific piece of ritual and symbolic activity. The aim of this task is to gather data about 'household change over two generations' or even 'changing western domestic symbolism'. I don't give examples so as not to anticipate their memory, but usually respondents think of mealtimes, the hearth, musical instruments or bathroom activities. Then I ask respondents to 'fast forward' into the present and imagine that they are in their current household (or again an equivalent example if their current situation is problematic) and consider the similarities and differences between their current and past households with regard to the symbolic value of their chosen ritual activity. They can 'dialogue' with any imaginary figures they encounter in their household. Usually, time permitting, I ask respondents to make a brief felt-tip picture of their imaginings and then share with the group, or in pairs, the symbols used and encountered and the preliminary explanations they have for such changes. Typically, respondents talk of changes in family structures, technological developments; gender and ethnic consciousness development; secularisation; changing consumption patterns; personal and public symbolism; a reflexive approach to the changing subject of experience. The group can then make a meta-analysis of the emerging themes.

As an example, I include two descriptions by participants who consented to share them in publication form. They come from non-English as first language speakers and I have retained the original writing.

> 1. My original and my present home is the same, only that I moved from my original home and came back after eleven years. The image manifested in travelling through my memories of living in my original home is the image of a room with a piano. There I spent my most imaginative and happy moments, hours and days of my childhood. I could remember the sounds and smells of the room, the light and the distant voices from the garden. Learning the music I discovered for the first time a magic touch of creativity and the happiness. The image discovered in my mind, connected with living in my present home (which is in the same house) is the image of my working room with my table and the computer on it. And again there is a strong feeling of happiness and creativity. Only this time there is not the music involved but writing different texts, letters, making concepts, dreaming, reading chapters etc. And again there is a keyboard. My English is not good enough to explain what I think is the meaning of my images. I can only say that they are of great importance for me and the finding of your exercise as well. What do they mean, two rooms in the second floor of our house? I need an entire life to pass from one room to another. First I was a child and now I am there with my family.

> 2. With a nice atmosphere precipitated by the introduction you made to this exercise, I found myself in the house of my childhood – the first family house I could remember and where I never 'came in' after I left (I was 10 then). The ritual activity that occurred to me was a family meal. We were all sat at the table and I could remember all the furniture inside it, even the

colour of the tablecloth. But I had a strange sensation of lacking of space in my place. Also it impressed me that this memory image had no movement, as if I was looking at a picture that stand still. Contrasting with the same ritual situation at my actual home, I saw myself moving. Always moving. In this case it was the activity that prevails over the scenery. I actually haven't paid much attention to the objects and furniture and colours (perhaps because they were very present in my memory) and the images that always were brought to my memory in this later case were all images of movement, where I played a strong role – bringing the food to the table, bringing water, for example (curiously I don't really do this as often as to justify this image of myself) mystery. In both cases the difficulty was to look at myself. Perhaps I was feeling the ambiguity of being inside and outside a situation and couldn't be able to assume both roles. That means I took the role of the observer but could only have the feelings of the observed – in the first case I had 'lack of space'; in the recent one I was always moving (escaping?). I think that image memories, like pictures, when we try to observe them are very helpful to practice the 'art of anthropology', and an essential part of our work as anthropologists is to observe and describe and analyse the observations we do.

Both of these responses show the quality of engagement of participants in the exercise and their ability to imaginatively recreate the 'sights' and feelings that they have for these emotional spaces of their selfhood. In the first example the participant muses over the 'journey' of his life seeming to be summarised by his movement between two rooms in the same family house. The respondent hints at deeper levels of discerned meaning, undisclosed due to language translation issues. Clearly significant, even profound, emotions have been generated which 'picture' his life as a journey between two rooms on the same floor. Whilst from this first example one might not be able to gather much by way of 'data' about changing ritual activities, for example, one could through follow-up interview and discussion develop ideas about his (and others) perceptions and concepts of identity and selfhood, including family membership, and the life course. The self, its felt identity and internal spatial knowing, is here emotionally activated as well as being conceptually present! Affective and intuitive, as well as cognitive, dimensions of the self are then manifested, generated and released. How different would the result of an interview be! The remembered movement of the person through their experience (in this case of a lifetime spent moving between two rooms) and then onto the verbal level reveals their intuitive understanding in a way that a solely cognitive engagement with a question doesn't. This is the benefit of an imagework process. Indeed, respondents may even become aware of their own deep perceptions which, hitherto, they did not quite consciously grasp; the unarticulated becomes articulated; the thought waiting in the wings, may even fly into the centre of the mind's theatre!

This example shows that participants will often interpret the task in the way they choose and so offer information perhaps about a slightly different research question; however at the very least I would contend the imaginative process opens them up for a depth of recall and evocative memorisation that will benefit any subsequent interviewing and data-collection process.

The second example shows a real contrast between the level and quality of the participant's engagement in the two remembered households; she describes this difference in terms of movement and lack of movement. Clearly follow-up discussion around the themes of 'lack of space' and family roles would possibly evoke deeper insights into her experience of childhood and adult family identity, family and gender roles and power and domestic space for example. As this was a training exercise for anthropologists in the methodology, this follow-up work didn't take place.

Spontaneous imagework

The third field I call spontaneous imagework. This consists of leading a group of respondents on an imaginary journey. Examples of these journeys are written up in Ernst and Goodison (1981), Glouberman (1989), and Markham (1989). A very typical exercise of this type is for the facilitator of the exercise, after an introductory relaxation exercise, to lead the participants on a journey. A classical form of this is to start the journey in a meadow and to lead participants over an obstacle and up a hill to a house on the hill where they meet a wise person whom they can talk to about any question that they have. An exercise like this (Ernst and Goodison 1981: 161), as found in my experience, can trigger disclosure of and work on important personal and social issues. For qualitative research purposes, this kind of exercise can be refocused to gain data concerning the subject of an enquiry. So, for example, if the researcher wished to gain data about respondents' views on any aspect of family life or social life, they would be asked to 'carry' this question in their mind and ask their 'wise old person' about this subject.

One recent imagework exercise I have adapted for use from Glouberman's 'sensing life choices, making life decisions' (1989: 168–86) I call 'crossroads'. In this exercise I suggest participants first develop a question about their life that is currently of interest to them; the question can be either a small one or a large. Then they imagine the choices they have with respect to this question and I ask them, following a suitable relaxation exercise, to visualise the different ways or paths that the different choices would offer. Then they can 'walk' down those different ways and encounter sometimes surprising material that subsequently in discussion they can relate to their intuitive expectation of life outcomes following particular decisions. Sometimes, as a variant, participants can, towards the end of this exercise, imagine themselves going up in a helicopter or a balloon above the different 'ways' and see for themselves how the different paths come together later or veer away from each other. Perhaps they all lead to the same place anyway! How can this exercise be used in a research context? Well any research question that involves the issue of personal and contextual decision-making, or risk assessment, is an obvious topic. People's perception of impending life changes and their expected and unexpected coping capacities and resources would manifest themselves well through such an exercise and probably in differing ways from a purely conceptual discussion. Participants can, for instance, visualise different courses of action and their imagined outcomes in relation to healthy and unhealthy lifestyles, relationship and career issues. Issues like perceptions of pregnancy, marriage, divorce, bereavement and even death, could be conjured up and worked with.

It is worth considering that we all anticipate and rehearse our possible futures during a large part of our daytime life, and possibly in our dreamtime too. We anticipate the day or evening or weekend ahead; where we might go on holiday if sufficiently time and money rich; who we might try and date; make friends with; in all these activities and countless others we are normally engaged in, we, excepting those very few who are not visual thinkers at all, imaginatively predict the possible outcomes; so anyway in an informal way we do the crossroads exercise many times each day, but usually we do it in a haphazard and somewhat undisciplined form and of course normally we do our imaginative rehearsal work on our own or 'chew it over' with a friend(s).

Some memory imagework exercises can involve spontaneous imagework characteristics. For instance the previously described exercise in which participants imaginatively 'journeyed' first back into their household of origin with a question or task, such as finding a 'ritual' activity, can have elements of spontaneous imagery, such as the contrast in the second example between her being immobile in the household of her childhood compared with her (slightly frantic?) activity in her current household.

Ethical and practices issues

Clearly the use of the different fields of the imagework method require familiarity with their use and skill in their application, though arguably a researcher could observe an imagework practitioner using such a method, rather than using it him/herself. The concern with careful use is important as such a method can reveal latent feelings and unrealised intuitions that have often only been partially made conscious or possibly even repressed. However, specific training programmes in these hitherto 'therapeutic' methods do now exist.[2] Moreover, introductory imagework is not difficult to use. A couple of training sessions with colleagues and a facilitiator should suffice.

The ethics of using such approaches are important. An imagework methodology should only be practised within accepted social science ethical guidelines. Christians (2000: 138–40) summarises the main codes of ethics for professional and academic qualitative research communities as consisting of four main guidelines: informed consent, opposition to deception, privacy and confidentiality, and accuracy. Any research activity using imagework and its associated techniques should meet normative requirements in these areas. Informed consent requirements can be met through the careful explanation of the processes to be involved, though it is important to note what Parse (1995: 82) has called 'lingering true presence' (see later). Deception is obviously important to avoid, and normal expectations of privacy and confidentiality can be maintained and are especially important in research activity that aims to elicit 'deep' data from respondents. Accuracy is likewise equally important.

Clearly some researchers will feel that the imagework method is unacceptably intrusive and raises power issues that are very problematic. However, whilst I would propose that an experiential method, such as imagework, has as its intention, the gathering of in-depth data, I would argue that any data-collection method involves intrusion and can provoke problematic self-disclosure. Even a simple interview can suddenly trigger a sensitive area for the respondent and leave the researcher with ethical considerations in terms of how to handle the resulting situation supportively. Johnson and Griffith (1998: 212) suggest that all interviewing technologies are primarily concerned with enabling respondents to 'open-up', particularly with respect to complex concerns. Some ethnographic methods, such as photo-elicitation in particular, seek, in a similar way to imagework, to open up the respondent to dimly perceived or remembered emotional depths (Collier 1967: 67). The methods I have outlined will sometimes be a catalyst for significant disclosure, yet the negative aspects of disclosure can be greatly prevented by making participation voluntary, by the sensitive explanation beforehand of the task and technique to participants, and by similar aftercare. Moreover, participants can be asked again, following an imagework exercise, if they wish their contribution still to be used as part of the research findings.

It is important to be aware that the creative, emotional and cognitive influence of an image may not be completed within the timespan of the session. Parse as part of her 'Human Becoming Theory', has called this after-effect, 'lingering true presence' (1995: 82). The evocative power of a symbol may engage the mind in an ongoing process of self-enquiry; therefore, it may be prudent for the researcher, as well as ensuring that their respondents finish the task at ease with any imaginative results, to make follow-up individual or group interviews available.

Some topics may be inappropriate for imagework, certainly in groups, and there is an appropriate literature on researching sensitive issues that would be relevant to the use of imagework methods (Renzetti and Lee 1993). However, one advantage of using imagework, and often following-up with artwork, is that it allows respondents to discuss potentially sensitive material in a coded way that allows them to retain their privacy. People can, for instance, verbally or in their accompanying artwork, refer to 'bad times' by using stereotypical images of unhappiness such as 'bad weather' and, as a result retain their privacy and their understanding of their meaning.

I outline a set of guidelines for this work.

Ethical/safe practice guidelines

- Explain everything beforehand: go through each part of the exercise, so there are no surprises 'on the way'.
- Give clear permission to people that they don't have to do the session if they don't want to.
- Ask, 'any questions' after introducing the exercise and before doing it.
- Develop trust from the beginning; open body gestures, clear quiet voice tone; reassure continually that 'they' are in control throughout the exercise and including during the sharing; it is their journey.
- Plan the timing of the session and have enough time for each part of it; don't try and do too much. Go through each part of the session in your mind beforehand. Prepare yourself.
- Practise with friends/colleagues beforehand, if you wish.
- If you feel really unsure about doing this exercise, as opposed to your 'normal' level of apprehension before doing a new type of exercise, then either don't do it, or choose a safer format.
- Talk through with respondents their 'self-care' issues first. Emphasise:
- They are in control of all parts of the process. They can guarantee their confidentiality by what they choose to share with others; symbols have many meanings and associations, and their multivocality is a real assset for both eliciting ideas and retaining confidentiality.
- If they are unhappy, ill, worried or preoccupied, then advise people not to do the exercise, or particularly look after themselves.
- Advise people that if they become distracted in an exercise then they can gently bring their wandering attention back to the subject.
- If someone encounters a 'difficult' memory or image then advise them that they have a choice either to go on with the exercise or stop and imagine something more pleasant. However, remind people that their images and accompanying feelings and thoughts are *their own*. Also, be clear that difficult feelings can be triggered by any 'outer' event also, for instance the look or smell of a flower. Moreover, this subject of difficult memory/image recall can be gone into in more depth, and discussion facilitated as to the possible long-term value of dealing with difficult memories that can suddenly intrude into consciousness at any time; is the 'unconscious' good at timing in all cases?
- Be 'around' afterwards, or have a colleague around, to provide support if needed, though my experience is that such support is rarely ever needed; watch carefully to see if anyone is looking upset at the end.
- Facilitate everyone sharing their feelings and experiences that have been evoked by the exercise, at least in pairs, so that each person has had the opportunity to tell 'their' story.
- Pace the visualisation process by doing the visualisation at the same time as the people you are facilitating. Make sure you leave plenty of time during the visualisation for people's imaginations to work.

- Don't allow any interuptions: put a very clear message on the door and even an object like a chair to block late entrants! There is nothing so disturbing as a late entrant in the middle of a visualisation exercise.

Conclusion

So the thesis of this chapter is that a 'new' research methodology such as imagework, offers the opportunity for researchers to further study the personal and social world of the respondent and so obtain a blend of cognitive, affective and intuitive material known, dimly known, implicit, suppressed and even repressed by the conscious mind. Overall the chapter has shown the way that imagework, one of several potential experiential research methods, offers researchers the means to access the latent knowledge and unexpressed feelings of respondents. The chapter has focused on presenting a description and classification of imagework as a novel research opportunity and located it within the potential range of methods of visual anthropology.

This chapter has not generally provided a detailed guide or manual for the beginning practitioner of the imagework method; rather, it has suggested a way forward for imagework practice as a part of the research process, and it has outlined a basic typological framework for imagework practitioners/researchers. Experiential research methods such as imagework can be utilised in part or on their own in research practice in such diverse fields as the social sciences, health and social care, education, development and even business and marketing. The imagework method is particularly effective in accessing participants' implicit awareness of such areas as personal and cultural identity formation and change; interpersonal dynamics; attitudes and ideologies, organisational culture; and individual and collective vision development. While the application of the imagework method may be considered innovative, the principles, ethics and practices governing the organisation and analysis of data derived from this method remain firmly within the established qualitative domain. The way is open for further studies using these methods, perhaps in controlled and cross-cultural studies, that would compare the value of such experiential methods against the use of more traditional research methods.

Overall, I advocate in this chapter that the field of imagework especially when objectified into artwork or other representational forms, become a particular focus or sub-field, of visual anthropology.

Notes

I should like to thank Dr Stephen Lyon, Department of Anthropology, University of Durham, for reading a draft of this paper. Of course, I am entirely responsible for the finished work.
1 A much earlier version of this chapter was published as 'The Imagework Method in Social Science and Health Research', *Qualitative Health Research*, 1999, 9(2): 198–211.

2 I occasionally run training courses; I am aware of an imagework training agency based in California, that offers distance and personal training in the use of 'Interactive Guided Imagery'. I have no direct experience of it (http://www.interactiveimagery.com).

References

Achterberg, J. (1985) *Imagery in Healing*, Boston: Shambhala.

Anderson, R. (1998) 'Intuitive Inquiry', in W. Baud and R. Anderson (eds), *Transpersonal Research Methods for the Social Sciences*, London: Sage.

Assagioli, R. (1965) *Psychosynthesis*, London: Mandala and Psychosynthesis Research Foundation.

Banks, M. (2001) *Visual Methods in Social Research*, London: Sage.

Braud, W. and Anderson, R. (1998) *Transpersonal Research Methods for the Social Sciences*, London: Sage.

Christians, C. (2000) 'Ethics and Politics in Qualitative Research', in N. Denzin and Y. Lincoln (eds), *Handbook of Qualitative Research*, 2nd edn, London: Sage.

Clandinin, D. (1986) *Classroom Practice: Teacher Images in Action*, London: Falmer Press.

Clandinin, D. and Connelly, F. (1994) 'Personal Experience Methods', in N. Denzin and Y. Lincoln (eds), *Handbook of Qualitative Research*, London: Sage.

Collier, J. (1967) *Visual Anthropology: Photography as a Research Method*, New York: Holt, Rinehart and Winston.

Corbin, H. (1966) 'The Visionary Dream in Islamic Spirituality', in G. Von Grunebaum and R. Callois (eds), *The Dream in Human Societies*, Berkeley: University of California Press.

De Mello, A. (1984) *Sadhana: A Way to God: Christian exercises in Eastern form*, New York: Image Books.

Denzin, N. and Lincoln, Y. (1994) *Handbook of Qualitative Research*, London: Sage.

—— (2000) *Handbook of Qualitative Research*, 2nd edn, London: Sage.

Edgar, I. (2004) *Guide to Imagework: An Introduction to Imagination-based Research Methods*, London: Routledge.

Eliade, M. (1964) *Shamanism: An Archaic Technique of Ecstasy*, New York: Pantheon.

Ellenberger, H. (1970) *The Discovery of the Unconscious: The History and Evolution of Dynamic Psychiatry*, New York: Basic Books.

Ernst, S. and Goodison, L. (1981) *In Our Own Hands: A Book of Self-Help Therapy*, London: The Women's Press.

Fern, E. (2001) *Advanced Focus Group Research*, Newbury Park, CA: Sage.

Glouberman, D. (1989) *Life Choices and Life Changes through Imagework*, London: Unwin.

Grimshaw, A. (2001) *The Ethnographer's Eye: Ways of Seeing in Anthropology*, Cambridge: Cambridge University Press.

Happold, F. (1963) *Mysticism*, Harmondsworth: Penguin.

Hunt, J. (1989) *Psychoanalytic Aspects of Fieldwork*, Newbury Park, CA: Sage.

Jennings, S. (1986) *Creative drama in groupwork*, Bicester, Oxon.: Winslow Press.

Johnson, J. and Griffith, D. (1998) 'Visual data: Collection, Analysis and Representation', in V. de Munck and E. Sobo (eds), *Using Methods in the Field: A Practical Introduction and Casebook*, Walnut Creek: Altamira Press.

Jung, C. (1959) 'Archetypes of the collective unconscious', in *The Collected Works of C. G. Jung*, vol. 9, Part 1, London: Routledge and Kegan Paul.

—— (1977 [1963]) *Memories, Dreams, Reflections*, London: Collins.

Markham, U. (1989) *The Elements of Visualisation*, Shaftesbury, Dorset: Element Books.

Morphy, H. and Banks, M. (1997) 'Introduction: rethinking visual anthropology', in M. Banks and H. Morphy (eds), *Rethinking Visual Anthropology*, London and New Haven: Yale University Press.

Okely, J. (1994) 'Vicarious and sensory knowledge of chronology and change: ageing in rural France', in K. Hastrup and P. Hervik (eds), *Social Experience and Anthropological Knowledge*, London: Routledge.

Palmisano, A. (2000) 'On the theory of trance: the Zar Cult in Ethiopia', *Kea: Zeitschrift für Kulturwissenschaften* 13: 119–36.

Parse, R. (1995) 'The human becoming practice methodology', in R. Parse (ed.), *Illuminations: The Human Becoming Theory in Practice and Research*, New York: National League for Nursing Press.

Pink, S. (2001) *Doing Visual Ethnography*, London: Sage.

Price-Williams, D. (1987) 'The Waking Dream in Ethnographic Perspective', in B. Tedlock (ed.), *Dreaming: Anthropological and Psychological Interpretations*, Cambridge: Cambridge University Press.

Renzetti, C. and Lee, R. (1993) *Researching Sensitive Topics*, Newbury Park, CA: Sage.

Riches, G. and Dawson, P. (1998) 'Lost children, living memories: the role of photographs in processes of grief and adjustment among bereaved parents', *Death Studies* 22: 121–40.

Rose, G. (2001) *Visual Methodologies*, London: Sage.

Rowan, J. (1993) *The Transpersonal: Psychotherapy and Counselling*, London: Routledge.

Smith, M. (1997) *Jung and Shamanism*, New York: Paulist Press.

Stuhlmuller, C. and Thorsen, R. (1997) 'Narrative picturing: a new strategy for qualitative data collection', *Qualitative Health Research* 7(1): 140–9.

Tulku, T. (1999) 'Lucid dreaming: exerting the creativity of the unconscious', in G. Watson, S. Batchelor and G. Clayton (eds), *The Psychology of Awakening*, London: Rider.

Yeshe, L. (1987) *Introduction to Tantra*, Boston, MA: Wisdom Publications.

Part II

Representing visual knowledge

Chapter 7

Putting film to work

Observational cinema as practical ethnography

Paul Henley

Any intellectual discipline will outgrow its early enthusiasms and change its methodologies . . . There is no need to argue exclusively for one method . . . This is obviously a waste of time. If different languages are being used, we just have to learn their rules to avoid confusion.

Colin Young (1995: 113)

Observational cinema and anthropology

The term 'observational cinema' has been applied to a range of different documentary film-making practices, some of which are based on mutually contradictory principles and strategies. At one extreme, it has been used to denote film-making in which there is no engagement with the subjects, who are filmed remotely, as if from a watchtower, in the interests of maintaining a supposedly 'scientific' objectivity. At another extreme, it can be used of television documentaries which feature slightly longer takes, slightly less commentary and slightly fewer interviews than is normal in such productions. However, the 'observational cinema' that I shall be concerned with in this article is the documentary practice that first developed in the late 1960s around the Ethnographic Film Training Programme at the University of California, Los Angeles (UCLA).

This variant of observational cinema falls somewhere between the two extremes outlined above. At the core of the approach lies the idea that through the rigorous observation of the minutiae of social events and interactions, it is possible to gain significant insights, not just into idiosyncratic personal motivations of the immediate subjects, but also into broader social and cultural realities of their social world. The film-making based on this process of observation lays particular emphasis on following the subjects' actions and recording them in their entirety rather than directing them according to some preconceived intellectual or aesthetic agenda. But, very importantly, despite the emphasis on observation, it also aims to be participatory in the sense that it should ideally take place from within a relationship of understanding and respect of the kind that can only arise when the film-maker has actively participated in the subjects' world for an extended period.

As this summary description makes clear and as has frequently been commented on before, observational cinema has much in common with the ethnographic method of participant observation that is conventionally one of the defining features of anthropological research. But there is also much common ground with respect to subject-matter since, like the majority of anthropologists, observational film-makers tend to be primarily concerned with 'ordinary' people in their everyday lives. Moreover, like most anthropologists, observational film-makers generally aim not to judge their subjects in any moral sense, but rather to present and analyse their world-view in such a way as to make it understandable to audiences with no direct personal experience of that world. Aesthetically too there is common ground in the sense that observational cinema, like most anthropological texts, is typically plain and unadorned stylistically.

Nor should the existence of this common ground be surprising since, although the principal proponents and practitioners of observational cinema have not themselves come from anthropological backgrounds, they have developed their approach in constant dialogue over the years with anthropologists, first in California, but subsequently in Britain as well as in other parts of Europe, Australia and elsewhere. The UCLA programme itself folded not long after its principal architect, Colin Young, returned to Britain in 1970 to run the National Film (and later, Television) School. But some years later, Young set up a similar programme in conjunction with the Royal Anthropological Institute and funded by the Leverhulme Trust. It ran at the NFTS from 1984 to 1987 and I myself was fortunate to be one of the participants.[1]

Observational cinema is certainly not the only method of film-making that is potentially appropriate to anthropological research, just as participant observation is not the only appropriate ethnographic fieldwork strategy. There are undoubtedly many situations and subject-matters to which other film-making approaches would be better suited. Indeed there seems to be no good reason to rule out in advance any particular film-making approach as inappropriate to anthropology. We can surely agree with Colin Young's view as expressed in the epigraph at the head of this chapter that such exclusionism is 'a waste of time'. Instead one need only require that the advocates of a given approach demonstrate its congruence or relevance to some aspect of the broader anthropological project. This opens the door to a whole range of possibilities, including poetic documentary and even fiction which, in any case, are no more than film-making terrains which have already been effectively colonised in the name of anthropology by the late Jean Rouch. But even whilst recognising these multiple possibilities, it remains the case that potentially there is a particularly harmonious correspondence between observational cinema and anthropology as it is presently constituted.

Yet whatever the compatibilities in respect of methodology and subject-matter or of ethics and aesthetics, in actual practice, observational cinema, in common with anthropological film-making generally, continues to operate in a sort of ghetto in which its proponents spend most of their time talking to one another rather than engaging in a broader 'conversation with anthropology'. As a result, the harsh truth is that despite the passing of more than three decades since the emergence of observational cinema, there is still a manifest lack of articulation between film-making and mainstream, literature-based anthropology.

There is a certain tendency amongst observational film-makers and their critical admirers to adopt the moral high-ground and suggest that this is due to various inadequacies of the text-makers. Academic anthropology generally is said to be somehow confused as to what to do with the visual, or perhaps worse still, 'iconophobic', positively afraid of the challenge that visual media pose to established methods and epistemologies.[2] Whilst there may once have been considerable truth in these assessments, personally I do not feel that there is any marked hostility towards the visual within the broader discipline at the present time. On the contrary, my sense is that as a result of the re-emergence of a general interest in ethnography in recent years, coupled with an enhanced concern with specific aspects of phenomenological experience, such as embodiment, performance, place and so on, there has been a simultaneously developing interest in visual representations of these aspects of social and cultural life. At the same time, reflecting their rapidly increasing importance in society generally, there has been an outburst of anthropological interest in visual media. However, in the anthropological exploration of such topics, the role of the visual has generally been merely to provide a small scrap of evidence on the basis of which an elaborate textual theorisation can be mounted. Film-making itself, observational or otherwise, has not been widely adopted as a means of investigation.

If this situation is to change, it is necessary for those working broadly within the observational cinema approach to demonstrate what film can do for text-making anthropologists, not just as a second-order visual aid in the classroom, but as a primary medium of research. But it is also important to ask in what ways the guiding principles of observational cinema itself may need to be reconsidered in order to make this conversation with the mainstream more productive. This need not only be a strategic matter: I believe that these adjustments could also result in richer, more interesting films for both specialist anthropological viewer and for cineaste alike.

In a recent article, Anna Grimshaw identifies observational cinema as a means of building upon the distinctive anthropological commitment to situated or experiential knowledge as exemplified by the centrality of fieldwork to the discipline. She also describes how her experience of teaching visual anthropology rapidly convinced her that 'anthropological film-making was not about adding film-making onto anthropology' but required instead 'a fundamental re-orientation of perspective such that the world is not primarily approached through language, explanation or generalization; but through a re-embodiment of the self as the foundation for renewed engagement with everyday life'. My own point of departure is rather different in that I consider that the contextual interpretation of social life, mediated through language and informed by comparative cultural awareness, to be of crucial and defining significance to the anthropological project as a whole. Moreover my own concern is not so much to effect a radical break with current text-based and language-based anthropological practice as to seek an accommodation between anthropological film-making and anthropological text-making, not by simply adding one onto the other, but by identifying points of articulation and interaction between the two, both conceptually and also in terms of the pragmatic practical processes of generating anthropological knowledge through the respective media. However where we appear to be in complete agreement is with regard to the potential of observational film-making to render the subjective and embodied aspects of human experience so frequently omitted from textual accounts. We also seem to agree that the key question with regard to the anthropological status of the knowledge generated through observational film-making is how this rendering of embodied experience 'can be made social', as she puts it, and which I would paraphrase as 'in what form can or should an interpretation be put upon this experience?' (see Grimshaw 2002: 11–12).

In the early part of this chapter, in line with my concern to identify points of articulation with the broader anthropological project, I will consider how film-making can be employed to enhance the generation of knowledge in the course of fieldwork whilst in the latter part, I will examine how this knowledge can be represented in ways that are sensitive to the social and cultural contexts of that knowledge. First though, in view of the many understandings and misunderstandings that the term 'observational cinema' generally evokes, I feel it is essential to begin with a brief summary account of the principles underlying the variant of observational cinema that I shall be concerned with in this chapter, at least as I myself understand them. Although this form of observational cinema has been progressively evolving and diversifying over the years, I would argue that there are still certain general principles that can be usefully identified, though no doubt every practitioner would have his or her own particular take on these. In attempting this synthesis, I shall be drawing extensively on certain key writings of two major figures, Colin Young and David MacDougall,[3] as well as on my own experience as a trainee observational film-maker at the NFTS under the inspiring tutorship of one of the pioneers of the approach, Herb di Gioia, then head of the School's documentary department.[4]

The principles of observational cinema

One of the first sustained formulations in print of the principles underlying observational cinema as defined in this chapter was Colin Young's contribution to the 1975 volume edited by Paul Hockings, *Principles of Visual Anthropology*, which is widely considered as the foundational text of the modern sub-discipline of visual anthropology (see Young 1995). The chapter was entitled, simply, 'Observational cinema' and was an attempt to summarise and explain the approach as it had developed up until that point to the emerging academic constituency of visual anthropologists. However Young himself was neither anthropologist nor documentarist: his immediate background was primarily in cinema studies, though he had a particular interest in a distinctively realist cinema tradition traceable from the Lumière brothers, through Jean Renoir to the post-war Italian neo-realists. In 1966, he was the Dean of Theatre Arts at UCLA and managed to establish the Ethnographic Film Training Programme by forging a series of alliances between his colleagues in the cinema department and those in anthropology and adjacent disciplines, such as sociology and ethnomusicology. One of these colleagues was the eminent ethnomethodologist Harold Garfinkel. Although he had no interest in the technical aspect of film-making, it was Garfinkel who encouraged Young to think of the film-making practice that he advocated as a *methodology* of ethnographic investigation rather than as simply a particular approach to documentary. Initially however, this methodology had no distinctive name; it was only a number of years after the establishment of the Film Training Programme that Young and his associates came to refer to it as 'observational cinema'.

Although participation was not referred to specifically in the new name, by this stage the involvement of the film-maker in the lives of the subjects was an integral part of Young's conception of the underlying principles of the approach. 'It must be based', he stressed in his contribution to *Principles*, 'on an intimate, sympathetic relationship between the film-maker and the subject – not the eye of the aloof, detached observer but of someone watching as much as possible from the inside.' Moreover he was quite explicit in insisting that no attempt should be made to hide this participation in the resulting film (Young 1995: 101–2, 110). However it seems that this emphasis on the notion of participation had not always been quite so marked. It is an emphasis that Young attributes particularly to David MacDougall, who along with his wife Judith was a graduate of the UCLA Film Training Programme. Together they had since become perhaps the most active practitioners of this form of participatory observational cinema. Comparing their 1972 film about the Jie pastoralists of Uganda, *To Live with Herds*, with those produced later in the same decade amongst Turkana pastoralists in Kenya, it is clear that being open about the participation of both subjects and film-makers in the construction of the film was becoming an increasingly prominent aspect of their work.

However, some misunderstanding seems to have arisen from the title of the chapter by David MacDougall in *Principles of Visual Anthropology*, immediately following Young's, in which MacDougall calls for the development of a film-making approach that he dubs 'participatory cinema'. Inspired by the example of Jean Rouch, this would be more open about the negotiation between film-maker and subjects in the construction of a film. The title of MacDougall's chapter is 'Beyond observational cinema' but the 'observational cinema' that MacDougall was aiming to go beyond here was not the variant as formulated by his former teacher in the preceding article, which already acknowledged the importance of participation, in part on account of MacDougall's own contribution to the debate about the still-emergent approach. Rather the 'observational cinema' that he was proposing to go beyond was exemplified by the work then being produced by film-makers such as John Marshall and Roger Sandall as well as by his own earlier work amongst the Jie. As it turned out though, the term 'participatory cinema' never really came to be widely adopted and whilst constantly seeking to develop the nature and degree of participation in the many films that he has subsequently made together with Judith, MacDougall has continued to identify his work within the general rubric of 'observational cinema' as formulated by Young.[5]

In this variant of observational cinema then, building on the participant observation methodology at its core, the film-maker should aim to exploit the distinctive capacity of synchronous sound film to communicate a sense of the lived experience of the events and situations observed. This is typically achieved through following, over a given period of time, the lives of a limited number of principal subjects whose personal circumstances throw some light on the broader issues with which the film-maker is concerned. In addition to the obviously necessary requirement that they themselves are interested in participating in the making of the film, the particular individuals chosen to play these 'leading roles' are generally selected on account of their eloquence and/or expressiveness of manner rather than on some principle of statistical representativeness. Through a process of identification and empathy with these particular subjects, the audience is encouraged to become interested and engaged with their world as a whole.

In practical film-making terms, the observational method seeks to effect this engagement between subject and audience through a cinematography based on an 'unprivileged' single camera that offers the viewpoint, in a very literal sense, of a normal human participant in the events portrayed. This camera should be mobile, following subjects and events rather than requiring them to be brought by prearrangement to be played out in front of it. Whenever possible or appropriate, long takes should be employed in order to preserve the integrity of events in the wholeness in which they spontaneously occur. To work effectively in this way requires a high degree of cinematographic skill, but stylistically the camerawork should be low-key: the observational cameraperson should take particular care that neither the distinctive temporal and spatial configurations of the events portrayed nor, more generally, the characteristic social and cultural aesthetics of their subjects' world are smothered by demonstrations of technical or aesthetic virtuosity.

However this concern with the integrity of the events represented should not be mistaken for any spurious claim to objectivity. Rather it arises from the observational film-maker's aspiration to communicate a sense of his or her subjective experience of 'being there' by showing certain moments of that experience in their entirety. But there is no pretence that this process of showing is anything other than highly selective. Nor does the observational method involve any denial of authorship: indeed, observational film-makers often claim authorship in a card that comes up immediately after the main title. However this method can be distinguished from more self-consciously authored approaches in the sense that it should, ideally, involve what David MacDougall has called a 'stance of humility before the world' that implicitly acknowledges that the subjects' story is more important than the film-maker's.

It is on these grounds then that there is a reluctance on the part of observational film-makers to intervene proactively in the events being filmed: not because it will somehow corrupt the evidence but rather because if subjects begin to think that they have to start performing in a particular way in order to meet the requirements of the film-maker, it will no longer be their story. At the same time, it reduces the possibility that they may open up interesting and entirely unanticipated avenues of enquiry. It is primarily as a corollary of this concern not to impose an external story that observational film-makers tend to frown on the formal interview or indeed on any kind of performance, however minor, which has been put on *at the film-maker's request*. This applies even to the re-enactment of an action that took place only a few moments before: if the film-maker has missed it, he should not ask for it to be repeated, but wait for something similar to occur. On the other hand, if a subject chooses to initiate a conversation, even a formal one, or put on a special performance of some kind for the camera, there is nothing wrong with this since, in this case, 'the mandate' – to employ a recurrent expression of Colin Young's – is coming from the subject, not from the film-maker.

If observational film-makers aim to respect the integrity of their subjects and events in the way in which they film them, they also aspire to do so in the way in which they assemble their rushes in the edit suite. Again, there is no attempt to deny that subjectivity and authorship will inevitably enter into the editing process in determining which sequences are preserved and which are not. But within the constraints of the material retained, the general aim should be to achieve a 'congruency between the subject as experienced by the film-makers and the film as experienced by the audience' (Young 1982b: 63). This means making an effort to retain long shots that capture the rhythms and spatial configurations of the social world represented. The same applies to the ambiguities, the vacillations and the repetitions that are integral aspect of everyday life but which can all too easily be excised by a conventional editor determined to eliminate redundancy at whatever cost. This cost can include eliminating the sense of contingency that is a crucial aspect of real experience.

Although observational film-makers will readily acknowledge that they share with other film-makers a concern to give a narrative shape to their films, these narratives should be adapted to the life rather than vice versa and the exploration of revealing detail should become a substitute for artificial dramatic tension. In general they should resist the temptation, as Young puts it, to play either the teacher or the artist, i.e. subjecting the rushes to such an imposing intellectual or aesthetic agenda that members of the audience can no longer draw their own conclusions about the significance of what they are seeing. On these grounds, extended explanatory voice-over commentary, music that is 'extra-diegetic' (i.e. from outside the action of the film) and dramatic special effects are all ruled out since they are considered not only to be external to the original material, and therefore stylistically inappropriate, but also to push the audience too strongly towards a given kind of reaction.

Observational cinema as practical ethnography

If these then are the basic principles of the observational approach emerging from the UCLA and NFTS programmes, we can now proceed to evaluate this approach to film-making as a means of practical ethnography. In order to do so, it is helpful to begin by distinguishing the potential of observational cinema as a means of *generating* anthropological knowledge from its potential as a means of *representing* such knowledge. For, in effect, the form of observational cinema with which I am concerned here involves two temporally distinct processes of discovery and participation: in the first place by the film-maker following the actions of his subjects rather than working to a predetermined script; subsequently by the audience as they are invited to locate their own meanings in the material that the film-maker presents to them. Or to put it another way, not only the film-maker and the subjects, but also the audience, become active participants in the construction of the meaning of the film. Whilst many anthropologists might identify with the first of these discovery processes, some might baulk at the idea of offering such a degree of interpretative freedom to their eventual audiences.

As far as the generation of knowledge is concerned, even those anthropologists who are favourably disposed to the use of film as a medium of ethnographic research often have a rather limited sense of its potential. Some continue to think of the camera merely as a data-gathering device, one that is rather more effective than a notebook in collecting and storing certain kinds of visual information which can then be analysed later. There is a lingering positivism in this view in that it implies that the gathering of facts and their interpretation can be separated from one another. As such, it harks back to the early days of visual anthropology when the camera was conceived of as a scientific apparatus analogous to the telescope or microscope.[6] But, as Colin Young himself put it long ago, what the camera certainly cannot do is rescue anthropologists from the subjectivity of their field notes (Young 1995: 100). What researchers choose to film and how they film it will obviously always remain similarly vulnerable to the contingencies of their particular interests and circumstances.

Such naivety as this may be increasingly rare, but there is a related notion, still advocated by some, that one should use a camera as if it were a notebook, more or less randomly compiling footage over the whole period of fieldwork without any clear purpose as to how it will be used later. But to use an analogy that has been deployed in a slightly different context, this is a method akin to keeping a store of good sentences in the hope that one day they can be shuffled into a book.[7] Technically speaking, it is surely a recipe for disaster since it will result in a large sprawling mass of material that will require months in the edit suite to sort out, and even then will probably lack focus and continuity both in terms of character and theme. Even cinematographically, it is likely to be sloppy and poorly framed. For if shooting becomes a banal everyday activity consisting simply of trawling for images that may one day prove useful, it is unlikely to be anything more than ordinary.

Usually underpinning these conceptions of the camera as data-gathering device is the more fundamental idea that the principal role of film-making should be no more than to provide a second-order illustration of understandings arrived at by other means. Anthropological film-making thereby becomes not so much a process of discovery as a means of providing confirmatory visual evidence for a verbal argument typically delivered through voice-over narration. In line with this assumption, certain colleagues have commented to me that they advise their doctoral students going on their first major fieldwork trip to leave making a film to some subsequent occasion on account of the 'danger' that it might interfere or distract them from their primary activity as researchers. Once they have made their discoveries and drawn their conclusions, it is implied, then they can go back and make a film in the light of these. But the idea that film-making should be put off until the real business of fieldwork is completed overlooks the capacity of film not just to illustrate an analysis but actually to generate it.

In one sense, my colleagues are undoubtedly right: film-making is certainly a distraction from other forms of research activity. Particularly if it is conducted in the observational manner, it requires intense concentration and commitment, and there is little room in the researcher's life for anything else. For this reason, I advise my own doctoral students to assign a distinct period within their fieldwork for film-making and focus on it exclusively during that time. Although every case will be different, as a rough index I suggest that this period should fall about two-thirds of the way through the fieldwork period: far enough in for the researcher to be well-informed, linguistically competent and socially integrated into the subjects' world, but still early enough for them to be able to pursue any additional lines of enquiry thrown up by the film-making.

This generation of knowledge through film-making can come about in a number of different ways. In a very general way, it can have an intensifying, catalytic effect on the conventional fieldwork processes of participant observation. Since there is often no second chance to film a particular event, anthropologist film-makers are obliged to focus precisely on what kinds of events it is that they wish to film, and on the circumstances in which these are likely to happen. Under these conditions, the disciplines of the observational method are particularly salutary, requiring acute observation and a total immersion in the event. If their films are not to be a series of disparate images strung together later around a commentary, even whilst in the field observational film-makers have to be constantly editorialising, asking themselves which sequences will be necessary to communicate their experience of the world that they are representing and then how one such sequence will influence another.

But this should not involve the mechanical shooting of a 'shopping list' of sequences according to some preconceived script. Instead it should be a continuously exploratory process that undergoes constant revision throughout the period of the shoot. Note-taking enables one to write everything down and think about it later. But with film-making there is an awareness that if one fails to film something when the opportunity presents itself in the field, one will not be able to recuperate it later through memory. And yet at the same time, one has to keep an eye on the tape stock and the camera battery life so as to make sure that one does not waste them on something that will not be useful. In short, like Dr Johnson's man condemned to hang in the morning, the observational film-maker's sense of the limited opportunity of the moment concentrates the mind wonderfully well.

Once one has returned from the field, the process of learning through intense observation can continue. Editing affords an opportunity for a second participative immersion in the events, particularly if one has shot the material according to the observational norms, i.e. long, considered takes, shot in an unprivileged style from the point of view of a normal human observer. In the absence of a formal editing script, observational editors (usually also the original film-makers) search for an appropriate structure within the rushes. It should not be an unguided search, since they should have in mind certain 'foreshadowed problems' to use that much-evoked Malinowskian phrase, namely those that arose in the field research. They are also likely to be oriented, almost despite themselves, by certain conventional narrative models. But they should also be open to learning new things about the material they themselves have shot: these can be purely factual matters, which they did not notice in the field. But in a manner analogous to the knowledge that can arise from the repeated revision and reclassification of field notes, this new knowledge can also consist of more abstract insights that derive simply from the repeated viewing of the rushes, or from the juxtaposition of sequences in preliminary assemblies.

The catalytic effect of film-making on participant observation can also involve the subjects of a film. First, in the discussions and negotiations with subjects about what the film should be about and how it should be made, the film-maker is likely to discover a great deal not only about the substantive content of the film to be made, but also a broad variety of other matters, such as the subjects' attitudes to visual media, the status of the visual in the subjects' social life more generally, ideas about social performance, the relationship of public to private areas of experience and so on. These discussions can be incorporated directly into the film or it may be more appropriate or practicable to explore them at greater length in print.[8]

Second, the presence of the camera itself, once it emerges from its case, can then have a variety of effects: in some cases, it may be no more than neutral, whilst in others, perhaps the majority, the presence of the camera leads the subjects to give what is, in effect, some sort of special performance. As we have seen, in the ideal–typical observational method, this is considered entirely acceptable provided the 'mandate' comes from the subjects. These performances motivated by the presence of the camera can be highly revealing, bringing to light aspects of personal identity, attitude, belief or fantasy that could otherwise remain hidden or unexpressed. The participation of the subjects in the making of a film can also take the form of reacting to a screening of the rushes. These reactions can then be taken into account in a further refinement of the film, a procedure that has a venerable ancestry in anthropological film-making.[9] Sometimes, they can lead instead to more abstract, theoretical reflections which can then further developed in a textual form, outside the film.[10]

Whilst any form of film-making might have these beneficial consequences to some degree, the observational approach is particularly effective. For it is the specific commitment to reproducing the original experience of the events filmed as integrally and as spontaneously as possible that requires film-makers in the field to become intensively immersed in the events being recorded, focusing their observations and sharpening their cinematography. Moreover it is the reproduction of the integrity and contingency of the events filmed which enables film-maker, and possibly their subjects as well, to relive and reinterpret that experience subsequently, be it the following day in the field or much later back in some distant edit suite. All this, I would suggest, provides a strong argument in favour not merely of film-making in general, but of film-making according to observational norms as a means of generating anthropological knowledge.

However, on the face it, it then seems rather strange, contradictory even, to conclude that having developed and refined one's knowledge and understanding of the events and situations recorded in all these ways, one should then subject them to no more than the most restrained manipulation in the edit suite before handing them over to the audience so that they can determine their ultimate significance. Yet this is one of the central tenets of the observational film-making approach, and one that is reiterated routinely in the writings of Young, MacDougall and others. All these sources stress that the observational film-maker must not present him- or herself as an 'expert' (a term which tends to be enclosed in sceptical inverted commas in their writings) and should refrain from any post-production strategies that might prevent the audience from seeing for itself. Cinema should be treated as a medium of suggestion and implication rather than of statement and description and the overall aim should be not to tell but to show. In this way, one ensures that a film remains not just an act of discovery for the maker, but also for the viewer who thereby participates actively in the construction of the meaning of the film.

This clearly poses a serious challenge to conventional strategies of representation in textual anthropology. For many anthropological authors would probably see their role as being precisely the opposite, namely, to provide a hermetic interpretative context for the material they are presenting. Having established the authority of their interpretation by various means at the beginning of their texts, they then typically seek to convince their audience of both its validity and comprehensiveness. To this end, they aim to elucidate any ambiguities and to counter all potentially competing interpretations, all with a view to eliminating any 'aberrant readings'.[11] So, even if we might agree that observational film-making closely complements an anthropological fieldwork practice based on participant observation, we might ask whether the norms of observational post-production are equally appropriate to the representation of that fieldwork to an anthropological audience.

A number of reasons have been offered by observational film-makers for their restraint in the editing suite. But for me the most convincing concerns the impact that overzealous editorial intervention can have on transmitting a sense of the experience of the events represented. For as Young puts it, when film-makers 'play the teacher or the artist', plastering over their images with an excessive explanatory commentary or indulging in overwhelming aesthetic devices, they pay a price in terms of diminishing the 'congruency between the subject as experienced by the film-makers and the film as experienced by the audience'. But to give up entirely on the aim of providing any interpretative context runs the risk of falling back on the lame assumption that a common humanity and some empathetic powers of intuition are all one needs to achieve an understanding of a film subjects' world that is different from one's own. Besides, the absence of interpretative context does not guarantee that the experience embodied in the filmic text will be more accessible: often quite the reverse is the case.[12]

One of the meta-themes of anthropology is surely that whilst empathy is certainly an advantage in achieving understanding across a boundary of cultural difference, it is certainly not sufficient. Films may allow one to communicate those human commonalities that lie beyond or beneath cultural difference very effectively, as MacDougall has persuasively argued.[13] But an analysis of how culture or variable social and political environments are inscribed upon those commonalities remains a defining concern of the anthropological project as a whole. The challenge then for anthropological film-makers working within the observational tradition broadly defined is to develop editorial strategies that will enable them to provide an appropriate interpretative context for the worlds they represent whilst at the same time ensuring that these do not fatally undermine the distinctive contribution that observational cinema can make to the development of an 'experience-rich' ethnography. As we shall see, the key to doing so is to provide that context as far as possible from within the film itself.

Issues of context

Considered as a means of anthropological representation, observational cinema poses issues of interpretative context on at least three different levels. First, there is the problem of the contextualisation of the events presented within a film: how does one event or situation relate to another, how do any of these events relate to cultural contexts, or bodies of knowledge or experience held by the subjects but lying outside the action of the film? Second, there is the problem of contextualising the film-making process itself: under what circumstances did it take place and within what network of relationships with the subjects, how does it relate to other aspects of the film-maker's research and her/his general intellectual agenda, how are the views it communicates constrained by other aspects of her/his personal subjectivity, such as institutional affiliations, political views, age or gender? Finally, there is the context of the use of the film: how should the film be related to previous anthropological productions – textual or filmic – on similar or related topics, what contribution does the film-maker feel that her/his work makes to the current general exchange of ideas within anthropology?

Observational film-makers have developed various strategies for dealing with the first of these levels. The juxtaposition of one sequence with another, or sometimes even just one shot with another, represents an elementary method of contextualisation and the choice as to which scenes or shots to juxtapose in this way can reflect particular anthropological ideas and interpretations. But more than this, many observational films are built around what turns out to be a fairly conventional narrative structure which, in effect, embodies an argument or at the very least represents the point of view of the film-maker(s). Although observational cinema advocates stress the importance of allowing audiences the freedom to construct their own meanings, this does not mean that they do not analyse their material and structure it accordingly. On the contrary, observational film-makers typically spend prolonged periods in the edit suite working on the ordering and weighting of the various component parts in order to give meaning and direction to their films. (This is made all the more difficult given their disinclination to use voice-over commentary.) But as David MacDougall himself has commented, 'It isn't just a case of presenting the material and allowing the audience to do what they will with it. It's always very much guided.'[14] Anthropologists making films in this way are clearly at liberty to guide their audience in directions that arise from or contribute to a contextualising anthropological analysis of the subject matter of the film.

Although interviews may be regarded with suspicion by some proponents of the observational cinema, they too can represent particularly effective means of contextualisation. In fact, notwithstanding the normative condemnation of interviews by observational pundits, in practice there is barely a film in the observational canon that does not involve conversational exchanges between film maker(s) and subjects that are interviews in everything but name. However, they tend to be informal in character, disguised in various ways and to be used sparingly. In contrast to a conventional 'talking-head' set-up, in which a whole film may be structured around one or more central interviews, the observational film-maker generally seeks to avoid returning to the same 'conversation' more than once, thus giving the impression that it is an exchange that arose spontaneously in the general flow of events rather than a formal interview as such. Sometimes the soundtrack from these may be laid over other images and used as voice-over commentary. Alternatively, subjects' reactions to the rushes may be recorded and this used instead as voice-over.[15] Employed in this way then, such 'conversations' can be used to provide the sort of contextualisations in which anthropological viewers may be interested without rupturing the general observational aesthetic of the film.[16]

However, all these devices primarily involve what one might call, adapting the vocabulary of Clifford Geertz, 'experience-near' contextualisation. That is, they involve contextualisation that is in some sense *emergent* from within the film itself, resulting either from the editorial ordering of shots and sequences or from oral comment by the subjects, be it in the form of unelicited spontaneous testimony or in the form of conversation with the film-maker. But one might also ask how and in what form within an ethnographic documentary one might achieve 'experience-distant' contextualisation, that is, contextualisation in terms that are external to the action of film itself and probably also alien to the subjects.[17] For example, could one use the commentary track to make theoretical allusions, draw out the comparative implications of the material presented or discuss methodological principles and procedures? If this were possible, the linkage to current themes and interests within anthropology as a whole would become much easier to establish.

But however desirable this might be, in trying to achieve such linkages one quickly runs up against a number of problems, both technical and stylistic. The most immediate is that 'experience-distant' commentary, as the term itself suggests, tends to undermine the whole purpose of using observational cinema as a means of anthropological representation in the first place, namely to restore some sense of lived, embodied experience to ethnographic accounts. The retailing of privileged information or understandings in a commentary can have the same effect as the privileged camera: it creates a sense of distance, of disengagement with the subjects. In the best case, an experience-distant commentary can seem merely patronising; in the worst case, even when it is well-intentioned and adopts a positive attitude towards the subjects, it can belittle and objectify them, making their world-views seem inadequate and clearly inferior to that of the commentator. This is particularly noticeable as the years go by: one need only look at ethnographic films made a mere twenty years ago to realise that the aspect that usually seems most dated is the voice-over commentary.[18]

But there is another, more technical, problem which is related to the fact that film is generally a very inefficient medium for communicating verbal information and analyses. The reason for this is very prosaic, namely, that it often takes much longer to make a verbal comment about an action or an event than it takes for that same action or event to occur. As a result, it is usually impossible within the time-frame of the duration of an action to provide a verbal commentary that elucidates anything more than a fraction of the relevant social or cultural significances of that action. In an attempt to fit it all in, it is only too easy to drown the image in words and/or cut the film up with a flurry of intertitle cards. Either way round, the characteristic rhythms and sounds of the world represented are submerged. In effect then, when one employs experience-distant commentary, one usually pays a price in terms of the objectification of the subjects and the loss of the sense of 'being there' without coming close to achieving a satisfactorily comprehensive contextualisation anyway.

Similar difficulties arise in relation to the second level of contextualisation identified above, namely the location of the film within the broader context of the work and person of the film-maker. As we have seen, the leading advocates of observational cinema certainly do not have any difficulty with the idea of revealing the presence of the film-maker within the filmic text itself. This provides the stylistic opportunity, as it were, for the film-maker to provide a reflexive meta-commentary in voice-over, describing such matters as his or her interests and motivations for making the film, the strategies employed and why, as well as more personal reflections on the experience of making the film and so on. Provided this voice-over is in the first person, the voice on the commentary track can effectively link up with the voice in the synch action, thereby giving the sense of emergence from the film itself. This is a device that could conflict in some degree with the 'stance of humility before the world' that many observational film-makers prefer to take. Given the time constraints of a film, any such reflexive meta-commentary has to be relatively restrained or it will soon overwhelm and outweigh the subjects' story as well as the general ethnographic content.[19] But, even taking these limitations into account, reflexive commentary by the film-maker could probably be used more effectively than it has been to date in observational film-making.

However, as with the first level of contextualisation, the more this reflexive voice emerges from the film itself, and the more it is couched in a vernacular, experience-near language, the less stylistically obtrusive it will seem. A reflexive account of the kind one might expect to find in the preface to an ethnographic monograph, detailing such matters as the film-maker's theoretical agenda, how the present work fits into the general trajectory of his or her intellectual project, or how it relates to other anthropological texts and representations would again run the risk of drowning the images and objectifying the subjects, thereby undermining the point of making an observational film in the first place.[20]

But even whilst one might recognise that it is both stylistically and technically problematic to incorporate experience-distant contexts directly into a film made according to observational principles, these contexts are still of legitimate interest to any anthropological audience, and must be addressed if this method of film-making is to become a genuinely effective means of ethnography. The most frequently proposed way of doing so is through the production of some kind of accompanying written text. In such a text, not only can theoretical, methodological and comparative issues be considered but it can also serve as a vehicle for any additional detailed ethnography that would have overburdened the film. It can be particularly useful for addressing the third level of context referred to above, namely situating the film in relation to previous anthropological works, textual or filmic, and generally identifying its relevance to current debates in the discipline as a whole.

But here too, practical difficulties have obstructed what appears initially to be an eminently sensible solution. First, despite many pious comments about the need to produce accompanying texts, in practice anthropological film-makers very rarely do so. Second, even when such texts have been produced, the film has still tended to circulate mostly by itself. Recent technological developments could overcome at least the second of these difficulties. With the coming of DVD and other electronic hypermedia, both film and text can be presented within the same medium. But in order to take full advantage of these technological developments, it will be necessary for anthropological film-makers to acquire DVD authoring skills, which is in itself no small undertaking. Navigational design of the DVDs will also need to be carefully considered if the distinctive potential of film as a means of communicating experience is not to be negated. For there is a risk, particularly in the proverbially word-based discipline that is anthropology, that these DVD compilations will result in the subordination of the visual materials to the role of merely providing supporting evidence for verbal or textual arguments.

However, there is no reason why this has to be so: in principle at least, it is readily possible to conceive of a DVD that is primarily constructed around a central film which, freed of the need for contextualisation by the presence of the accompanying texts, could be even more purely observational than one that is free-standing. At the same time, the presentation of these contextualising textual or verbal materials could be designed so that they could be read either before or after watching the film rather than being consulted during the course of it and thereby rupturing the engagement of the viewer. Nor need texts be the only additional materials presented. Depending on the capacity of the DVD, it should also be possible to present additional visual sequences, sound recordings or indeed complete minor accompanying films that would have unbalanced the narrative or unduly prolonged the running time if they had been incorporated into the principal film. Only time will tell if this new medium for anthropological representation will fulfil its promise, but there are already some encouraging beginnings.[21]

The renewal of observational cinema

For many, both inside the academic world and beyond, observational cinema is now decidedly past its sell-by date. In television, it has been entirely displaced by highly manipulated films based on a profusion of short takes, dramatic reconstructions and interviews, usually bound together with music and/or commentary. Some of this work is interesting and certainly highly skilled, and the techniques and methods on which it is based could perhaps be moulded to anthropological purposes also. But whilst not wanting to discount these methods, I would maintain that the participatory variant of observational cinema as defined in this chapter continues to be a particularly appropriate film-making strategy for anthropological research. All too often – perhaps because 'observational cinema' can mean so many different things – those academic commentators who dismiss it as passé have signally failed to understand its basic premises, frequently misreading it as being based on some sort of naive positivism.

However, even whilst continuing to advocate the basic approach as a means of practical ethnography, I am not convinced that it is necessary to remain slavishly tied to the most stringent interpretation of its norms. Certainly we should be actively exploring all possible ways of relating the films we make to the broader anthropological 'conversation', be it through seeking more specifically focused narratives that address contemporary issues in anthropology, by developing the emergent contextualising strategies described above and/or by co-opting the possibilities offered by DVD technology. Nor should these norms be treated as if they were commandments set in stone for all time. Indeed in my own film-making practice, I have sought to adjust my primary formation as an observational film-maker to a variety of circumstances and subject-matters.

As Colin Young observes in the epigraph at the head of this chapter, any intellectual discipline is bound to outgrow its early enthusiasms and change its methodologies, and there is no reason why observational cinema should be an exception. Indeed, no sooner had the principles first been formulated than David MacDougall was suggesting a means for going beyond them, whilst his subsequent film work together with Judith MacDougall could be interpreted as a prolonged and meticulous exploration of how to mould the approach to a wide variety of cultural contexts and topics. All those who aim to use this form of cinema for the specific purposes of anthropological research should be similarly imaginative in renewing observational cinema by adapting its principles to meet both present and future needs.

Notes

1 The other participants were John Baily (now teaching at the Department of Music, Goldsmiths College, University of London), Marcus Banks (Institute of Social and Cultural Anthropology, University of Oxford) and Felicia Hughes-Freeland (Department of Sociology and Anthropology, University of Swansea). Subsequently, in a sort of further extension of the scheme funded by the Granada Centre for Visual Anthropology, University of Manchester, Anna Grimshaw attended the School in 1991–2 following her appointment to a lectureship in the Centre.
2 See e.g. Taylor 1996, MacDougall 1997.
3 Amongst the most important primary textual sources have been Young 1982a, 1982b, 1995, the essays collected together in David MacDougall's book, *Transcultural Cinema*

(1998), most of which have been previously published, as well as MacDougall's commentaries (1999, 2001) on his most recent project, a series of films shot in the Doon School in India. See also the 'conversation' with MacDougall conducted by Anna Grimshaw and Nikos Papastergiadis (1995) and mine with Colin Young, conducted in 2001 and due to be published shortly (Henley, forthcoming a). Of secondary sources, both Peter Loizos (1993) and Anna Grimshaw (2001) dedicate important chapters of their respective general books on anthropological film to a critical assessment of certain key films in the MacDougall *oeuvre*. Another good secondary source is Lucien Taylor's introduction to *Transcultural Cinema*.

4   As an observational film-maker, Herb di Gioia is perhaps best known for his work with the late David Hancock on *Vermont People*, a series of intimate portraits of neighbours and friends in his home State shot in the early 1970s. Another well-known joint work is *Naim and Jabar* (1974), a film about the friendship between two Afghani teenage boys as their lives threaten to take them on different paths into adulthood. This was part of one of five film-making projects in the American Universities Field Staffs series produced by Norman Miller. In the absence of any direct sources, an article by Hancock reviewing Granada Television's *Disappearing World* series (1975) is valuable here since he uses it as a vehicle for the ideas about observational cinema that he and di Gioia were presumably working out together at the time.

5   MacDougall has explained (pers. comm.) that at the time *Principles* was going through the press, he was in East Africa working on the *Turkana Conversations* trilogy. So the first time that he became aware that his title might lead to his contribution being misread as a critique of Young's preceding article was when the book was already published and it was too late to do anything about it. In a post-script added in the second edition of *Principles*, MacDougall acknowledges that he had perhaps over-stressed the borderline the between the earlier forms of observational cinema and the proposed 'participatory' cinema. For a discussion of the MacDougalls' development of ideas and strategies of participation, see Grimshaw and Papastergiadis 1995, particularly pp. 40 ff.

6   The *locus classicus* for this point of view is Margaret Mead's opening chapter in *Principles of Visual Anthropology* (Mead 1995). This was originally published in 1975 but echoes are still to be found in later works.

7   The distinguished observational editor Dai Vaughan used this analogy in relation to the preoccupation of some anthropologists to preserve out-takes at all costs, but it can be applied with equal force to the shooting of unmotivated material in the first place (Vaughan 1992: 114).

8   See the interesting reflections by Amanda Ravetz (2002) about her experience shooting her observational doctoral film *The Bracewells* in a Pennine town and by Rosie Read (forthcoming) about filming observationally within the 'scopic regime' of the Czech prison-cum-geriatric hospital which was the principal location of her doctoral film *Domov*.

9   Flaherty used the technique with Allakarialak (aka Nanook) and his fellow Inuit in 1920 to work out the ongoing development of his shoot. Thirty years later, in the 1950s, Jean Rouch introduced a further development which was to record his subjects' feedback and then use this as voice-over commentary. Thirty years after that, in the 1980s, the MacDougalls were using a similar technique of 'interior commentary' recorded in the edit suite with Australian Aboriginal subjects.

10 See Howard Morphy's perceptive account of both his own and his informants' re-actions to the completed version of *Madarrpa Funeral at Gurka'wuy*, a film which he made in conjunction with Frances Morphy and the director Ian Dunlop, and which concerns the funeral rites of the Yolgnu people of Yirrkala in northeast Arnhemland (Morphy 1994).

11 Since the 'literary turn' in anthropology, there have been many analyses of the way in which authority is established in ethnographic texts, but amongst the most frequently cited are Marcus and Cushman 1982, Clifford 1988, Geertz 1988.

12 The objectification of the subjects that occurs in certain conventional forms of ethno-graphic film has been described by Marc Piault as the 'entomologist's perspective' (Piault 2000: 146). This is an allusion to the well-known rebuff directed at Jean Rouch by the Senegalese author and film-maker Ousmane Sembène, namely, that 'you look at us like insects'. However, significantly, Sembène relates this criticism specifically to Rouch's early omnibus film about the peoples of the Niger, *Les fils de l'eau* (1955), in which, Sembène claims, African rituals are presented without explanation (Prédal 1982). This serves as a powerful reminder that *under*-explanation can be just as objectifying as *over*-explanation.

13 See particularly the concluding eponymous essay of *Transcultural Cinema*, 1998: 245–78.

14 See MacDougall's remarks in Grimshaw and Papastergiadis 1995: 49, and Colin Young's on a similar theme in our 'conversation' in Henley (forthcoming a). See also my longer discussion of narrative in ethnographic documentary in Henley (forthcoming b).

15 See n. 9 above.

16 The MacDougalls have made use of these informal 'conversational' exchanges as contextualising devices throughout their career and in David's most recent work in the Doon School, they play an important if discreet role. I have discussed the role of interviews in observational cinema and ethnographic film more generally in a recently published article (Henley 2003). Here I make the point that in addition to their strategic value as contextualising devices, interviews can also be very revealing of culturally variable norms of oral performance.

17 Geertz himself borrowed the distinction between experience-near and experience-distant concepts from the psychoanalyst Heinz Kohut. As Geertz explains, 'An experience-near concept is, roughly, one that someone – a patient, a subject, in our case an informant – might himself naturally and effortlessly use to define what he or his fellows see, feel, think, imagine, and so on . . . An experience-distant concept is one that specialists . . . employ to forward their scientific, philosophical, or practical aims. "Love" is an experience-near concept, "object-cathexis" is an experience-distant one' (Geertz 1993: 57).

18 See Jean Rouch's amusing remarks on the history of commentary styles in anthro-pological film-making (1995: 92). However, his awareness of their ready tendency to anachronism has not inhibited him from using extensive narration himself!

19 As Brian Winston, the eminent documentary film commentator, has wittily sug-gested, if every documentary is to be comprehensively reflexive, then there is a risk that the subject-matter of every documentary will be the making of a documentary (Winston 1993: 51).

20 Perhaps the most enthusiastic advocate of the need for a reflexive positioning of the film-maker within the filmic text itself has been Jay Ruby. But as he himself

comments, comprehensive reflexivity of the kind that he envisages is very rarely achieved. This is true even of written anthropological texts, despite all sorts of routine statements as to the importance of being methodologically reflexive from Malinowski onwards. As far as film is concerned, Ruby cannot think of a single example in the hundred-year history of ethnographic film-making that has entirely satisfied his requirements, including it seems such an extensively reflexive work as the Edgar Morin and Jean Rouch classic *Chronicle of a Summer* (see Ruby 2000: 156–7). This fact alone suggests that he may be too ambitious for filmic reflexivity given the nature of the medium.

21 Although they were both produced a considerable time after the making of the original film, two relatively recent electronic film–text packages demonstrate future possibilities: they are the CD-based *Yanomamö Interactive*, the reworking by Peter Biella, Napoleon Chagnon and Gary Seaman (1997) of the Tim Asch and Chagnon classic 1975 film *The Ax Fight*, and the DVD/text package released by Robert Gardner and Ákos Östör (2001) concerning their much-discussed 1989 film of funerary practices in Benares, *Forest of Bliss*. See also Pink 2001, especially pp. 162–71 for a more developed discussion of the potential of ethnographic hypermedia.

References

Biella, P., Chagnon, N. A. and Seaman, G. (1997) *Yanomamö Interactive: The Ax Fight*, New York: Harcourt Brace College Publishers.

Clifford, J. (1988) 'On ethnographic authority', in J. Clifford, *The Predicament of Culture: Twentieth-Century Ethnography, Literature and Art*, Cambridge, Mass. and London: Harvard University Press, 21–54.

Gardner, R. and Östör, Á. (2001) *Making Forest of Bliss: Intention, Circumstance and Chance in Non-Fiction Film*, Cambridge, Mass. and London: Harvard Film Archive.

Geertz, C. (1988) *Works and Lives: The Anthropologist as Author*, Stanford, CA: Stanford University Press.

—— (1993) ' "From the native's point of view": on the nature of anthropological understanding'. in C. Geertz, *Local Knowledge: Further Essays in Interpretive Anthropology*, London: Fontana, 55–70.

Grimshaw, A. (2001) *The Ethnographer's Eye: Ways of Seeing in Anthropology*, Cambridge: Cambridge University Press.

—— (2002) 'Eyeing the field: new horizons for visual anthropology'. *Journal of Media Practice* 3(1): 7–15.

Grimshaw, A. and Papastergiadis, N. (1995) *Conversations with Anthropological Filmmakers: David MacDougall*, Pamphlet no. 9, Cambridge: Prickly Pear Press.

Hancock, D. (1975) '*Disappearing World*: anthropology on television', *Sight & Sound* 44: 103–7.

Henley, P. (2003) 'Are you happy? Interviews, 'conversations' and 'talking heads' as means of gathering oral testimony in ethnographic documentary', in J. Wossidlo and U. Roters (eds), *Film und Interview. Volkskundliche und ethnologische Ansätze zu Methodik und Analyse*, Münster, New York, Munich, and Berlin: Waxmann Verlag.

—— (forthcoming a) 'The origins of observational cinema: conversations with Colin Young', in B. Engelbrecht (ed.), *Memories of the Origins of Visual Anthropology*, Frankfurt, New York, Bern and Brussels: Peter Lang.

—— (forthcoming b) 'Narratives – the guilty secret of documentary?', in M. Postma (ed.), *Reflecting Visual Ethnography: Using the Camera in Anthropological Research*, Aarhus: Intervention Press.

Loizos, P. (1993) *Innovation in Ethnographic Film: From Innocence to Self-Consciousness 1955–1985*, Manchester: Manchester University Press.

MacDougall, D. (1995) 'Beyond observational cinema', in P. Hockings (ed.), *Principles of Visual Anthropology*, 2nd edn, Berlin and New York: Mouton de Gruyter, 115–32.

—— (1997) 'The visual in anthropology', in M. Banks and H. Morphy (eds), *Rethinking Visual Anthropology*, New Haven and London: Yale University Press, 276–95.

—— (1998) *Transcultural Cinema*. Princeton University Press.

—— (1999) 'Social aesthetics and the Doon School', *Visual Anthropology Review* 15(1): 3–20.

—— (2001) 'Renewing ethnographic film. Is digital video changing the genre?', *Anthropology Today* 17(3): 15–21.

Marcus, G. E. and Cushman, D. (1982) 'Ethnographies as texts', *Annual Review of Anthropology* 11: 25–69.

Mead, M. (1995) 'Visual anthropology in a discipline of words', in P. Hockings (ed.), *Principles of Visual Anthropology*, 2nd edn, Berlin and New York: Mouton de Gruyter, 3–10.

Morphy, H. (1994) 'The interpretation of ritual: reflections from film on anthropological practice', *Man* 29: 117–46.

Piault, M.-H. (2000) *Anthropologie et cinéma: passage à l'image, passage par l'image*, Paris: Éditions Nathan.

Pink, S. (2001) *Doing Visual Ethnography: Images, Media and Representation in Research*, London: Sage.

Prédal, R. (1982) 'Une confrontation historique en 1965 entre Jean Rouch et Sembène Ousmane', in R. Prédal (ed.), *Le griot gaulois, CinémAction* 17: 77–8.

Ravetz, A. (2002) 'News from home: reflections on fine art and anthropology', *Journal of Media Practice* 3(1): 16–25.

Read, R. (forthcoming) 'Scopic regimes and the observational approach: ethnographic film-making in a Czech institution', *Visual Anthropology* (due to appear in 2004).

Rouch, J. (1995) 'The camera and man', in P. Hockings (ed.), *Principles of Visual Anthropology*, 2nd edn, Berlin and New York: Mouton de Gruyter, 79–98.

Ruby, J. (2000) 'Exposing yourself: reflexivity, anthropology, and film', in J. Ruby, *Picturing Culture: explorations of film and anthropology*, Chicago and London: University of Chicago Press, 151–80.

Taylor, L. (1996) 'Iconophobia: how anthropology lost it at the movies', *Transition* 6(1) no. 69: 64–88.

—— (1998) 'Introduction', In D. MacDougall, *Transcultural Cinema*, Princeton: Princeton University Press, 3–21.

Vaughan, D. (1992) 'The aesthetics of ambiguity', in P. Crawford and D. Turton (eds.) *Film as Ethnography*, Manchester: Manchester University Press, 99–115.

Winston, B. (1993) 'The documentary film as scientific inscription', in M. Renov (ed.), *Theorizing Documentary*, New York and London: Routledge, 37–57.

Young, C. (1982a) 'MacDougall conversations', *Royal Anthropological Institute Newsletter* 50: 5–8.

—— (1982b) 'Vérité – the true story', Edinburgh International Television Festival, Programme no. 7, 58–65.

—— (1995) 'Observational cinema', in P. Hockings (ed.), *Principles of Visual Anthropology*, 2nd edn, Berlin and New York: Mouton de Gruyter, 99–113.

Chapter 8

Revealing the hidden

Making anthropological documentaries

Victoriano Camas Baena, Ana Martínez Pérez, Rafael Muñoz Sotelo, Manuel Ortiz Mateos

> It is time for ethnographic film-makers to stop being so concerned with making 'important' films and to become more interested in how their work affects the people they portray and those who view the images.
>
> (Ruby 2000: 221)

The idea of 'co-operatively produced' or 'subject generated' films has been discussed to some extent in the existing literature. As Jay Ruby characterises them such documentaries might be 'dissimilar to the dominant practice' and 'offer the possibility of perceiving the world from the viewpoint of people who lead lives that are different from those traditionally in control of the means of imaging the world' (2000: 196). This chapter describes and discusses the work of *A Buen Común*, an interdisciplinary Spanish ethnographic film-making unit. *A Buen Común*'s distinctive approach offers an alternative to the observational ethnographic film styles that developed in the late nineteenth century. *A Buen Común's* work is interdisciplinary, democratic and collaborative. In each documentary project film-makers, social researchers and the protagonists work together. Its members view social science and film to be instruments of social transformation, working towards a fairer and better society.

Below we outline *A Buen Común's* research and production processes vis-à-vis the case studies of two recent films: *La piel del monte* and *Mujeres invisibles*. Both documentaries were produced by the unit in collaboration with local Andalusian protagonists.

Epistemology

A Buen Común[1] was formed in mid-1998, after producing an ethnographic documentary of the same name on *jornalero* (labourer) identity and work culture in Bujalance (a village in Cordoba, Andalusia). Some of the unit's members are from the Taller de Antropologia Visual or TAV[2] (Visual Anthropology Workshop), which since 1992 has concentrated on applying audiovisual methods to social research mainly in social and cultural anthropology. Following the

TAV ethnographic documentary production is seen as either a coherent research project in itself that is independent of written documentation and analysis, or as a visual synthesis of a broader research project. *A Buen Común* also incorporates the approach of the scientific–cultural association Centro de Relaciones Inter-personales de Córdoba (Cordoban Centre for Interpersonal Relations) that works with individuals, groups and institutions from a multidisciplinary 'psycho-socio-anthropological' perspective. Here for over twenty-five years, we have carried out psychotherapeutic projects (with individuals, couples, families and groups), work with training groups, as well as anthropological, psychosocial, sociological and oral history projects. Some of the Centre's members are also involved in new audiovisual activities, especially video and television. All of us – whether film-makers, social researchers or film subjects – are driven by four main epistemo-logical and ideological ideas:

1   The desire to research and work towards social change leading to a fairer society based on self-management and solidarity among persons and groups.
2   A (self-)critical passion for revealing hidden aspects of ourselves and our society.
3   The conviction that social change will only follow individual transformation, and that this is best achieved through group work.
4   To ensure that the achievements of our individual and group subjects work to reduce negative entropy.

The use of media by cultural activists has become established around the world, including interventions in how indigenous people are represented by state media institutions (Ginsburg 1997: 119). For us social research is a form of intervention, rather than merely methodological practice. Its ethical–ideological approach should help dissolve the barrier between researcher and researched. Both should be on the same epistemic level and share the entire decision-making process as equal partners. We see the social sciences and film-making as tools for social transformation towards a fairer, inclusive society that will not ignore the shadows and incoherencies that surround us. Our documentaries engage with the issues and problems faced by their subjects: identities in crisis, social or work exclusion, work cultures dying out in front of us, etc. Because our informants raise these issues before we commence each new project, in our research social intervention is instituted through this initial needs assessment. Our first negotiations introduce us to the problems afflicting the film's main characters, and from this point onwards they become full members of the research and film-making process.

In order to work in this way it is imperative that no person or institution, including the film/research team, sets the agenda on the basis of their financial contribution, therefore it is a prerequisite that our documentaries are self-funded. As David MacDougall (2001) and Jay Ruby (2000) have recently commented ethnographic film-making needs to be freed from the limits imposed on it by broadcast television funding. We work with people who have requested our intervention rather than on a commission. Whereas mainstream social research and audiovisual productions are usually separate activities our method allows protagonists, researchers and film-makers to all be integrated in the film/ research process. Similarly whereas popular associations of knowledge and power tend to subordinate informants (and sometimes audiovisual technicians too) to academic researchers, we aim to blur the distinction between 'experts' and 'lay persons'.

The themes of our documentaries are 'marginal' in that they are distant from the audiovisual and research spotlight. They are obscure parts of ourselves and our society that the powers-that-be are interested in keeping hidden. Our main objective is to *reveal the hidden* and to stimulate change in two ways: by asking the film's viewers to recognise the existence of 'hidden' realities; and by encouraging the protagonists to re-appropriate their own history, their worth as persons and their right to demand and achieve what is theirs. For example, in our first documentary (*A Buen Común*) we wanted to show not simply who *jornaleros* from the village of Bujalance are and what they are like, but to demonstrate that there are other ways of understanding work and life. In contrast to written text documentary video is especially good at revealing 'marginal' social realities because it usually remains beyond the scope of social analysis (see Lapassade 1973: 143). It is only after it has been socially revealed that a material or discursive reality can dialectically confront the instituted. Therefore it should be the film subjects themselves who request the project (or participate in it) and drive its narrative. It is they who should relate their life experience and transmit their knowledge to contribute to the social dynamic that has hereto excluded them.

The dissemination of the videos also involves all team members. The image professionals seek ways of reaching television and cinema outlets, competitions, etc.; the social researchers try to access educational institutions and academic circles; the protagonists work in their own social milieus (neighbourhoods, town halls, nearby localities with similar problems). At every screening we try to ensure that all subgroups are represented during the presentation and discussion – not only because the work is co-authored, but so that it enriches the debate by providing audiences with emic and etic viewpoints.

Of course this method is not problem-free. Once the protagonists and research/production team have agreed the aims and procedures a key difficulty in making aesthetically and 'psycho-socio-anthropological' acceptable documentaries is co-ordinating the research and audiovisual work. Our heterogeneity usually enriches the group and its work, but can also threaten team spirit and the quality of the work if research and audiovisual interests are not negotiated and co-ordinated. For example an interview with an informant may be unusable if she has to wait too long and becomes nervous, losing her spontaneity while technicians prepare the setting and equipment. Likewise her contribution would be worthless if its technical quality was insufficient for it to be edited and disseminated. Because both aspects are necessary to reach our common goals 'a documentary (like any other collaborative endeavour) can only be made if interdisciplinary boundaries are respected and decisions are made jointly – an obvious point to make in so far as teamwork is but one form of human relation' (Martínez and Ranera 1999: 169).

Before discussing our work methods in more detail, first we describe two of our recent films *Mujeres invisibles* (2000) and *La piel del monte* (2002) to outline the shape our projects take and the impact they can have.

Mujeres invisibles (Invisible women)

Throughout most of 2000 in Cordoba (Andalusia) the Yerbabuena Women's Assembly was busy preparing the umbrella 'Spanish Feminist Association' conference to be held that December. Meanwhile, since 1998, various neighbourhoods in the city had been developing the 'Positive spaces of equality' project sponsored by the regional government (*Junta*) of Andalusia and the women's department of Cordoba's city council (*Ayuntamiento*). Two grassroots initiatives were also participating in this project: equality campaigners from Promotoras para la Igualdad (Women for Equality) and trainers from Encuentro en la Calle (Street Encounters). Both groups aim to bring social services to disadvantaged women in marginal urban neighbourhoods, rather than asking the women to leave their neighbourhoods to access central services. These associations already knew our work and called a meeting to request a new documentary. In institutional analysis terminology this first meeting was a 'needs analysis': they outlined the task and we began to negotiate the project's remit. These initial collaborators would later become our mediators vis-à-vis the 'invisible women' protagonists of the film. The researchers/ film-makers, mediators and protagonists are the three essential components in our documentaries.

In their everyday work the social workers and feminists encounter many women whose perseverance and struggle deserves society's recognition. Since one of our objectives was to reveal these hidden aspects of social reality we proposed to disseminate the life stories of women whose experiences would both be representative and provide a basis for reflection. The personal histories related in *Mujeres invisibles* are unfortunately too common in marginal urban neighbourhoods. They nevertheless represent a reality that usually remains hidden or at best forgotten for the comfortable educated consumerist urban middle classes. Moreover, in Spain women who usually participate in debates about the situation of our gender use a feminist theoretical discourse that describes identity according to homogenised, 'ethnocentric' variables that sometimes exclude other ways of being a woman. Launching this feminist conference with the accounts of these 'invisible women' was not only a daring act for the Yerbabuena Assembly but a rallying call for all of us who believe in social change. Although these women are invisible for much of society, they are clearly visible and necessary for the neighbourhoods and families they come from.

The filming took place over four intense days following a plan designed by the project mediators. Each day was programmed with a number of interviews attended by: the 'invisible woman' protagonist conversing with the interviewer and, silent but not absent, her social worker and the cameraperson. We aimed to create the most intimate atmosphere possible to help the women relate events that were transcendental and often painful to recall. The interviewer would explain the work process, stressing that there could be discrepancies between the actual interview and the final edited version. As such the protagonists gained confidence in their roles, each woman being the most appropriate person to talk about her own life. It was her voice that should be heard, neither a voice-over nor the interviewer's voice should replace her first-hand account of her own life. Each interview followed an open-ended script that represented the turning points in each woman's trajectory: her childhood and her relationships with her partner and children. Finally we asked them what they understood feminism to be. As we viewed the interviews we realised that these people did not perceive their gender identities simply as women as opposed to men, but rather as women who were daughters, partners, mothers and women. Because it was neither confrontational nor seeking equality, their feminist discourse turned out to be more naturalised than ours. If there is one thing that distinguishes them from males it is their motherhood. Despite the heavy burden of raising numerous children, rather than hampering their fulfilment as women and persons, it is precisely their children who endow them with their gender identity. Each of the six 'invisible women' spoke about her way of being a daughter, partner, mother and woman, concluding by addressing all other women.

We pay attention to the feedback generated by each viewing of our documentaries. When researching a group's image we always include that group's own reaction to the work we have created. The first people to see the edited documentary were the protagonists and the mediators. The protagonists' reactions were an awkward mixture of embarrassment and pride, confirming that they had been treated with respect and dignity. We were pleased with these results as we had made the documentary in their interests. We were also keen to know what the response of the three thousand women who would attend the opening of the Feminist conference would be. Given that the people in this audience would have lived their identities as women in quite different ways from the film's protagonists, we wondered how their reaction might reflect these and other contrasting interpretations. However after the screening the audience cried out in unison 'long live the women's struggle'. What was interesting about this was not only that it surprised us but that the common denominator between such different women was the struggle, and not the motive for struggling or the position from which one was doing it. Socially and economically the situations of the older of the protagonists, Paca who is 88, and Amalia who is 26 are similar. Perhaps the true difference is that today we can find an audience willing to recognise itself in the testimonies of these women. In contrast in the Andalusia of 1936 when Paca was Amalia's age, there was neither a women's forum nor a wider context shaped by a century of feminist struggle that would accommodate such testimonies. Thanks to documentary film-making we have been able to contribute, on a small scale, to make visible the lives of some women who do not deserve to be anonymous.

The impact of *Mujeres invisibles* also extended beyond the Cordoba conference, both geographically and in the impact it had on the lives of its protagonists. Amalia and Carmen are both gypsy women who live in two marginal neighbourhoods in Cordoba. They had only ever left their city to visit relatives who were in prison in other parts of Spain. In May 2001 we were invited to present *Mujeres invisibles* at the Bideo Mostra de Donosti–San Sebastian.

This was the first time Amalia and Carmen had been on a high-speed train, travelling across Spain to be greeted at the other end by the local authorities of Donosti (San Sebastian) and to speak in front of an auditorium full of people who would applaud their words. So many things surprised them that we film-makers asked ourselves if we really inhabited the same world. Looking around in the streets they asked where they 'city's poor' were, as they couldn't see them in the doors of the church or in the bars, they concluded there couldn't be any poor people in Donosti. The menus in the restaurants also made us think that we must come from different cultures. We read out the names and ingredients of each dish, but as they did not recognise most of them they did not want to

Figure 8.1 Carmen and Amalia with some members of the film-making team during the trip to present *Mujeres invisibles* at the Bideo Mostra de Donosti–San Sebastian. From left to right: Rafael, Ana, Carmen, Maria Luz, Amalia, Encarna and Manolo.

risk ordering something that they wouldn't like and would have to leave. One day faced with the difficulty of choosing from the menu they looked at each other and Carmen said 'look at us, so poor and so delicate!'.

La piel del monte: nature and culture at the Jimena de la Frontera (Cádiz) cork oak forest

La piel del monte (The skin of the hill) is a research and ethnographic documentary project about the residents of Jimena de la Frontera (Cádiz), their identity and relationship to the work culture in Alcornocales Park. Jimena de la Frontera is a village whose inhabitants have a close relationship with their natural environment – the cork oak forest. The forest is a source of employment for many local men and some women.

Closely linked to its cork oak production, the forest has further economic uses as a hunting ground, for cattle grazing, mushroom-picking, beekeeping and contemplation. The great forest also, with its 35,000 metric tonnes of annual cork production, attracts growing numbers of rural tourists. The work culture built around cork is based on gathering and preparation of raw materials that are later transformed in to cork in Portugal and Catalonia. We are interested in the symbiotic relationship that local inhabitants have created with their environment, a model of identity built on the work culture of cork bark. We have also documented how they feel they need to increase the proportion of raw material transformed locally – at present this stands at only 16 per cent. These local people's long-standing, balanced relationship with their natural milieu could be a model of conservation at the turn of the millennium.

This ethnographic documentary links the duality nature–culture to the identity of the people we worked with. First, as regards *the relationship of human beings with their environment* (Alcornocales Park) through the *work culture* associated with that environment. It was important to show how it has only been possible to preserve this environment over centuries (there are no known cases of arson) through appropriate work practices and a profound knowledge, love and respect towards the forest. This is manifested in their anthropomorphisation of the forest ('the forest is a living being', cork oak trees 'feel, laugh, fall ill, are happy or unhappy, have backs, bellies, feet, blood, mothers, they tell you what they need', etc). We aim to send a message to prevent this situation from deteriorating either through overexploitation, local people distancing themselves from the forest, or the uncontrolled growth of rural tourism (all threats pointed out by most of our informants).

Second, knowledge about the forest and its lifestyles is disseminated via *oral transmission*, through an *intergenerational relationship* which is part of this local culture. In this way, local identity is manifested through a profound *identification with the land* – a model that has helped, and still helps, to maintain the nature–culture duality in balance. This harmonious relationship with the environment is in line with contemporary social movements, with tourism and environmentalism being particularly influential. In this respect, the documentary also wants to highlight the cooling of Jimena's relationship with their chief means of livelihood. This cooling disrupts the process of experiential and identity transmission from one generation to the next. It is 'alarming', as the protagonists themselves put it, that young local people will take up work in the building or tourist industry in the nearby Costa del Sol rather than enter as cork 'novices' (*novicios en la saca de la corcha*). Responsibility for this seems to fall on the youths, wealthy landowners, the various administrations, local bosses and the cork labourers themselves. In fact, there is widespread agreement that a solid local cork-processing industry is urgently needed, for it would create employment, protect existing jobs, and stimulate other job-creating activities, such as handicrafts and services. The underdevelopment of Andalusia (a non-industrialised country dependent on the export of raw materials) is once again apparent.

The documentary is, therefore, a joint response to a question we asked the protagonists: What does this cork oak forest, the Alcornocal, mean to you? Through their stories our informants (cork extractors, muleteers, entrepreneurs, bank staff, craftsmen, environmentalists, proprietors, local politicians, hoteliers) together paint a huge fresco whose main characters are identity and nature in the eternal transit from tradition to modernity. As a counterpoint to this line of argument, and in parallel to it, we follow the work process 'from *corcha* (cork bark) to *corcho* (finished cork)', that is, the preparation, collection, transport and transformation of the raw material.

The two-stage shoot took place in April and in the first week of July 2000. The first stage was an initial encounter with the research subjects/objects. We also developed the needs analysis that had been initiated months earlier and found the settings and cutaway images (scenery, village, natural and human context). In the period between the first and second stages, we sketched out the open-ended script from which to resume production. The second stage was the main one, as it coincided with the cork harvest, known as the *saca*. Whilst for the first stage we used a single film crew, for the second we had to employ two crews and plan each day of shooting in painstaking detail.

We usually film each documentary with a shooting script and edit list, both of which are open ended and are developed through constant feedback provided by team members and informants. This process is time-consuming but rewarding, slow but participatory, and the final work is developed out of everyone's ideas. With *La piel del monte* we were surprised to discover that one of the main protagonists was not satisfied with the final video. After watching and discussing the film with him we concluded that he did not like how he came across and, worse still, he was worried about the repercussions his words could have on his public image in a community of less that 1,000 inhabitants. The camera was perceived as an enemy when it began to portray aspects of each character that did not fit with the image that they had of themselves or that they wanted to communicate to other villagers. In the end after much negotiation we came to the consensus that if someone had spoken certain words in front of the camera it was because that is what they had felt at the time, but knowing that at any time they could paralyse the editing process and eliminate the fragments that were most compromising for them.

The team: themes and dynamics

Invading other people's lives so that one can know them well enough to show them to others is a delicate operation. If documentary film-making and fiction can be distinguished at all, it is in their conceptualisation and treatment of characters. In a documentary, characters are themselves before, during and after the film is made. In fictional films characters have no real life beyond the studio. The relationship between the camera and character is another distinguishing feature. Whilst in documentary film-making the camera serves the action and protagonists, in fictional films the reverse is true: actors work for the camera. This awareness of the character as a person whose life is independent from whether or not a film is built around him brings documentary-making and anthropological research closer. Qualitative research in the social sciences – especially in individual and group psychology as well as in social and cultural anthropology where the research/intervention is based on participant observation – always entails an immersion in the life and behaviour of those we study. Some researchers seek to define fieldwork 'objectively' in terms of observation rather than participation (e.g. Emmison and Smith 2000) and in the Spanish methodology literature some still critique the participatory, committed approaches that they deem 'subjective and unscientific' (for a critical survey of this problem, see Camas Baena 1996). Such authors fail to recognise that a research process neither begins nor ends with fieldwork, just as making a documentary is more than filming. In fact an emphasis on subjectivity is crucial in ethnographic documentary making since as MacDougall puts it 'Filming . . . produces an object in which the filmmaker's interaction with the film subject is explicitly inscribed. Rather than simply running their course, their experiences intersect permanently in the fabric of the film' (1998: 56). This relationship between film-makers and subjects is therefore decisive in shaping the nature of the final documentary. The production of alternative media 'involves collective action and entails the expression of group interests' often resulting in 'collaborative and organised democratic participation (see Anderson and Goldson 1991: 61, cited by Ginsburg 1997: 118). Our work achieves this in a particular way. In *A Buen Común*'s projects our engagement is two-sided: our protagonists become integrated in the production process and also adopt the position of participant observers in the project. For this they require basic knowledge of both the documentary-making process, and the repercussions of their request. This is achieved through a series of preliminary meetings in which we explain the process step-by-step: what an interview consists of, the uses of cut away shots, and so on. Thus a mainstream documentary interviewee or socio-cultural research informant is transformed into a participant, another collaborator in a joint project. Two processes thus unfold: on the one hand, their everyday life, on the other, the audiovisual representation we will construct on behalf of that life.

MacDougall has suggested that 'what is finally most important about film, apart from communicating with the viewers, is that it provides a way of communicating with the subjects – a way for each to show the other what otherwise cannot be shown, in a statement that is irrevocable' (1998: 56). In the work of *A Buen Común* this two-way engagement (of the researchers/ producers in the life of the protagonists and vice versa) is a form of teamwork. This process is dialogical, involving constant negotiation of the theoretical assumptions, personal agendas and the various elements that will constitute the final product. The first priority is the group *dynamics* involving all the persons in a given context; the *theme* is less important as our work serves our relationship with the people, and not the other way round. Hence it would be better to cancel a recording session if this will avoid conflict. Our aims are, first and foremost, social – only secondarily are they artistic. Since we create in order to intervene in society and our protagonists are persons and not personas, we privilege oral-pretechnological to visual-technological discourse.

One unusual aspect of our work model is the figure of 'contrasting observer' (*observador contraste*). In the making of each documentary, one of us will take up a more distant position so as to act as a contrasting observer, i.e. someone who observes the group dynamics while participating in them. This is usually a newcomer to our team who is still undergoing a period of training. In a sense, all of us carry out this task insofar as all observations are intrinsically participatory and all observers affect the field of observation, not least when lumbering heavy filming equipment. To us it is more a case of becoming involved in each situation instead of 'seeing, listening and keeping quiet'.

In social research, the contrasting observer is a bridge between the social context and the team. In contrast, in a documentary team she will embody the figure of viewer. When we think in images we translate ideas into visual discourse as they come along. This process has the built-in difficulty of not offering a materialised discourse until the very end. The contrasting observer is not a receptor ignorant of the work process, but neither is she fully immersed in the audiovisual creative process, hence her go-between function.

Functions within the *A Buen Común* team are usually precisely defined, although the same person may take on one or more different functions if required. Thus, we shall now outline the main division of tasks and functions within our film crew during the second, main phase of production. Every film crew comprises a *cameraman*, a *film-maker-cum-assistant cameraman*, a '*contrasting observer*' and an *interviewer*.

The *cameraman*'s specificity makes him irreplaceable. He deals with everything concerning the camera, light and focus with a degree of creative freedom so he can apprehend elements from the reality or person being filmed. The cameraman is continually engaged with the images transmitted to a monitor, with the film-maker-assistant cameraman, as well as with the contrasting observer and interviewer. He works with both eyes and ears wide open, taking his own decisions as a film-maker and not merely as a cameraman awaiting further instructions. His assistant corrects the light, the brilliance, the focus, the framing. From his field monitor he studies the panoramic views, the camera pans and watches his movements, so that he can indicate when to repeat a given take. He undertakes film-making duties in a strict sense in that the monitor picture is always sharper than that of the best camera viewfinder. The contrasting observer constantly follows the work progress as well as keeping the camera log – a variant of the anthropological field diary that captures the time codes of each tape and scene. The narrator is not greatly involved in the camera log since it is, above all, an index of the recorded scenes. Yet the observer, in addition to documenting the scenes and work already carried out, helps to foreshadow future activities, as he will brief each camera crew on the work carried out by the other from the perspective of a viewer. Finally, the contrasting observer will often suggest framings and camera angles. He is in charge of sound, holding the microphone pole during interviews or field recordings. The interviewer is fully involved with the persons or groups she is interviewing. Her main function is to 'connect' with the interviewees assisted by the contact persons. Although she concentrates on the human dimension, she also takes part in decisions regarding framing and camera positioning.

The Process

Our ethnographic documentary making begins with a needs analysis parallel to a period of research and documentation that is necessary to develop a script. This period starts when the protagonists are able to tell a story audiovisually, both requesting it and being willing to assume narrative responsibility. Once the spatio-temporal context and narrative are agreed upon, we create a research team (*dynamics*) and organise ourselves into a documentary film crew (*theme*).

The pre-production, production and post-production phases in an ethnographic film are complex. First, as our work can only take place within a group, we ensure that part of our task centres on the team's own dynamics. Shooting a film is above all an experience of group interaction – the entire project depends on this interaction. Second, we are dealing with a social inquiry translated into images in which the protagonists contribute their vision and social worlds. As we noted above we do not take commissioned work, which means that our informants are part of the decision-making process. Working with open-ended scripts complicates matters further. To this we should add that the documentary characters act as team members and that all of us take part in the making of each phase.

Our teamwork centres on the task whose aim is to act to resolve the difficulties arising from within the group space-time.[3] Thus, both task and dynamics take place in three phases that can be compared to those of the audiovisual work process. In the dynamic sphere, the *pre-task* focuses on analysing and solving the project's resistances, conflicts, expectations and ghosts. The *task* is the time devoted to following up and resolving problems and difficulties (of a technical or personal nature) originating during the shooting. Finally, during the *project* we analyse and tackle problems (e.g. with the protagonists, the team, the broadcasting or dissemination institutions, etc) that may hinder the planned operative strategies towards an intervention. In this way, the *theme* (the explicit audiovisual domain) complements the *dynamics* (the implicit, hidden domain of the group activity).

As regards image production, pre-production is devoted to developing the idea to be filmed. From the initial request we look for ways to turn the ideas into images as they arise. We research the topic, getting to know the characters who will aid our task and introducing our 'privileged informants', i.e. the protagonists, to the work process. We do not develop a detailed shooting plan because our script must be as open-ended as possible. Our main characters are not actors learning their lines by heart. They are playing themselves and express themselves freely as the interactions during shooting or production occur. Shoots are excellent settings for social researchers observing group dynamics. First, they are shared stretches of space-time whose purpose it is to create an audio-visual product as well as a social intervention in the socio-cultural context we wish to portray. Whilst in social research process prevails over product (i.e. an instant is a meaningful whole in its own right), in audiovisual communication the opposite holds true: the only *raison d'être* of a concrete moment is its insertion in post-production – product prevails over process. The script is adapted as a result of the shooting, once the 'raw' tapes have been viewed. The story we wish to tell is nonetheless present throughout the entire process. It operates as an open script subject to the changes resulting from the interaction between team and protagonists. Therefore we treat both shooting and editing as contexts where emic and etic discourses are negotiated between the protagonists and those of us who act as narrative mediators. Table 8.1 represents our work plan.

Social impact and intervention

The two documentaries discussed above have been involved in both critiquing social policy and in helping to develop new feminist engagements in policy-making. As we have noted our aim is to reveal aspects of social reality that remain hidden, and thus our documentaries are initiated when we agree to work with people who have asked us to make their story public. The extent to which this can influence policy-making cannot be measured. Instead, in seeking to 'reveal the hidden' each documentary potentially has a personal and social impact. For example when Antonio, who has now passed away, and who was one of the protagonists of our first film (also titled *A Buen Común*), saw the film for the first time he said 'now we can die in peace'. His son, Juan, another of the characters in the film asked us to make the film public because it seemed

Table 8.1 Work plan

Phases	Themes	Dynamics
Pre-production/ pre-task	Needs analysis Data-gathering and localisations Contacting human resources Pre-script writing Shooting plan Fund-raising	Analysis and resolution of resistances and conflicts (expectations and ghosts) surrounding this phase's tasks
Production/task	Shooting of contextual images Interview recording	Solve relevant problems Daily follow-up and analysis of work process
Post-production/ project	Viewing of 'raw' materials Script adjustment Film montage First viewing with protagonists Distribution and showing/ broadcasting Fund-raising	Discuss possible interventions of final product

that the current government was going to cut the subsidy provided for Andalusian labourers. When the labourers demonstrated against this by walking all the way from their Andalusian village to Madrid holding a banner some people came up to them and told them that they knew them because a film had been made about them. They were very proud that people knew their story, and this is our commitment: to make such stories public.

However our task is not always easy; not everyone wants to know the stories of marginal people in Spain. When we sent out films to a television broadcaster that specialises in documentaries, the director told us that they were interested in social issues in Asia, South America or Africa but not in Europe and even less in Spain. This motivated us to continue our work. It demonstrated to us that in Spain such official channels want certain realities either to remain hidden or to be told by the people they appoint themselves. However, there is always a network of associations and civic and educational centres where our work is disseminated.

Summary

Ethnographic documentaries can and perhaps ought to have some impact on the worlds they represent and are viewed in. *A Buen Común* aims to work with informants/protagonists to 'reveal the hidden' in ways that incorporate their own narratives and represent their voices, stories, issues and problems. Each project the unit embarks on is not solely an ethnographic documentary that aims to represent the culture and experience of a particular people in a particular space and time, but a social intervention, and a critical commentary on aspects of our society. It is intended to be, in Ginsburg's terms, 'transformative' and as such to exploit the potential of visual media in the way producers of indigenous media have, 'by renarrating, from their perspective, the relationship between indigenous histories and cultures and the encompassing societies in which they live' (1997: 123). In order to achieve this *A Buen Común* follows the methodology set out above. Its emphasis on teamwork, defined roles, continuous negotiation and collaboration aims to ensure that the documentaries produced are not simply visual products that might have a given social impact. Rather it seeks to turn the video-making process itself into a type of intervention that serves the documentary's protagonists. In doing so it requires that each documentary is produced out of a democratic and collaborative teamwork process – a process that is as much about the team and their work together as it is about the topic of the documentary itself.

As such *A Buen Común's* work seeks to offer a new way of producing ethnographic documentaries that is based in collaboration. Ruby has argued that 'For a [film] production to be truly collaborative, parties involved must be equal in their competencies or have achieved an equitable division of labour (2000: 208) Moreover, in order for a film to be classified as 'collaborative' he requires the following to be fulfilled:

> Is the collaboration to be found at all stages of the production? Have the film-makers trained the subjects in technical and artistic production skills, or are the subjects merely 'subject-area specialists' who gauge the accuracy of the information and pass upon the political and moral correctness of the finished work? Who had the idea of the film in the first place? Who raised and controls the funds? Who operates the equipment? Who is professionally concerned with the completion of the film? Who organizes and controls the distribution? Who travels with the film to conferences, festivals and other such events?
>
> (Ruby 2000: 208–9)

Ruby remarks that he knows of no films that meet these requirements (2000: 209). Perhaps because, as he points out himself, if film subjects became skilled enough to collaborate at this level then they would have little need for film-makers with whom to collaborate (2000: 12). Given that Ruby's ideal is unattainable, *A Buen Común's* film-making process takes a realistic approach to collaboration that allows film-makers and subjects to employ and share with each other their respective expertise. The film ideas are initiated by their subjects and developed jointly with the film-makers, the decision-making processes involve both film-makers and subjects throughout. Funding and dissemination activities again involve both and when possible both film-makers and subjects attend their films' public screenings.

The work of *A Buen Común* aims to transform both individuals' lives and experiences and to promote social change. Its third challenge is to the way ethnographic films had 'traditionally' been produced, rejecting the idea of making films 'about' other cultures in favour of developing, producing and disseminating documentaries collaboratively with their subjects.

Notes

1 *A Buen Común* is a documentary inspired by Victoriano Camas Baena's doctoral thesis, *Identidad y cultura del trabajo en el olivar de Bujalance: la historia oral como espacio interdisciplinar en la investigación social* (Work culture in the Bujalance olive grove: oral history as an interdisciplinary space for social research). Made by Victoriano Camas, Manuel Cerezo, Jean-Vital Consigny, Ana Martínez and Manuel Ortiz, it is an audio-visual study of *jornalero* identity and work culture based on the statements of five persons from different age-groups. All were labourers from Bujalance (Cordoba), a village where the chief economic activity is single-crop olive-growing.

2 The Taller de Antropología Visual (TAV) was created in 1992 by Dr Carlos Mª Caravantes García of the Department of Anthropology of America (Faculty of History and Geography, Universidad Complutense de Madrid (UCM)). One of its members (Manuel Cerezo Lasne) graduated from this department, while another two members (Ana Martínez Pérez and Penélope Ranera Sánchez) have doctorates from the Department of Social Anthropology (Faculty of Political Sciences and Sociology, UCM).

3 We are borrowing from the theory of groups a model developed by Enrique Pichon-Rivière. It is known as 'operative group' (*grupo operativo*) (Pichon-Rivière 1985).

References

Anderson, K. and Goldson, A. (1991) 'Alternating currents: alternative television inside and outside of the Academy', *Social Texts* 28: 56–71.

Camas Baena, V. (1996) *Nuevas tendencias en la observación participante*, in *Actas Del V Congreso De Sociología*, Granada: Fes.

Emmison, M. and Smith, P. (2000) *Researching the Visual*, London: Sage.

García, M., Martínez, A., Pitarch, P. *et al.* (1996). *Antropología de los sentidos: la vista*, Madrid: Celeste.

Ginsburg, F. (1997) ' "From little things, big things grow": indigenous media and cultural activism', in R. G. Fox and O. Starn (eds), *Between Resistance and Revolution: Cultural Politics and Social Protest*, London: Rutgers University Press.

Lapassade, G. (1973) [1963] *La entrada en la vida. Ensayo sobre la no-terminación del hombre*, Madrid: Fundamentos.

Lourau, R. (1975) [1970]. *El análisis institucional*, Buenos Aires: Amorrortu.

MacDougall, D. (1998) *Transcultural Cinema*, Princeton: Princeton University Press.

—— (2001) 'Renewing ethnographic film: is digital video changing the genre?', *Anthropology Today* 17(3).

Marinas, J. M. and Santamarina, C. (1999) *La historia oral: métodos y experiencias*, Madrid: Debate.

Martínez, A. and Ranera, P. (1999). 'Cronotopo y mitiario: dos exploraciones del taller de antropología visual', *Revista De Antropología Social* 8: 159–81.

Pérez Tolón, L. and Ardévol, E. (1995) *Imagen y cultura. Perspectivas del cine etnográfico*, Granada: Diputación Prov. De Granada.

Pichon-Rivière, E. (1985) *El proceso grupal*, Buenos Aires: Nueva Visión.

Pujadas, J. J. (1992) *El método biográfico: el uso de las historias de vida en ciencias sociales*, Madrid: Centro De Investigaciones Sociológicas.

Ruby, J. (2000) *Picturing Culture: Explorations of Film and Anthropology*, Chicago: University of Chicago Press.

VV.AA. (1995) *Historia, antropología y fuentes orales*. 18. *Voz e imagen.*-Vv.Aa. (1999) *Revista De Antropología Social*, 8. Madrid: Universidad Complutense.

Filmography

A buen común (1999). An audiovisual approach to labourer identity and work culture in contemporary Andalusia through the statements of five people of different ages – men and women labourers from Bujalance (Cordoba), a village where the main economic activity is single-crop olive cultivation.

Mujeres invisibles (Invisible women) (2000). Six life histories of Cordovan women aged 26 to 88. They retell in front of the camera their experiences and silent everyday struggles to raise their children and improve their living conditions. They see themselves primarily as 'fighting women'. It is from this perspective that they construct their gender identity and address all other women.

La piel del monte (The skin of the hill) (2001). A collective answer to the key question, 'What does the *Alcornocal* (cork oak forest) mean to you?' The informants (cork extractors, muleteers, entrepreneurs, bank staff, craftsmen, environmentalists, proprietors, local politicians, hoteliers) together paint a huge fresco whose main characters are identity and nature in the eternal transit from tradition to modernity.

Al compás de los sueños (In time to the rhythm of dreams) (2003). A project co-funded by the Cordoba city council and the regional government of Andalusia. The aim is to tell through dreams the current realities of people suffering from, or at risk of, social exclusion. Children from marginal neighbourhoods in Cordoba sing flamenco and bring music to their dreams, whilst adult men and women and social workers from the association, Encuentros en la Calle (Street Encounters), relate their life trajectories to demonstrate that it is possible to integrate an excluded group.

Documentary making team

Victoriano Camas Baena
Manuel Cerezo Lasne
Jean-Vital Consigny Perignon
Pablo López Calle

Lorenzo María Hormigos
Ana Martínez Pérez
Rafael Muñoz Sotelo
Manuel Ortiz Mateos

Chapter 9

Drawing the lines

The limitations of intercultural *ekphrasis*

Manuel João Ramos

What do I see in you?

The present paper offers the reader a brief personal reflection on the ekphrastic relations between visual and written imagery in anthropological research, followed by a self-critical reading of the possibilities and shortcomings of using visual recording techniques in the field (drawn from my own experience in Ethiopia, where I have been working both as anthropologist and as graphic illustrator).

By writing, anthropologists recreate transmitted social memories for the benefit of their readers and, in doing so, the literary nature of their endeavour becomes manifest. Much like a novelist, when the social scientist produces and publishes a written text, he/she offers the public a fictional reality shared between the transmitter of a memory and the reader's intellectual reception and aesthetic response. This shared reality is, in the proper sense, an imaginary universe that is summoned by the author (Atkinson 1990: 57–81; Hammersley 1992: 22–8; Iser 1980: 53–85).

Anthropology has traditionally been a literary activity deriving its self-legitimacy as a 'reproductive' device from a constant rhetoric contrast with the oral conditions of ethnographic enquiry (Atkinson 1990: 88–103; Sperber 1982: 32–3). Furthermore, anthropological language, style and argumentation have depended heavily on visual and geometric metaphors. That is, to analyse social life, we tend to use words that are imbued with imagistic powers. Anthropological discourse has always relied heavily on what we could call its ekphrastic value (from Gk. *ekphrasis*, 'description'). But we frequently talk about 'centre' and 'periphery' in societies, 'high' and 'low levels', 'position', 'perspective', 'space', 'framework', 'dimension', etc., without generally considering what is implied in such recurring metaphors (Ramos 2001: 97).

The word 'ekphrasis' was originally used by Greek classical rhetoricians to qualify a description with great visual content. Its special use in the European history of art relates to the *ekphrasein* of ancient Greek paintings of sculptures that have since disappeared (Heffernan 1993; Hochmann 1994; Krieger 1992). A more recent meaning of 'ekphrasis' reflects both a stress on the intricate relations between the visual arts and literature, and on the possibility of using the imagistic capacity of literature as a methodological lever to analyse art. A derivative use of the expression can be found in the study of the complementarities between travel literature and travel iconography.

In any case, 'ekphrasis' is conceived as an important tool in the study of the aesthetic impact of a description in the reader's/spectator's mind. In an article called 'From lies to truth: colonial *ekphrasis* and the act of cross-cultural translation', Thomas Cummins focuses his attention on how pictorial images were an important factor of multicultural translation (and evangelising) in the New World conquered by the Spanish. While a mutual learning of linguistic codes of communication served as a means to register and spread information and ideas, pictorial images were especially important to establish a common cognitive ground between colonisers and colonised (Cummins 1995: 172). Likewise, because they are designed to have an immediate aesthetic impact upon the spectator, pictorial or graphical images can be useful tools in interactive procedures of ethnographic construction.

Today, image-processing techniques have become increasingly available and popularised as research and discursive tools in the reinvigorated classical field of 'visual anthropology' (Pink 2001: 24–9), the fast expansion of which grows out of the widespread post-modern conception that a century-old obsession of asserting discursive legitimacy, in 'literary anthropology', may have hindered its heuristic potency. By connecting their (written) words with a variety of graphic devices (from opposition tables and kinship schemes to analytical diagrams, drawings, photographs, filmed data, computerised multimedia, web design, etc.), researchers are now offered a range of complementary possibilities of reporting on different social and cultural realities, and may indeed feel obliged to explore new ways of retrieving and managing such data.

Still, because such devices and techniques are material extensions of one's mental perspective, they very much abide to the rule that anthropological strategies of interpreting/reinventing social worlds are a measure of imposing the researcher's own cultural background on them (Pink 2001: 18–9, 24). At the end of the day, when anthropologists use 'visual' means of recording social and cultural data, they are, as ever, still dependent on their literary world-view, which, coincidently, is marked by the above-mentioned set of metaphorical operations (based on 'objectivity', 'observations', 'points of view', 'perspectives', 'dimensions', etc.).

To be conscious of the virtues and shortcomings of the 'ekphrastic' endeavour is an important requirement in the search for a cognitive and aesthetic common ground between subject and researcher in anthropology, 'visual' or otherwise. In this respect, it is of little consequence whether the preferred tool for registering, mastering and treating visual data is the latest digital technological novelty or the humblest of pencil drawings. Personally, I tend to prefer the latter medium, since it relates better to the traditional craft-quality of anthropological practices and discourses. In fact, for some years now I have pursued two distinct, but increasingly convergent careers – as a researcher in Anthropology and as a graphic illustrator (see Ramos 2000, 2002). My training and practice in these two areas have caused me to pay special attention to culturally meaningful visual elements, in connection with my written (and oral) productions. I personally tend to make an extensive, albeit prudent, use of graphic means of recording and interpreting my field experiences and to use them as a window for intercultural dialogue.

During fieldwork research, I have found that a trained eye and a skilled hand are useful instruments for documenting both material culture aspects and varied instances of social life. Yet, drawing is not merely a documenting activity but also an important and creative tool for interacting with and relating to human beings, of different cultures and languages. I have been using my meagre drawing skills in quite a systematic way while travelling and doing fieldwork. It generally strikes me that, whereas taking photographs or using a video camera frequently creates a barrier between me and the people I work with, when drawing I become the subject of a more benign form of curiosity, by many of those that I address. When travelling, I continually use a sketchbook as a noting tool, where I draw everything that catches my eye. I am generally aware that by drawing in such places as in the middle of a cereal field, in a collective taxi, a religious festival or in a café I'm bound to attract people's curiosity. This habit has led me to all sorts of situations, some very gratifying, some disturbing, some life-imperilling (Plate 9.1).[1] The act of drawing can, then, be more than just a pastime or an exercise of visual discipline: being a source of interaction that helps to humanise me in other people's eyes, it becomes part of the anthropological process of tentatively bringing together observer and observed.[2]

Honi soit qui mal y peint

It would, of course, be naive to think that the practice of producing images for intercultural communication can be taken lightly, and that one doesn't have to be careful with how such images are perceived, handled and interpreted. In the following pages, I describe a situation where my willingness to interact through my own handmade images in a different culture was cut short by the negative expectation that such images might be interpreted in such way that could contribute to jeopardise my fieldwork. This situation will, I hope, offer a lesson of prudence, both in terms of one's interactions in the field and with regard to the epistemological limits of 'visual anthropology'. During a two-month stay in Ethiopia in 2002, where I was collecting ethnographic data, I was, quite unexpectedly, asked to produce two sets of paintings for the new display of the ethnographic collection of the Institute of Ethiopian Studies (Addis Ababa University). The new display's curators, Carmen Porras Goméz (a Spanish anthropologist) and Natalia Hirsch (a French art historian), who challenged me to make that contribution, were already familiar with some of my artwork on Ethiopia: two years before, I had published an illustrated travel and ethnographic account on Northern Ethiopia (Ramos 2000) and participated in the art show that marked the opening of the new Harari Cultural Centre, in the south-eastern town of Harar.[3]

The commissioned work was (a) a set of 12 square painted canvases occupy-ing the total space of 3 × 2m., with a rendering of the legend of Makeda, the Queen of Sheba, and (b) a 2 × 1.5m. diptych, equally on canvas, about the *buk* cult of the Nilotic Nuer. Regarding the first painting, I was particularly inter-ested in producing a narrative sequence of the Ethiopian version of the Queen of Sheba story in a way that would evoke the popular painted strips (Plate 9.2), which are one of the most common objects in Ethiopian 'airport art'. My idea was to produce a modernised version of the Sheba legend that would reflect my personal views on present-day Ethiopian society. The board of the IES accepted my proposal and I began toying with the script, until I settled on the story of a country girl who would become a beauty queen in Addis Ababa (Plate 9.3); when visiting her kin in Israel, she would somehow fall in love with a mysterious arms dealer conveniently called Solomon; their son Menelik would later turn out to be a shrewd politician whose goal would be to bring multi-ethnic Ethiopian society under his despotic wing.

The second painting was more straightforward than the first but was still challenging, albeit at a different level: the requested subject was the fertility cult of the *buk*, of the Nuer[4] and my task would be to illustrate its different ritual and symbolic aspects, according to the classical rules of ethnographical inter-pretation. I was only too aware that my knowledge of Nuer ethnography was mainly literary and, although I was in contact with Nuer immigrants in Addis Ababa, I had never been in Nuerland. As soon as I began referring the project to some Ethiopian friends and acquaintances, I started noticing a muted dis-comfort regarding my idea for the Queen of Sheba painting – whereas, they were basically unresponsive regarding the Nuer piece. The hints that I shouldn't go ahead with the Sheba painting became stronger, and I finally decided to give up that part of the project. In the end, only the Nuer piece was put up for the opening of the new display, but not without some grumbles, as I was later informed (I had left Ethiopia a few weeks before the opening).

According to rumours reported by a friend, some members of the Society of Friends of the Institute of Ethiopian Studies (SOFIES),[5] once having seen the painting, had apparently suggested it should either be removed during the show's opening or, at least, hung in a discreet place. They were worried about the possible disapproval of its contents from both the general (Ethiopian) public and the (Ethiopian) patrons of the collection. It was feared that the central upper part of the diptych would hurt people's feelings of propriety, since it pre-sented a black-and-white realistic scene of a naked black (Nuer) woman giving birth to a whitish baby, under the moonlight (Plate 9.4; inspired by photo-graphs of Sharon Hutchinson, in Hutchinson, 1996: 194–5, pls 17 and 18). Two rather sketchy sections flanked this central section: on the left-hand side, the blood sacrifice of a spotted ox, and, on the right, a landscape of a Nuer village and field under heavy rainfall.

The three upper sections represented three complementary forms of manifestation of the *buk*, the white and black fertility spirit that the Nuer traditionally
associated with rivers and streams: sacrificial blood, birth blood and rainy
season water symbolically connected the upper to the lower part of the painting.
The latter was further divided horizontally in two sections: the top one was a
blood-red band bathing the blue silhouettes of various river animals (fishes,
snakes, crocodiles, river birds, frogs, etc.) and water insects; the bottom section
was a hydrographical and orographical map of a sun-scorched Nuerland, serving
as background to a realistic representation of a pied crow, an animal avatar of
the *buk* spirit (Evans Pritchard, 1956: 31–3, 45–6, 81, 125–7; Hutchinson,
1980: 224–7). The painting was meant to be an ethnographically accurate
painted interpretation of a traditional Nuer 'belief', and there was not much
'artistic' licence in the portraying of the birth scene – that I chose to do a
'photo-like' portrait was stressed in the option of using only black, grey and
white tones in the upper central section.

Some people were not very comfortable with the presence of the painting in
the ethnographic display, but there wasn't any special stir about it. Of course,
I knew from the outset that it was unlikely that many Nuer would visit the
exhibition. In fact, Nuer immigrants in Addis Ababa, more often than not a
socially marginalised and politically voiceless community, are not the most frequent of visitors to the ethnographic displays of the IES – or to any highbrow
'cultural event' of the Ethiopian capital, for that matter.[6] The main challenge
of producing and displaying the *buk* painting was that a relevant number of
the expected public (Ethiopian and foreign) of the IES display either has a
training in anthropology and 'knows' about the Nuer, or is familiar with ethnographic museums and 'knows' that painted canvases are very rarely used to
convey information about indigenous material or immaterial cultures. That said,
the risk I felt I was taking was mainly epistemological: questions aroused in
my mind as to what was the value, the meaning and the validity of painting and
displaying (not in Nuerland but in Addis Ababa) a piece based on obvious
ethnographic clichés. Also, what made me give up the Queen of Sheba project
but not the *buk* one? With that other painting, I wouldn't be portraying aspects
of the traditional culture of indigenous peoples whom many Northern Ethiopians still today derogatorily designate as *shankilla* ('slaves', 'black', or 'primitive' peoples), but I would rather be directly impinging on the ideological core
of Abyssinian nationality.

The striking characteristic of the Ethiopian elaboration of the biblical story of
the 'Queen of the South', known as Makeda in Ethiopia, and Bilkis in the Arabian
versions, is that it establishes a very special alliance between Yahweh and the
abasha. The fruit of the brief union between her and the Israeli King Solomon,
Menelik I, brings the Ark of the Covenant from Jerusalem and is crowned in
the holy city of Aksum as the first king of the Solomonic dynasty in Ethiopia.[7]

This fabulous narrative is used to explain the historical connection of the
Amhara and Tygrinean with the Semitic world, and, until recently, to legitimise

their political hold of the country. My proposed version was a somewhat satirical portrait of the present, post-socialist, Ethiopia, where the political tensions that result from the federal system now put in place are expressed through the language of ethnicity. The feeling of many Ethiopians today is that the federal government structures have been taken over by the members of the TPLF, a Tygrenian-based guerrilla movement that fought the socialist dictatorship with the military, political and financial support of foreign governments such as the United States of America – now explicitly consolidated in the good diplomatic relations of the Ethiopian government with both the USA and Israel.

Of course, had I finished the Sheba painting, it wouldn't have been the first non-traditional interpretation of the legend. The lobby of the Hilton Hotel, in Addis Ababa, displays in permanence a late 1960s personal interpretation of the story by the Ethiopian painter Eskender Boghossian (of Armenian origin). On the other hand, the love story of Sheba and Solomon, already known in medieval Europe and popularised in the Renaissance, became a very fashionable artistic motto in the late nineteenth century, as an epitome of orientalist romance.[8]

In present day Ethiopia, Makeda is a very popular iconic figure, just as Solomon is a key figure in popular wisdom and medicine (Mercier 1992: 138). The references to their love story are, actually, a recurring element in many instances of Ethiopian social life, not least because of its linkage with the Christian liturgy: the *tabot*, i.e. the Ark of the Covenant, representations of which play a central part in the public ceremonies of *Fassika* (Easter) and *Temqat* (Epiphany), is said to have been brought from Israel to Ethiopia by Menelik, the son of Makeda and Solomon, as already mentioned. The 'airport art' paintings that circulate in souvenirs and handicrafts shops (see Plate 9.2) echo the vitality with which oral popular culture has developed and transformed the old literary legend of the *Kebra Nagast*: the love story is collated with the myth of the great serpent Arwe, Menelik has a half-brother of *shankilla* descent, and it is the queen, and not Solomon, who is depicted with the Lion of Judah.

Still, as far as I am aware, it would have been a novelty in Addis Ababa for a *ferenj* (pl. *ferenjoch*; a 'Frank', or 'white person'), if not to go about painting the Solomon–Sheba story, at least to actually display it in one of the most visited museums of the Ethiopian capital. That, in fact, had been the reason why I was, in the beginning, so wilfully drawn to accept the proposal: I felt I was simultaneously being offered a unique chance to evaluate the social impact of introducing both a variation of meaning to the Abyssinian national myth and a new mode and style of visual representation unmistakably foreign to the customary 'cultural paintings', as Ethiopians call (in English) their traditional/airport art.

Contacting my friends and acquaintances in Addis Ababa, I soon recognized that, seductive as it seemed, the project could unfortunately imperil my professional status in Ethiopia. The painting would most likely be subjected to levels of reading and appreciation beyond my control, with the risk of provoking a negative reaction from either the Ethiopian Church authorities or some political and intellectual circles – or even, as I knew had happened before, a popular outburst of anger towards a *ferenj* (see below).

That the intention of producing a modernised version of the Sheba story could be read as insulting by Orthodox Christians was specially worrying to me, since the feeling one has is that the Orthodox Christian Church feels it is somehow under constant threat and tends to react defensively against any further erosion of its traditional hold over Ethiopian society. That could definitely be the case with a 'heterodox' painting relating to the most sacred of Christian Ethiopian traditions: that of the coming of the Ark of the Covenant to Ethiopia, in the hands of Menelik, the first-born son of Solomon and the 'Queen of the South'. It must be noted that the present social context of the country is one of great competition between the Ethiopian Orthodox Church and, on the one hand, an increasingly self-affirming Muslim community, on the other, growingly popular Protestant alternative sects – a situation that is enmeshed with the new political situation created by the change of regime, in 1991, that led to the present federal, regionalised and ethnicised state.

Blinding

I should state that part of my research work in oral history has been carried out in Northern Ethiopia, in predominantly Christian areas, where I tend to collaborate with local Church people (priests and deacons, laymen, erudites, etc.; see Ramos 2000). Thanks to my friends' somewhat muted advice and the total lack of enthusiasm they invariably expressed each time I'd mention the project, it became growingly clear to me that nurturing (even if involuntarily) a reputation as an *agent provocateur* in Addis Ababa could actually harm my anthropological research, in the very conservative areas of the North Amhara region – either because the necessary letters of authorisation could be hard to come by or simply because people would prefer not to talk to me if they were informed (through a newspaper column or by way of mouth, for instance) that I was the author of a painting that seemed to insult Abyssinian *affatarik* ('traditional history'). Moreover, I was conscious of the fact that, in previous instances, not long before, other *ferenjoch* had been in trouble for having, in one way or another, been involuntarily caught in situations where their behaviour was considered insulting to the Ethiopian state and/or society. The most telling of the cases that came to my knowledge was the following.

In 1994, a German couple living in Addis asked the renowned Harari artist Tibebe Terrfa to paint their car and the gate of their house. He acquiesced and decided to make a strongly expressionist depiction of a multitude of distorted and anguished human faces. For a westerner, these were somewhat reminiscent of Munch's *The Cry*, but for Ethiopians the more immediate reading was that they represented evil *zar* spirits or *ganen* demons. According to rumours that spread quickly in the 'Old Airport' neighbourhood (the quarter of Addis Ababa where the couple lived), the paintings were read as evidence that satanic rites were taking place in the *ferenjoch* house.

Unfortunately for the Germans, the completion of the paintings coincided with the publication of the results of the referendum in which the Eritreans chose to become independent from Ethiopia, an event that many Ethiopians saw as immensely traumatic, and so people's emotions were running high in Addis Ababa. In the day when Eritrea became effectively independent, an angry mob concentrated in front of the house's gate, and started shouting accusations of Devil worship against the Germans, clearly intent on sacking the house and expelling the owners, in front of a television camera. The police finally intervened and the Germans managed to get out of the situation physically unharmed. A few weeks later, unable to deal with the negative social pressure, the couple painfully decided to leave Ethiopia for good.[9] As the above-mentioned episodes remind us, a possible outcome of an intercultural 'ekphrasis' is what one could call the *Salman Rushdie Syndrome*[10] – a contextual combination of interpretations that concur to bring the meanings of an intended action totally out of the control of the one who promoted it. There are things that ought not be said, done, shown or seen, in certain circumstances, lest misunderstanding prevails, research is hindered and understanding is denied. Such, in a way, is a precious lesson to be learned from Andersen's tale *The Emperor's Clothes*. Our ingrained desire, as humans, to communicate, to expose our convictions, to say something, put us sometimes on the oblique tracks of gullibility, misunderstanding or conflict.

For this reason, and in order to satisfy a possible (and legitimate) desire of my western readers to see the abovementioned, not displayed, version of the legend of the Queen of Sheba, without unnecessarily annoying their Ethiopian counterparts, I decided to reproduce the painting here, duly covered in black ink and without the corresponding legends (Plate 9.5).[11]

Notes

1 Specially in Muslim regions, where many coach and taxi drivers cannot repress their curiosity and tend to turn their head back, or sideways, to be able to see what I'm drawing.

2 A very interesting experiment in this regard is Deena Newman's use of a comic-strip structure to narrative the web of rumours surrounding the strange death of a *bahtawy* ('hermit' or 'anchorite') in Addis Ababa (Newman 1998).

3 The Harari Cultural Centre is located in what was formerly a rich indian merchant's house. Although Arthur Rimbaud never lived there, the Centre was baptised by the French Cultural Co-operation as the 'Maison de Rimbaud' – the Centre is locally known as *Rambo bet* or 'Rambo house'.

4 E. E. Evans Pritchard, who raised the Nuer to anthropological fame, has done his fieldwork among the Western Nuer, from Sudan. But it is the material culture of the Eastern Nuer, who live across the border, in Ethiopia (in the administrative region of Gambela) that is represented in the IES collection. The civil war in Sudan caused

an eastwards flow of refugees, who settled in refugee camps in the Gambela region. Addis Ababa also harbours a growing migrant population from Nuerland.

5 SOFIES was founded in 1968 to support the Institute of Ethiopian Studies, then under the auspices of Emperor Haile Selassie. SOFIES has always been a very active fundraiser for the IES library, archive and museum, and is to this day an independent organisation with obvious influence in the decision-making processes of the IES.

6 It should be mentioned that, due partly to the presence of a large and mixed expatriate community of diplomats (from more than seventy embassies), members of a variety of international organisations and NGOs, Addis Ababa has a surprisingly cosmopolitan feel about it.

7 The oldest surviving document that relates this legend is the *Kebra Nagast*, or the 'Glory of Kings', a fourteenth-century manuscript contemporary of the rise of the so-called Solomic dynasty in Ethiopia (Munro-Hay 2001; Wallis-Budge 1932).

8 An early version of the story appears in the Qur'an and in old Arabic folktales as well as in Jew post-biblical literature (in the *Targum Sheni*, the *Midrash Mishle* and in the *Midrash Hachefez*). In European lore, it appears in the guise of the 'Queen with an ass's foot' and in the tales of the Sybil. The encounter of the Queen of Sheba and Solomon is depicted, among others, in a panel painting by Tintoretto, in Rubens' *The Visit of the Queen of Sheba*, in Veronese's *The Queen kneeling to Solomon* and in Lorrain's *The Embarkation of the Queen of Sheba*. The theme became quite popular in dramatic literature and music (from Calderon de la Barca's *The Oriental Sybil* and Rider Haggard's *Queen of Sheba's Ring* to Goldmark's and Gounod's operas, to Respighi's ballet, and Yeats' poems).

9 These events were first referred to me by Tibebe Terrfa himself, during a taped interview, and later confirmed by a number of other sources.

10 As a reminder to the situation of extreme disconfort that the writer Indian-born Salman Rushdie had to endure for several years as a result from having been the subject of a *Fatwah* pronounced by the hardline Iranian religious authorities, after the publication of his novel *Satanic Verses.*

11 See *Secret Painting*, by the British conceptual art group, Art & Language (1967–8), and the short story 'Tafas' by Jorge Luis Borges and Adolfo Bioy Casares (in *Las Cronicas de Bustos Domecq* 1967); these are recent refinements of an old motif in European art and literature, that of the invisible painting (from *Father Amis*, by Stricker and Juan Manuel's *exempla* about the king and the weavers, to Cervantes' *El retabulo de Maravilla*, Stendhal's *Le chef d'oeuvre inconnu* or even Magritte's *Ceci n'est pas une pipe*).

References

Atkinson, P. (1990) *The Ethnographic Imagination. Textual Constructions of Reality*, London: Routledge.

Cummins, T. (1995) 'From lies to truth: colonial ekphrasis and the art of crosscultural translation', in C. Fargo (ed.), *Reframing the Renaissance. Visual Culture in Europe and Latin America 1450–1650*. New Haven and London: Yale University Press.

Evans Pritchard, E. E. (1956) *Nuer Religion*, Oxford and New York: Oxford University Press.

Hammersley, Martyn (1992) *What's Wrong with Ethnography. Methodological Explorations*, London: Routledge.

Heffernan, J. A. W. (1993) *Museum of Words. The Poetics of Ekphrasis from Homer to Ashbery*, Chicago: Chicago University Press.

Hochmann, M. (1994) 'L'*ekphrasis* efficace. L'influence des programmes iconographiques sur les peintures et les décors italiens au XVIe siècle', in O. Bonfait (ed.), *Peinture et rhétorique. Actes du Colloque de l'Accadémie de France à Rome 10–11 Juin 1993*. Paris: Réunion des Musées Nationaux.

Hutchinson, S. (1980) 'Relations between the sexes among the Nuer: 1930', *Africa* 50(4): 371–88.

—— (1996) *Nuer Dilemmas: Coping with Money, War and the State*, Berkeley and Los Angeles: California University Press.

Iser, W. (1980) *The Act of Reading, A Theory of Aesthetic Response*, trans. by the author, Baltimore and London: Johns Hopkins University Press (orig. Munich 1976).

Krieger, M. (1992) *Ekphrasis. The Illusion of the Natural Sign*, Baltimore and London: Johns Hopkins University Press.

Mercier, J. (ed.) (1992) *Salomon et les maîtres du regard. Art et médecine en Éthiopie*, Paris: Réunion des Musées Nationaux.

Munro-Hay, S. (2001) 'A sixth-century Kebra Nagast?', *Annales d'Éthiopie* 17: 43–58.

Newman, D. (1998) 'Prophecies, police reports, cartoons and other ethnographic rumors in Addis Ababa', *Ethnofoor – Anthropologisch Tijdschrift*, 11(2/2): 83–110.

Pink, S. (2001) *Doing Visual Ethnography. Images, Media and Representation in Research*, London: Sage.

Ramos, M. J. (2000). *Histórias Etíopes. Diários de Viagem*. Lisbon: Assírio & Alvim.

—— (2001) 'Nem Mais nem Menos: Literalidade e Problematização em Antropologia', in M. Catedra (ed.), *La mirada cruzada en la cultura ibérica. Perspectivas desde la antropologia social en Portugal y España*. Madrid: Catarata.

—— (2002) *Traços de viagem*, http://reporter.clix.pt/tracosdeviagem/tracosdeviagem/index.html.

Sperber, D. (1982) *Le savoir des anthropologies*, Paris: Hermann.

Wallis-Budge, E. A. (trans. and ed.) (1932) *[Kebra Nagast] The Queen of Sheba and her only son Menelek (I), being the 'Book of the Glory of kings'*, Oxford: Oxford University Press.

Plate 9.1 Snapshots (Addis Ababa), by Manuel João Ramos, 2002 (from Ethiopian Sketch-book 6).

Plate 9.2 The Story of the Queen of Sheba, by Jembere Hailu, n.d. (collection: Manuel João Ramos).

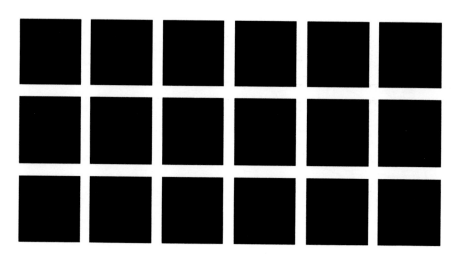

Plate 9.5 Arwe/Makeda (not yet displayed), by Manuel João Ramos.

HISTÓRIA DE MAKEDA + ARWE

- PINTOR QUE PINTA FRESCO COM HISTÓRIA DE ARWE - EJACULAÇÃO NO RIO
- NASCIMENTO DE RAPARIGA E DE SERPENTE
- FRESCO DE IGREJA DE OFERENDA A ARWE
- CHEGADA DE AGABO - CONCELHO DE ALDEIA
- AGABO ENVENENA CABRA
- AGABO TRANSPORTA-A P/ ARWE
- NOVA PINTURA DE IGREJA - OU
        ENTÃO PINTURA DE AEROPORTO
        (PINTOR PINTANDO): ARWE
        MORRE COMENDO A CABRA
- AS TRÊS POSSIBILIDADES: AGABO ENVE-
                            NENA
                    - MAKEDA QUEIMA
                            (TEF)
                    - RAINHA É MAKEDA

CONTAR POR ESCRITO]
         ← IMITAÇÃO DE
            PERGAMINHO

- "RAINHA" DE ADDIS ABEBA - MISS IN SHERATON
ETC. A VINDA DA ARCA PARA A   GIGI LIKE
ETIÓPIA PODE SER PINTURA EM
ESTILO GONDARINO INSERIDA

- QUANTOS QUADRADOS?

SALOMÃO:
- ISRAELITA
OU AMERICANO?

(BIG QUESTION)

CAFÉ

EL-AL
TABOT

SHERATON

6 + 6 + 6		

1,5 X 3 METROS

ARCA PELO CÉU NAIF

[KEDUSSE MIKAEL OU AVIÃO?]

ARWE - COM PINTURAS TRADICIONAIS

MAKEDA - NASCIMENTO DE
MENELIK: VIRGEM COM
MENINO, À
ETÍOPE
(HIPÓTESE HIRSCH)

MENELIK A CAVALO

NAIF ESTELA ITALIANA

MENELIK

* VERNISSAGE NA ASNI GALERY?
(MENELIK VÊ-SE NA PINTURA)

* FICÇÃO CIENTÍFICA APOCALÍPTICA - RUÍNAS E MEMÓRIAS DO PAS-
                                        SADO EM UNIVERSO FUTURI!!
+ TEMPO PRESENTE - A.A.   + A
☉ IMAGENS RURAIS   [OU ENTÃO + : FIN DE SIÈCLE
                            * : TEMPO PRESENTE]
- LEGENDAS EM AMÁRICO   MENELIK = AGABO ≠ SALOMÃO

- MENELIK: POLÍTICO OU BUSINESSMAN? [MELES OU ALAMUDI]

Plate 9.3 First sketches of the painting *Arwe/Makeda*, by Manuel João Ramos, 2002 (from Ethiopian Sketchbook 6).

Plate 9.4 Buk (Nuer), Manuel João Ramos, 2002 (collection: Museum of the Institute of Ethiopian Studies, Addis Ababa).

Plate 10.1 Captain José Caravela © Olivia da Silva.

Plate 10.2 Vic and Anne Willoughby (Grimsby) © Olivia da Silva.

Plate 10.3 Angelina Sousa (Matosinhos) © Olivia da Silva.

Plate 10.4 Antonio Pinhal (Matosinhos) © Olivia da Silva.

Plate 10.5 Alf Hudson (Grimsby) © Olivia da Silva.

Plate 10.6 Kurt Christman (Grimsby) © Olivia da Silva.

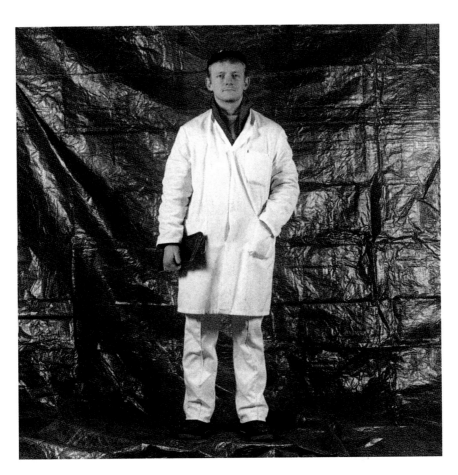

Plate 10.7 Nelson Hunter (Grimsby) © Olivia da Silva.

Plate 10.8 Joaquim Santos (Matosinhos) © Olivia da Silva.

Chapter 10

In the Net
Anthropology and photography

Olivia da Silva and Sarah Pink

My interviews with Captain José Caravela (see Plate 10.1) produced two types of narrative: formal information about the history and politics of fishing; and informal knowledge about individual histories and details of professional and personal life. When I used sophisticated video equipment and lighting it discouraged José from being informal in front of the camera, exacerbated by his having recently been interviewed by local television and radio stations. This transformed him into an ambassador for the whole of the (Portuguese) Matosinhos fishing community, rather than creating a space for the more intimate negotiations that can form part of the interaction between photographer and photographed. To achieve the latter I worked closely with the subjects of my portraits as they lived out their everyday lives in the port. As a participant observer I integrated myself into their everyday lives to access the personal and domestic arenas of fishing communities and to record individual histories and narratives. José's answers to my questions enabled me to include not just a photograph of a generalised fisherman, but a portrait that combined important cultural icons with a personal narrative. The fishing boxes that comprise the background are used in the sardine industry. The book of António Botto's poems that José holds was banned by the Portuguese political regime until 1974. The author, Botto, was from Matosinhos himself, but this particular volume found its way into José Caravela's hands and my portrait via a Brazilian fishing boat. Poetry is also part of José's personal narrative. For three months of the year, while the boats were being serviced, José devoted himself to a life away from fishing, to his family and his poetry, a characteristic that sets him apart from many of his fellow captains.

Introduction

Foster suggests anthropology appeals to contemporary artists because it 'is prized as the science of *alterity*', 'takes culture as its object' and 'is thought to arbitrate the *interdisciplinary*'. Ethnography offers the contextualisation that artists seek, inspiring some to do fieldwork, and a 'critical ethnography' offers both reflexivity and paradoxically preserves a certain 'romanticism' (1995: 395). Some artists innovatively engage with communities 'ethnographically' for example 'to recover suppressed histories that are sited in particular ways, that are accessed by some more effectively than others', however such interdisciplinary borrowing concerns Foster. He is sceptical about artists' potentially 'psuedoethnographic role' that he fears will neither attend to nor question the principles of participant observation effecting only 'limited engagement of the sited other' (1995: 306) thus losing the critique of ethnographic authority (1995: 307) and using the so-called ethnographic to *establish* authority. This chapter, by the photographer Olivia da Silva (in tinted boxes) and the anthropologist Sarah Pink (standard font), suggests how photography might go beyond this superficial engagement with alterity, reflexivity, culture and context. It discusses da Silva's *In the Net* – a documentary photography project informed by visual ethnographic research and anthropological concepts, represented in Plates 10.1 to 10.8 in between pages 156–157.

Anthropology and photography

Recent discussions of anthropology and photography suggest how anthropologists might learn from contemporary photographic practice. Elizabeth Edwards discusses how 'expressive', as opposed to 'realist', documentary photographs might represent anthropological ideas, arguing that expressive images might fracture the positivist assumptions that inform realist 'visual notebook' approaches to ethnographic photography. In dialogue with Elizabeth Williams' close-up photographs of fragments of Bedouin people and artefacts, Edwards argues that ambiguity is implied by each image being incomplete and difficult to comprehend. For Edwards such photography has a parallel with anthropological fieldwork methods because 'The fragmenting nature of the photographs . . . relate[s] very directly to anthropological practice', since 'Participant observation in anthropology has stressed the minutiae, not out of desire for wholeness *per se* but of the realisation that what looks insignificant to one way of thinking and perceiving may be singularly significant to another', arguing this concept is fundamental to non-realist anthropological photographic practice (1997: 68).

Allison James and Jo Booth also note parallels between anthropological and photographic agendas, as contemporary approaches to documentary practice recognise 'photography is fundamentally subjective' about the 'representation' of the visual and 'acknowledges the thoughts, feelings, preferences and ideologies of the photographer'. Analysing documentary photographer Martin Parr's images of people in contemporary cultural contexts they stress Parr's subjectivity as photographer/author – how his images ' "speak" clearly about the feelings he has about culture and identity', and how he 'positions himself as a cultural commentator' and observer (James and Booth 2000). This focus on the photographer's agency as author parallels anthropological concerns. However, like anthropology, photographs are also the result of a 'complex process of liaison' (James *et al.* 1997: 11) between the photographer and subject. Indeed recognising the photographer's – at the expense of the subjects' – subjectivity raises ethical issues. For instance having a camera 'suddenly thrust at you like an offensive weapon', which Jacobson associates with Parr's method: 'I go in very close to people because it's the only way you can get the picture. You go right up to them. Even now, I don't find it easy. I pretend to be focussing elsewhere . . . I don't try to hide what I'm doing – that would be folly' (Parr, quoted by Jacobson 2000: 2). Whether such negotiations between photographer and subject should be made explicit, and the terms they should be conducted on, are ethical questions that some might consider more appropriate for anthropologists than artists. However some documentary photographers and critics are also addressing these issues. Mark Durden discusses Richard Billingham's *Ray's a Laugh* (1996) – a series of 'photos of his [Billingham's] close family: his unemployed alcoholic father, Ray, his mother Elizabeth who hardly drinks and likes pets and things that are decorative; his brother Jason who was taken in care when he was eleven, but is now back with Ray and Liz again' all living in poverty in their Birmingham council flat (1996). Billingham's work is situated within the intimate context of his family relationships. Durden describes it as 'to an extent autobiographic' and it is similar to what Renov calls 'domestic ethnography' which 'engages in the [video] documentation of family members or, less literally, of people with whom the maker has maintained long-standing everyday relations and has thus achieved a level of casual intimacy' (1999: 141). Billingham's images are uncaptioned, and like domestic ethnography emerge from a photographic encounter with Ray, Liz and Jason's everyday life. They shock as they bring private lives into a public domain (common in anthropology) but according to Billingham his family's response to his book was that 'Neither I nor they are shocked by its directness because we're all well-enough acquainted with having to live in poverty. After all, there are millions of other people in Britain living similarly' (Billingham quoted in Durden 1996). *Ray's a Laugh* shares anthropological concerns since it attends to the detail of everyday life, represents fragments rather than wholes, is unapologetically selective, and makes explicit the photographer's relationship with his subjects. While Parr comments on culture by representing unnamed individuals in images pronouncing his own world-view, Billingham engages with the intimacy of his family's everyday experience. Both emphasise difference, using comparison to represent contemporary English culture. However, neither claim to do ethnography.

Interdisciplinary exchanges should be carefully situated. Anthropologists' photographs, designed to participate in *anthropological* discourses, might fare badly under the scathing gaze of art critics. Similarly photographers do not become anthropologists by virtue of informing their photography with anthropological methods and concepts; their work will not necessarily participate in anthropological debates. Instead, acknowledging the parallel concerns of anthropological and photographic practice, this chapter explores how anthropologists might learn from innovations in documentary photography to suggest new ways of representing ethnography photographically.

In the Net: comparison and collaboration

Olivia da Silva began her career as a photojournalist for *Público*, a Portuguese national newspaper. Shifting her focus to documentary photography she began to explore new aspects of photographic production and representation, developing themes of identity and cultural difference in *8/2*, a project comparing Portuguese and English market traders.[1] These experiences attracted her to visual anthropology to inform her understanding of the communities she worked with, the methods she researched her photographic projects with, and to explore the intersubjectivity, negotiations and collaborations between herself and the people she photographed. *In the Net* (1997–2000)[2] continued this, using photography to explore and represent photographically concepts of place, culture, identity, difference and gender in the Grimsby (England) and Matosinhos (Portugal) fishing communities. *In the Net* consists of interviews on video and minidisk, two CD-ROM projects, a set of portraits and a written text that situates Silva's photographic practice and images in relation to existing photographic projects about fishing communities. *In the Net* also develops two key anthropological themes.

First, it is based on long-term participant observation and visual ethnographic methods (Pink 2001; Banks 2001), reflecting the insistence on reflexivity and intersubjectivity that characterises recent anthropological work (James *et al.* 1997), especially visual anthropology (MacDougall 1998; Ruby 2000; Pink 2001). Since the 'writing culture debate', attention to the relationship between anthropologist and informant has become paramount, as: 'The making of anthropological representations can therefore be seen as the final outcome of a complex process of liaison between the informant and the researcher, each of whom is engaged in similar, though often separate attempts to generate interpretations which can encompass the multiplexity of everyday life' (James *et al.* ibid.). By using visual ethnographic methods to research individuals' identities and visual cultures of fishing communities, collaborating with her subjects, and interrogating the relationship between photographer and subject in photographic production, da Silva's portraits are informed by ethnographic knowledge and anthropological theory and explicitly constructed to represent individual identities and local cultures. As an exhibition *In the Net* was developed in consultation with its subjects, and included sound and video. Its final portraits were taken in various contexts (studios created in fish markets, ports, homes, bars and work spaces) over the two years da Silva spent with the fishing communities.

Second, *In the Net* is a comparative project concerned with culture and identity. As Gingrich and Fox note, anthropology's original comparative projects of 'ethnoscience, neo-evolutionism and holocultural methodology' have been critiqued and largely abandoned. Recent work has rethought comparison in contemporary anthropology identifying diverse plural comparative projects (2002: 12) including the study of regional variations (2002: 20) and insisting comparison is not essentially connected to grand theory construction (2002: 5). Comparison of similar activities, categories and cultural contexts across Europe can indicate how change (globalisation for Gingrich and Fox 2002: 6–7) affects different individuals and communities differently. Da Silva demonstrates how the fishing communities she worked with incorporate new fishing technologies and regulations in different ways and how this is manifested in individual actions and self-representations. In contrast to Allan Sekula's *Fish Story* (1995), probably the best-known comparative photographic project about fishing, *In the Net* does not explicitly support a grand theory. *Fish Story* combines writing and photography to argue for 'the continued importance of maritime space in order to counter the exaggerated importance attached to that large metaphysical construct, "cyberspace" and the corollary myth of "instantaneous" contact between distant spaces' (1995: 50), a point da Silva agrees with (2000: 68). Sekula's photographs of water and industrial areas, usually without people, compare global ports to represent his own visual and theoretical viewpoint (see da Silva 2000b: 67). Conversely *In the Net* draws from ethnographic experience to represent members of two self-defined fishing communities as individuals who participate in particular local cultures that are affected by similar global trends, sometimes in different ways.

Visual ethnography in the ports

I began by collecting examples of old photographs that people had stored away or hung on the walls of their homes. This included old and new photographs of places I had visited, such as family houses, fishing museums, market halls, chapels, public houses and cafés. I spent time hanging around, integrating myself into their space by visiting them in their homes, having a coffee or a beer, and being prepared to listen to them and to come away from a meeting 'empty handed' and not see this as wasted time. During my first interviews I took some photographs of people using a Polaroid, 35 mm and/or digital camera. I wanted to be able to present the sitter with something immediate in return for their co-operation and I hoped this might be the start of an ongoing relationship that would permit me to develop my portraits and my analysis of intersubjectivity. This technology was less intrusive and was comfortable to operate in the busy market place. Later I introduced the recording equipment and video camera, and when the time was right I suggested a visit to their home where I photographed people individually or in groups. Next I invited people to come to my studio in the Paulo Adriano warehouse in the Docapesca (docks) area of Matosinhos, or the fish market in Grimsby.

My studios were close to the harbour, fishing boats and trawlers. I intended to become an integral part of a space frequented by fishermen to establish a close relationship with them. It also gave me easier access to the individuals and objects that were part of my photographic work without unduly interrupting the daily routine of the fish market. After taking the first studio portrait I showed the sitter a print and we discussed it in relation to the objectives we had initially agreed on. Sometimes one or both of us was unhappy with the photograph.

My research created a fragmented collection of images and interviews. To make sense of this information I produced several small exhibitions and two CD-ROMs of work in progress. The exhibitions were held within the fish market and were an invaluable source of reflection. The CD-ROMs were valuable in providing an initial platform from which to look at the relationship between my interviews and my images. The finished work was finally first exhibited in Porto (Portugal) in 2000. In the exhibition the video and minidisk recordings of interviews and the everyday sounds of the fish markets and ports both reveal the photographers' working methodology and are integral to the viewer's experience of the portraits.

Ethnographic comparison, visual representation

The Grimsby fish auction is held from Monday to Friday, at 7.00 to 8.30, once trawlers and refrigerated lorries have arrived from across the United Kingdom. The fish are weighed, crated and sold by men in white coats and boots, notebooks in hand. The traditional sale of fish in a market equipped with all types of modern equipment creates a pleasant atmosphere. It is a blend of the old and the sterile new, accompanied by the tune of male voices calling out the prices. It was here that I set up my studio. The space I had been given in Matosinhos was in a warehouse where the fishermen worked daily on their nets and which was littered with objects relating to the sea. The room I was given in Grimsby was quite different – simply a garage for the machines used to transport fish from trawlers or lorries to the port where it was sold in the market.

Therefore I decided to add a new background that was figuratively related to the sea (since oilskins are used to cover objects on board fishing boats). I hung a blue oilskin from two rafters and spread it over the floor to isolate my subjects from the rough cement walls of the storehouse and create a studio environment. Nelson, the first person I photographed in the studio was relaxed and friendly, he looked directly into the camera and our relationship was pleasant and easy. I photographed him against a blue background, trying to make him stand out as he was wearing his white coat – the compulsory uniform of the fish market. Notebook in his right hand, pencil in pocket, he expressed some of the typical character-istics of the fishmongers. In a sense Nelson presented himself as a metaphor for the Grimsby fishing industry. He was dressed to meet health and hygiene regulations that had little to do with the traditions of catching and selling fish. He stood for a Grimsby almost divorced from the sea and it was fitting that he found himself in front of an equally metaphoric backcloth.

The market fishmongers highlighted the relationship between old and new in the same environment, creating a unique atmosphere. The male voices calling out the price of the fish and the old black notebooks are signs of times past that still endure in the will of each of these individuals. These men, inserted in a sterile hall, forced to wear white coats, and very often white boots and hats, were selling their wares in the old-fashioned way. Unable to resist EEC regulations they made a stand against digital auction equipment. Ironically in contrast in Matosinhos the men wear whatever they like but turn up to a digital auction each day.

In the Net

Departing from the observational styles of other documentary photographers, *In the Net* represents culture differently. Its deliberately constructed images compare change in Grimsby and Matosinhos fishing communities and icons of individual and cultural values and experiences. Their very constructedness indicates their status as self-conscious products of the negotiations between photographer and subject.

Da Silva's portraits are explicitly constructed. Like Williams' photographs of fragments (Edwards 1997) and like Parr's and Billingham's photography they attend to detail – they do not pretend to represent whole truths – but they do so differently. Whereas Parr's work 'collect[s] the detail of contemporary culture and make[s] spectacle out of the ordinariness of everyday life' (James and Booth 2000), da Silva's portraits situate individuals in relation to metaphors for their culture and everyday life. Her portraits combine individuals with living or material elements of their lives to evoke aspects of their experience, the contexts they inhabit and their cultural values and beliefs. As she describes for José Caravela's portrait (above), she learnt about him from interviews and informal conversations. Through collaboration and negotiation they produced a portrait that represents elements of his personal and professional experience. The portrait includes important icons – fishing boxes, a poetry book – that represent José's identity as a poet and family man, distinguishing him from other captains. Thus da Silva implies the intersubjectivity between people and their material cultures, suggesting how the narratives of individuals and objects intersect. However da Silva's methodology appreciates that meanings are not made simply through the photographer's creativity and intentionality and contained in the image, but are interpreted by viewers. During her research da Silva exhibited her portraits in the communities they represented, to evaluate their responses and understandings of the work, and ensure their appropriateness.

Da Silva's portraits, constituted of fragments that imply a wider context of personal and cultural knowledge and experience, respond to the demands of a reflexive anthropology. First they critique the realist notion that one can visually record wholes, inviting viewers to consider relationships between components of the image, to create a story from them. Second her exhibition refers to inter-subjectivity in ethnographic and photographic processes by using tape recordings and video to evoke the experienced reality of interviews, ports and markets. Da Silva goes beyond questions of her own subjectivity, making her subject's contributions in the form of objects they brought explicit as elements of the composition of their portraits.

New ideas for anthropological photography

In the past anthropologists have enlisted photography as a realist support for positivist anthropology (e.g. Collier and Collier 1986); however it is now recognised that written anthropological representations 'do not offer a copy of the original' and neither do photographs because although they 'might appear to constitute a more "faithful" representation' they are 'framed' and 'represented' themselves when exhibited or published (James *et al.* 1997: 11). Nevertheless photography and writing make different contributions to anthropology and for photography to make a 'concrete contribution' to anthropology, anthropologists need to 'harness those qualities peculiar to the *medium* of still photography' (Edwards 1997: 53). Recently some excellent works have demonstrated how realist ethnographic photography might have an anthropological and applied impact (see Kratz 2002). The example discussed here suggests how deliberately constructed expressive photography might also support the project of an anthropology that reveals the processes and intersubjectivity by which knowledge and representations are produced and constructed.

Notes

1 MA in Photography project, University of Derby, UK.
2 A Ph.D. project, University of Derby, supervised by Sarah Pink, Mark Durden and Karen Forbes and funded by the Gulbenkian Foundation, Portugal.

References

Foster, H. (1995) 'The artist as ethnographer', in G. E. Marcus and F. R. Myers (eds), *The Traffic in Culture: Refiguring Art and Anthropology*, University of California Press.

Banks, M. (2001) *Visual Methods in Social Research*, London: Sage.

Billingham, R. (1996) *Ray's a Laugh*, Zurich, Berlin and New York: Scalo Press.

Collier, J. and Collier, M. (1986) *Visual Anthropology: Photography as a Research Method*, Albuquerque: University of New Mexico Press.

Da Silva, O. (2000a) *In the Net*, Porto, Portugal: Rainho & Neves Lda. Exhibition catalogue.

—— (2000b) *In the Net*, Ph.D. thesis, University of Derby.

Durden, M. (1996) 'Family photographs: Richard Billingham', in *Portfolio* 24: 58–9.

Edwards, E. (1997) 'Beyond the boundary: a consideration of the expressive in photography and anthropology', in M. Banks and H. Morphy (eds), *Rethinking Visual Anthropology*, London: Routledge.

Gringrich, A. and Fox, R. (2002) *Anthropology by Comparison*, London: Routledge.

Jacobson, C. (2000) 'Magnum Farce', in *Zonezero* Magazine http://www.zonezero.com/magazine/articles/jacobson/magnum1.html

James, A., Hockey, J. and Dawson, A. (1997) *After Writing Culture*, London: Routledge.

James, A. and Booth, J. (2000) 'Anthropology meets photography on the Internet', in *iNtergraph: journal of dialogic anthropology* (1)1 http://www.intergraphjournal.com/enhanced/articles/article2/photoframes.htm

Kratz, C. (2002) *The Ones That are Wanted*, California: California University Press.

MacDougall, D. (1998) *Transcultural Cinema*, Princeton: Princeton University Press.

Pink, S. (2001) *Doing Visual Ethnography*, London: Sage.

Renov, M. (1999) 'Domestic ethnography and the construction of the "Other" self', in J. M. Gaines and M. Renov (eds), *Collecting Visible Evidence*, Minneapolis: University of Minnesota Press, 140–55.

Ruby, J. (2000) *Picturing Culture*, Chicago: Chicago University Press.

Sekula, A. (1995) *Fish Story*, Germany: Richter Verlag.

Chapter 11

Conversing anthropologically

Hypermedia as anthropological text

Sarah Pink

Moving images, written words and the anthropology of gender

Visual anthropologists have recently argued for a (re)integration of the visual into mainstream anthropology and the incorporation of anthropological aims into ethnographic film-making. This would give the visual a critical role in revising the categories through which anthropological knowledge is produced (MacDougall 1997: 292, Grimshaw 2001: 173) by introducing the visual as an alternative way of understanding and route to knowledge about social phenomena. Moreover it suggests a new agenda for ethnographic film-making to produce films according to anthropological, rather than broadcast television, agendas (MacDougall 2001; Ruby 2000a). Two other chapters in this book suggest how departures from observational film (Henley) and a collaborative film-making endeavour (Martínez *et al.*) might achieve this. Here I suggest that to close the divide between visual and mainstream anthropology requires not simply new ethnographic film forms but also anthropological texts that combine and mutually situate visual and written ethnographic materials with anthropological theory. Hypermedia offers one route towards such an anthropology that allows the visual to make critical insights that inspire us to rethink the way anthropological arguments are conventionally constructed. Such texts would aim to combine visual and written knowledge and representations so each might communicate in the way it is best at. In doing so anthropological hypermedia texts might intervene in the debates and theories of mainstream anthropology in ways ethnographic film cannot.

In this chapter I discuss the relationship between written and visual anthropology by drawing from examples from the anthropology of gender. Taking the relationship between written and filmic anthropologies of gender as an example of the unsatisfactory relationship between film and text in anthropology I examine how anthropological hypermedia texts might combine image and writing to resolve this.

Ethnographic film and written anthropology: a one-way conversation?

In her historical analysis of academic anthropology and documentary cinema in the post-war twentieth century Grimshaw shows how the two developed different 'ways of seeing'. Anthropology became increasingly established as an academic discipline that 'saw the world as an object to be scientifically invest-igated and represented' while cinema was 'predicated on the interrogation of notions of reality and the means of its apprehension through the development of a new relationship with the world'. Initial ethnographic film projects of the 1960s and 1970s were aligned with the aims of anthropology's scientific endeavour. However the later films of Rouch, the MacDougalls and Llewelyn-Davies developed the techniques and ideas of cinema and television, forming 'an important counterpoint to the textual preoccupations of their anthro-pological contemporaries in the academy' (Grimshaw 2001: 87–9). This gulf between written and filmic ethnography set a context in which the two genres infrequently conversed with one another.

Mainstream written anthropology has recently departed from a scientific paradigm to favour reflexivity, subjectivity and the questioning of truth claims, allowing film and writing to share theoretical and ethnographic concerns and goals. Nonetheless a substantial dialogue has not developed between the two. While 'all documentary films exist in an intertextual relationship with other films and with written literature' there is still work to be done so that rather than producing written study guides for films, film and text might be 'alternative representations' within the body of work of an anthropologist/film-maker, that are 'brought into an analytically constructive dialogue, rather than one passively supporting the other' (Banks 2001: 151). At present however the relationship between filmic and written anthropology tends to flow in just one direction, since: 'If a film viewer wishes to, or is instructed to, she can find an academic literature that does not necessarily "support" the film, but which can provide an alternative representation' (Banks 2001: 151). Written ethnographies infrequently direct their readers to films (with the exception of introductory course texts e.g. Hendry 1998). There is therefore in general a lack of conversation between film and written text in anthropological research publications, which is substantiated when we look at specific sub-disciplines (e.g. the anthropology of home – see Pink 2003). Neither is a dialogue between visual and written anthropological representations often established within ethnographic regions and area studies. In part this lack of conversation can be explained in terms of the differences between ethnographic film and writing, as Henley defines them, characterising the former as descriptive of particular cases but inevitably informed by anthro-pological theory and the latter as explicitly 'concerned with general theoretical issue about human culture and society' but usually referring to particular cases in doing so (Henley 2000: 217). Film and writing tend to communicate dif-ferent types of anthropological and ethnographic knowledge in different ways.

Below as an example I discuss two recent ethnographic films that represent Spanish gender to explore their relationships to the corresponding written anthropology.

Mujeres invisibles (*A Buen Común* 2000) is an ethnographic video based on a long-term collaborative project with women in Cordoba (Andalusia), including a book (Martínez 2000). The film and its making are discussed in Chapter 9. Having done fieldwork about gender in Cordoba (Pink 1997) I interpret *Mujeres invisibles* as an ethnographic film that interweaves a set of interviews with local women to represent their individual biographies, everyday lives, aspirations and needs. The film explores these women's interpretations of their own femininity, and what it means to them to be women in the contemporary context they live in. It is about their consciousness, and enables what MacDougall has coined as the potential of visual representation 'to make possible a view of social actors responding creatively to a site of open-ended cultural possibilities, rather than being bound by a rigid framework of cultural constraints' (1998: 271). *Mujeres invisibles* implicitly responds to a theory of plural gender and provides a new challenge to the problematic binary models of Spanish gender as an honour and shame system formulated by anthropologists such as Gilmore (1987). Like recent work by Spanish (Sanchiz 1992) and Northern European (Pink 1997; Thuren 2000) anthropologists *Mujeres invisibles* focuses on women's experience, whereas past studies of Andalusian gender were largely by male anthropologists and represented a masculine standpoint (cf. Loizos 1992). It shows how local women skilfully both comply with and depart from traditional gendered relationships to survive economically and emotionally in difficult circumstances. The film is also an ethnography of those who were silenced in past anthropologies of Spanish gender, of ordinary women living in poor urban neighbourhoods. We learn about what MacDougall has called 'a convergence of the personal, historical, and material at a particular place and time' rather than about 'culture as a discrete set of structures' (1998: 271).

Sonia Herman Dolz's *Romance de Valentía* (1994) is a documentary film about the Spanish bullfight. It is informed by Garry Marvin's anthropological research on bullfighting (Marvin 1988) and Marvin worked on the film. It represents a 'traditional' discourse about the hegemonic masculinity of the bullfighting world and the iconography, values and relationships that inform and are informed by this (Pink 1999). This film provides an excellent representation of bullfighting culture as it is described in traditional discourse, and as such represents the binary gender system this discourse promotes. Whereas *Mujeres invisibles* is made from interviews and contextualising footage, *Romance de Valentía* is overtly constructed through a range of different scenarios, using actors and a leading bullfighter to represent the experiences of a bullfighter and the world he inhabits. This film is about traditional Spanish gender and resonates well with representations of gender segregation in the existing ethnography. In contrast to *Mujeres invisibles* it represents the individual within the order of established cultural models. It seeks to evoke experience, but not so much the personal experience of individuals as the culturally defined generalised experiences that are associated with the bullfight.

Mujeres invisibles and *Romance de Valentía* are different types of film that explicitly represent different ethnographic experiences and implicitly represent particular theories of Spanish gender. *Mujeres invisibles* implies plural gender and difference, comparing the women who speak in the video with one another and with the experience of the viewer. *Romance de Valentía* describes a gender-segregated model of the Spanish bullfighting world based on a binary model of gender. Neither is a conventional observational ethnographic film (see Henley this volume) and both seek alternative ways to communicate anthropologically. Both films disseminate anthropologically informed ideas to a wider public. *Mujeres invisibles* makes important points about women's experiences in Southern Spain; its relevance goes beyond the anthropology of gender. For example, its première was at the Journadas Feministas del Estado Español in Cordoba in 2000 and in 2001 it was screened at the Videomostra del Ayuntamiento de Donostia–San Sebastian and the Videoteca del Ayuntamiento de Madrid. *Romance de Valentía*, produced by VPRO-television in the Netherlands, was intended for a popular audience. It has been shown on television internationally, was screened at the Amsterdam and London Film Festivals in 1993 and awarded the Golden Hugo for Best Documentary, Chicago 1994 and the Best Documentary, Troy 1994. In contrast their impact as anthropological texts beyond their intertextual relationship (Banks 2001) with Marvin's (1988) and Martínez's (2000) written representations is limited. Indeed neither film is anthropological in the sense that they explicitly expound anthropological theory. Although both films can be understood in the context of theoretical debates about Spanish gender, and in my view make important comments on these, they do not intervene in written debates. Moreover although gender debates are implicitly represented in film, these debates gain their momentum in anthropological writing. Ethnographic film about Spanish gender is not in continuous dialogue with writing on the anthropology of Spanish gender. Written anthropological texts about Spanish gender share a concern with representing everyday ethnographic experiences and reflexivity (see especially Sanchíz 1992, Pink 1997, Martínez 2000). However in written work these are represented in explicit relationship with theory.

Other discussions of the relevance of ethnographic film about gender to written anthropology of gender also indicate that generally film has little impact on written debates. For example, Grimshaw's (2001) discussion of the feminist anthropological television of Melissa Llewelyn-Davies focuses not on what the anthropology of gender has learnt from Llewelyn-Davies' films but on how the film-maker's Maasai women film cycle developed as feminist anthropological television. Grimshaw notes the gendered qualities of this work and argues that 'The refraction of her changing ethnographic concerns through the prism of feminism makes Llewelyn-Davies a critical figure in the creation of a different kind of [feminist] anthropology' (2001: 170). However Grimshaw does not demonstrate the wider impact of these films on anthropological writing and the question remains of how much Llewelyn Davies' television work (produced between the 1970s and early 1990s) has influenced the development of a gendered academic anthropology. A review of subsequent key English-language publications on the anthropology of gender, including edited collections (del Valle's (1993) *Gendered Anthropology*, Goddard's (2000) *Gender, Agency and Change*, and Cornwall and Lindisfarne's (1994) *Dislocating Masculinity*) and Moore's *A Passion for Difference* (1994) as well as her more recent work on gender (e.g. Moore 1999), shows these works do not engage with ethnographic film or video representations of gender either theoretically or ethnographically.

Nevertheless written texts and ethnographic films about gender are not irrelevant to one another, as the Spanish case shows often they are interested in similar themes or questions. Moreover, the specificity of ethnographic films represents their unavoidable commitment to the study of concrete localities in ethnographic regions or of individuals in particular cultures. Combining film and writing provides an excellent opportunity to address wider anthropological questions such as that of gender using both language and images. As I have shown above, films about gender can be interpreted as implicitly representing ideas also found in written anthropology. However film and writing tend not to directly reference or engage with one another in their representations of anthropological and ethnographic ideas. To do so would be difficult for several reasons. First, it would involve a form of 'translation' between knowledge that has been represented filmically or in words. Even if anthropological commentary is added as voice-over to ethnographic film it is infrequently satisfactory in its depth of theoretical engagement and more likely to be explanatory or didactic. Second, direct references to complex written theoretical debates would break the linear visual narrative of a film, it might require the viewer to stop viewing and read a text. Third, descriptions of scenes or dialogues from ethnographic films included in written texts are not wholly adequate because they lack 'understandings that may be accessible only through non-verbal means' (MacDougall 1997: 292). In short, film and written text have difficulties in conversing with one another that cannot necessarily be resolved simply by producing 'better' films and texts. I am not arguing that we should stop making ethnographic films, but that to achieve a dialogue between the visual and written that facilitates the critical role envisaged for the visual (see MacDougall 1997; Grimshaw 2001) we need to explore new media.

Visual ethnography and anthropological representation

In my own ethnographic work, involving video footage, participant observation and tape-recorded interviewing, the question of the relationship between film and writing is also important. Since 1999 I have been working on a visual ethnographic project about gender and the home in England and Spain. This included one-hour videotaped interviews with individuals in their homes, conceptualised as a 'video tour': a collaborative exploration of the home where we discussed how the home is used, maintained, cleaned, designed, and the meanings of objects in it. We looked in fridges and wardrobes, and at photographs and paintings, smelt their perfumes, and 'smelly' parts of the home, we touched surfaces and 'felt' the floor under our feet, and listened to their CDs and to the squeaking of bats that lived in the eaves. These ethnographic videotapes can be interpreted largely within the terms that MacDougall discusses for the reflexivity of film and its focus on the individual and consciousness rather than on culture as a system. They represent 'deep' as opposed to explanatory reflexivity. The former inscribes the relationships through which the video was produced whereas the latter takes place after the event is more common in reflexive ethnographic writing (1998: 89). Simultaneously the tapes represented my informants' individual views and experiences of their home decoration and housework and the specific strategies they employed to undertake these gendered practices.

In 1999 when interviewing I envisaged how an ethnographic 'film' might develop, and some informants gave me permission to use their tapes in visual publications. A film would have allowed me to reflexively represent individual informants' unique gendered, embodied and sensory experiences of and in their homes. It would have facilitated the emphasis on consciousness (both my own and my informants') that MacDougall has proposed would be a feature of the visual anthropology of the future (1998: 271–4). It would have allowed me to evoke experiences of emotion, embodied experience, smell, touch and sound in ways that are untranslatable into written words. Rather than situating my informants' views, actions and experiences within a 'culture' through abstract theoretical discussion, it would have focused on the continuities and differences between them as individuals performing their own gendered identities through their everyday practices. Thus exploiting what MacDougall has described as the benefits of ethnographic film. However working with these materials anthropologically I realised that, although I could use them to represent my informants' voices, experiences and embodied actions and a reflexive take on the research, I also needed to use language to represent much that I wanted to express about and with them. My analysis of these tapes is situated within existing academic discourses about gender, agency, performativity theory and home. Moreover my analysis of my informants' experiences, views, actions and strategies focuses on the question of how I and they see them as departing from conventional gendered behaviours and roles. I cannot participate in these written academic discourses without writing. One option would be a film and a written text. However, were my films screened at a film festival I doubt many would read my accompanying book. If I published my work in a journal my film would not be distributed with it. In short my potential film would exist in a similar relationship to the anthropology to gender to those films I have discussed above. As I began to produce theorised anthropological (as opposed to descriptive ethnographic) representations from this work its visual and video aspects remained inseparable – one was always contingent on the other and although I had already decided to write a book *Home Truths* (Pink, forthcoming) based on this work in which I would inevitably have to resort to written description and transcripts to represent video, I wanted to explore other options. Seeking a solution I began to develop this work as CD-ROM hypermedia projects that combine still and moving images with written words. Ruby has expressed similar concerns regarding his 'Oak Park Stories' digital video project (see Ruby 2000). As Ruby's research developed he began to doubt that film was the answer: 'I was determined not to do what others had done – produce a "film" that depended upon accompanying written materials to make it a "complete" ethnographic statement.' Instead he envisaged a text needing 'an audience of one' sitting at a computer and assuming 'the activist stance that is the norm for people working with a computer and not passively waiting to be amused by the television', leading him 'to explore ways in which I can combine text, photographs, audio recordings, and video footage into a coherent package' that might be delivered on DVD (Ruby 2001).

My CD-ROM projects combine written words, video, and stills. They attempt to communicate anthropologically using multiple media and to draw from and engage with discourses from both a reflexive visual anthropology and gendered (mainstream) anthropology. I aim to create an anthropological text that converses with both written and visual anthropologies, and thus to bridge the gap between the two. For such a project to work I propose it needs to have two components, a theorised and considered relationship between images and words and an ability to respond to rather than simply reflect the existing discourses of anthropological film and writing.

Hypermedia as anthropological text

Hypermedia ethnography is fast becoming an established form, of interest to anthropologists and sociologists, used in teaching and learning and in ethnographic representation (see the Introduction to this volume). Such work is increasingly prominent in visual anthropology conferences, film festivals and on-line. Simultaneously a new literature discusses the development and value of hypermedia ethnography, how technological possibilities facilitate anthropological and sociological argument and representation of ethnographic realities (e.g. Biella 1994, 1996, Banks 1994, 2001). I have begun to reflect on these questions in recent work (Pink 2001, 2003), arguing that hypermedia allows us to produce new anthropological texts that are multilinear, multimedia, interactive and reflexive. Sociologists have recently come to similar conclusions (e.g. Mason and Dicks 2001). Such texts might meet the demands of a reflexive anthropology by making visual and written fieldwork materials directly available to the user through hyperlinks or as embedded in the text. By including fieldwork videotapes they can come closer to representing what MacDougall calls 'deep' reflexivity (1998: 89). They can combine written and visual text and ethnography and theory (thus integrating more closely mainstream written and visual anthropology). Through their multilinearity they can represent multiple and simultaneous voices (of anthropologists and informants), having more than one linear narrative. Their interactivity can empower their viewers with new ways of learning from text and images, allowing them to follow their own, albeit guided, but sometimes unpredictable, pathways (see Pink 2001).

Hypermedia offers us the exciting prospect of combining ethnographic film and anthropological writing. However in addition to promoting the virtues of its capacity to do so, we need to theorise how such a combination may function as anthropological representation. To produce effective anthropological hypermedia, the use of images and words needs to be supported by an analysis of what each is best at and how the types of knowledge represented in each can best be used. MacDougall demarcates different but interrelated roles of writing and film in anthropology where the 'challenge of images' is a challenge to the concept of culture and an invitation to the particular and the 'transcultural' (1998: 259). Writing, he argues, is more disposed to 'cultural explanations in that it allows the writer to represent a society from within, based on the participatory experiences of fieldwork' and 'more often emphasises basic structures such as those of kinship or exchange' (1998: 256). Writing also, importantly, allows us to theorise experiences and behaviours, to be explicit about our anthropological ways of interpreting them and to engage in dialogues with other anthropologists about these. The 'challenge' of the visual is important, but to have its full effect it should be integrated with and thus work in *direct* relation to written anthropology (rather than challenging it from the distance of a big screen or video monitor). Moreover, now ethnographic writing has begun to represent the individual and the particular with more enthusiasm, the visual might not be regarded as a challenge so much as a welcome collaborator. Working with my own visual and written materials I aimed to combine video and words to represent particular individual gendered embodied experiences and consciousness in relation (and resistance) to traditional gender models and discourse. Moreover I wanted to do this in relation to an explicit written theory of gender.

Below I reflect on theoretical and technological aspects of this to examine how one might create an anthropological hypermedia text that is conversant with both ethnographic film and a gendered anthropology by discussing an experimental CD-ROM project I am working on: *Women's Worlds*. The objectives of the project were twofold: first, to represent the relationship between femininity and home; second, to explore the potential of hypermedia representation for moving beyond both text and film and bridging the gap between them.

Women's Worlds

My wider project on gender and the home examines how gender is changing in Britain and Spain. I explore this ethnographically in the home though a study of men's and women's approaches to home decoration, creativity and housework. Theoretically I examine these questions through notions of gender performativity, the sensory aspects and experience of home and notions of human agency, consciousness, and the creative individual. I argue that changing gender is (at least partially) driven by the everyday actions of human agents, creative gendered individuals who interact with the sensory homes they inhabit in ways that transgress what they (and anthropologists) see as 'traditional' gender roles. In doing so they are establishing new gendered identities. In this ethnographic and theoretical project the individual, the embodied and the particular that MacDougall refers to are necessarily present.

Women's Worlds also explores the relationship between gender performativity, agency and the sensory experience and creation of home by examining how women represent their homes and themselves in their homes. This project is an experiment in producing an anthropological text akin to an article, but unlike on-line journal articles (see for example *Sociological Research Online*) that follow the conventional linear styles of printed articles it has a series of alternative

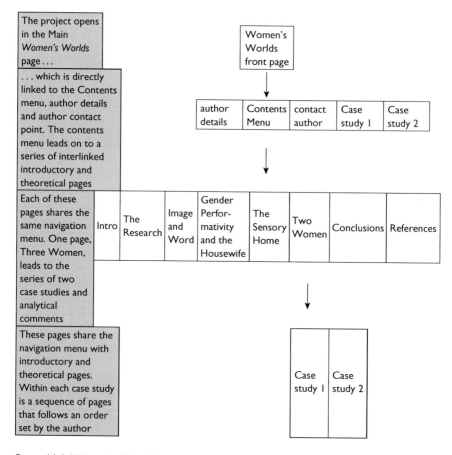

Figure 11.1 Women's Worlds: project map.

routes and uses different strategies to communicate anthropological and ethnographic ideas including, video, written text, colour, layout and linkages. In terms of its content *Women's Worlds* includes theoretical written texts, descriptive ethnographic writing and ethnographic video clips and quotations from interviews. Its case-study narratives focus on two women of different ages, neither of whom sees herself as a 'housewife', who have different relationships to their sensory and material homes, and create 'home' in different ways.

Structure and navigation

Navigation and the degree of control offered to hypermedia users are important issues. There should be sufficient guidance to ensure the author's argument is communicated, while allowing enough autonomy to empower users to control how they produce knowledge from the text (Pink 2001; Mason and Dicks 2001). I wanted the user to be able to navigate *Women's Worlds* at multiple points in its structure. Therefore each page shares the same navigation menu (see Figure 11.2) which, in combination with the Internet Explorer navigation toolbar, the viewer uses to navigate between different narratives. The project was created using Dreamweaver Ultra Dev 4 software. By using a web-page design and browser I aimed to make the structure and composition of the text explicit.

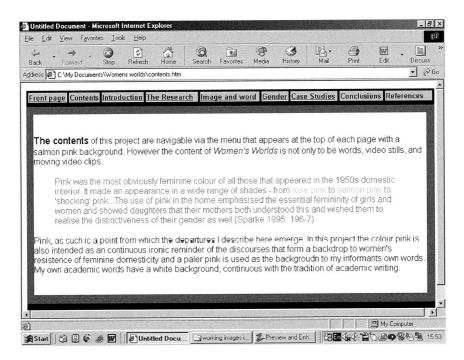

Figure 11.2 The contents page of the CD.

Thus I intended to encourage users to make informed decisions about their routes through the project while making my own intentions clear through the hyperlinks on offer. At all times each narrative of the project is available via the heading navigation menu, allowing multilinear access to the key strands of the text. The case studies are accessible only as linear texts presented on a page-by-page basis. Nevertheless the case studies and written texts are interconnected both explicitly through hyperlinks and implicitly through their use of the same ethnographic materials. The written texts draw from the case studies as a source of examples to demonstrate how the theoretical approaches developed might frame our understandings of specific aspects and experiences of gender and home represented in the research materials. Therefore whichever order users read these different types of narrative in they should gain a sense of their interwovenness and the interdependence between ethnography and theory.

Colour, writing and background

Colour contrasts can be used to represent different voices or ways of speaking, but in printed academic publications 'social scientists rarely get the opportunity to explore this area because of the expense involved' (Chaplin 1994: 249). However hypermedia offers new opportunities. In *Women's Worlds* I developed ideas from existing literature to explore how colour might be used as an ironic and critical metaphor to support the academic argument framing the project.

Existing literature about the relationship between gender and domestic interiors has focused on a symbolic and empirical relationship between woman and home, and embodied in the idea of 'woman as home'. For example, Morley (2000: 75–8) argues that because there is 'nostalgia' for the traditional nuclear family we might assume most women play traditional feminine roles in their homes. However, survey and statistical sources (see *Social Trends*) show the number of women living in nuclear family units, and playing housewife roles is declining (only 30 per cent of the population now live in nuclear families). In this context many women's everyday activities, experiences and identities vary from the housewife model and their relationships with their homes are subsequently very different from those prescribed by symbolic analyses that gender the home as feminine. My research explored this changing context: I interviewed women living alone, in house-shares, working full-time, and who did not consider themselves housewives. I have argued that the home is not essentially a feminine space and women are not always the makers and keepers of home. Rather, women's relationships with their homes are more complex. In *Women's Worlds* I discuss how such women make their homes on their own terms and not as housewives living in nuclear families. To emphasise this I use colour ironically to give this argument a continuous presence on pages where it is not explicitly expressed in written words by giving all the pages of *Women's Worlds* a salmon pink navigation bar. Pink was selected to represent two themes, one theoretical and the other ethnographic: my critique of theories of 'woman as home'; and my informants' non-conformity with a 'housewifely' femininity. As the contents page of the CD (Figure 11.2) explains the colour was selected as a result of my literature review.

Through this use of colour I intended to embed my argument about plural gender and individual resistance to housewifely identities through visual design of the project. Indeed the two women who feature in the case studies have very different ideal colour schemes involving purple, green and futuristic chrome designs. In addition I have used colour to represent the different types of text in the CD. Anthropological writing and my own commentaries are in black print on a white background, corresponding to the presentation of the discourses they seek to engage with. Interview transcripts continue to play on the theme of the gendered home, using black on a pink background.

Video

One option would have been to edit a short ethnographic video and include this on the CD-ROM. However as Mason and Dicks (2001) have pointed out existing software does not facilitate the easy creation of hyperlinks to written text via video. The video would have been included as a linear documentary video, and as a narrative that would be isolated from (and that could possibly be viewed to the exclusion of) the project's written texts. As such it might have shared the fate of the films I discussed above because it would not engage fully with anthropological writing. Instead I attempted to reference film in two ways:

1   By treating the case-study sections as film narratives, borrowing as Marcus (1995) has suggested a montage style from film. Grimshaw's (2001) book, itself an experiment of basing writing on film styles (in her case montage and *mise-en-scène*), demonstrates that montage can be a successful strategy for written anthropology. It would seem equally appropriate for hypermedia narratives.
2   By embedding video clips in the written text. These acknowledge a reflexive film-making style but depart from usual uses of ethnographic film.

The edited, digitised video clips in *Women's Worlds* last up to three minutes. Technically this is because longer clips take longer to load and the storage capacity of the CD-ROM has limited the amount of video used. In *Women's Worlds* these video clips have a dual role, as both a reflexive device and a medium for representing examples of the diverse practices, opinions and experiences that form part of different women's every day lives in their homes. As video and *not* film they also serve to link fieldwork and representation. As MacDougall has argued, video is 'not simply a replacement for film but a medium with its own capabilities and limitations' (2001). In particular, working alone with digital video is more akin to a fieldwork than a film-making situation, and a process that produces subjective footage that represents that context. Video is a medium

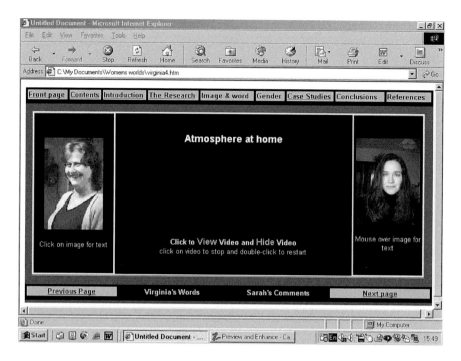

Figure 11.3.1 A case study page.

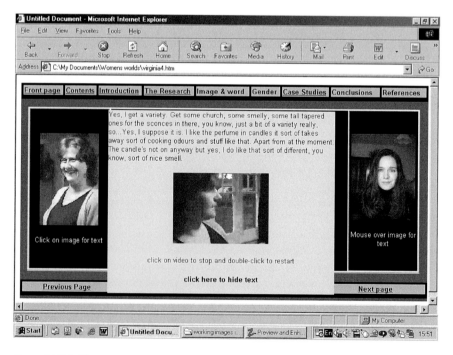

Figure 11.3.2 The same page with Virginia's words and video showing.

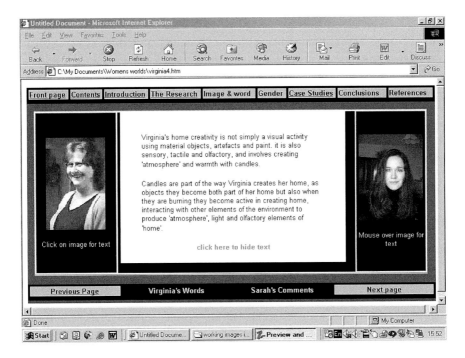

Figure 11.3.3 The same page with my commentary.

and technology used both to explore and to represent ethnographic experiences and informants' self-representations. However such video is never *only* about its own making; it is also a narrative device that uses metaphor to represent emotions, experiences and actions. In *Women's Worlds* these video clips also communicate my informants' descriptions, practices and emotions as I had recorded them through their spoken words, embodied actions, facial expressions and the objects and space in which our encounter had taken place.

Images and words in the ethnographic case studies

In the case studies I wanted to represent my informants' stories and perform-ances as they unfolded in the context of our collaborative video interviews. To do this I developed montage essays that combined written description, interview quotations and video clips. I wanted to create a text that, like *Mujeres invisibles*, compares the subjectivities and biographies of individual women, to explore notions of femininity and what it might mean to be a woman in a contemporary context. In the case studies, because our interviews started with a tape-recorded interview, my informants' introductions of themselves only exist in transcripts and not on video. Without shooting extra footage, it would have been difficult to edit a coherent ethnographic documentary 'film' to include on the CD. Instead I produced each informant's story by combining quotations of their transcribed words, video clips and my own descriptions. For example, Holly's pages begin with a still portrait of her and a quotation from her interview where she describes herself in terms of her biography of moving home and the sort of person she sees herself as. The following pages go on to combine my own descriptions with more quotations and video clips. The case-study pages are designed to juxtapose video, quotations and my own commentaries. Allowing a combination of what MacDougall has called 'deep' (video) and explanatory (writing) reflexivity and simultaneously a representation of my informant's story of her life as a unique, gendered individual in a particular home. I sought to create a dialogue between video and printed words as different forms of representation, as having potential to represent different sorts of knowledge and as being able to reference and engage in different debates and discourses. Within each page the montage style is employed: each page is made up of a combination of different visual and written texts and voices represented in layers that the user can move between using a navigation system internal to the page.

Images and words in the anthropological texts

In the written sections of *Women's Worlds* my objective was to engage with conventional anthropological academic writing in a way that integrated the visual to recognise the intersubjective and performative origins of ethnographic insights theory might be applied to. Where appropriate hyperlinks take the user to relevant pages of the case-study sections that serve as examples. For example the written text on gender performativity and the housewife has hyperlinks to pages of the case studies that demonstrate everyday performativity and resistance to housewifely knowledge and identities. By shifting the relationship between words and images, and writing and video in the case studies and anthropological written texts, I aimed to indicate how meaning might be created differently when the relationship and balance between these components is altered, and to emphasise the constructedness of the relationship between experience, representation and theory.

Hypermedia, writing and film: bridging the gap

At the beginning of this article I discussed some of the limitations that ethnographic film encounters in participating in mainstream anthropology. The films I discussed are informed by anthropological theories of gender and specifically refer to traditional southern Spanish gender models. *Mujeres invisibles* shows how women must negotiate these models and how some individual women resist them in their everyday lives. *Romance de Valentía* shows the ideal models and how gender is ideally experienced through a ritual performance in a particular cultural context. However to interpret these films I relied on my experience of fieldwork and theoretical literature about the topics they covered, Spanish gender, women's agency and bullfighting culture. To a non-specialist these themes might not be so immediately obvious. The films are only indirectly engaged with existing written anthropological theory. A more direct engagement with literature on gender would have required a more explicit communication about gender theory that would have been able to situate the experiences and discourses represented in the films in relation to specific arguments about how gender is experienced and lived out in both everyday life and ritual contexts. In *Women's Worlds* I have tried to bridge this gap by combining and interlinking video and written representations of everyday experience with more abstract discussions in the same text. My aim has been to surpass some of the limits of film and writing to create a text that combines abstract theory with experiential reflexivity. Film brings the individual to the fore (MacDougall 1997). In doing so film introduces the most fundamental element in anthropology, the relationship of an individual fieldworker to individual informants, as it unfolds. It focuses on the specificity of the experiences through which ethnographic knowledge is produced and offers a 'deep' reflexivity that cannot be achieved in the same way through the 'explanatory' reflexivity of writing (MacDougall 1998). If ethnographic film is seen as almost opposed to anthropological writing, in terms of distinctions such as specific/general, the individual/the abstract and anthropological theory/ethnography, then the visual will appear to challenge the coherence of an abstracting science. Instead in *Women's Worlds* I have made the individual a welcome component, a necessary part of the relationship between research and representation and a means of creating links between fieldwork and theory. In *Women's Worlds* the visual is actually incorporated into the written texts to anchor the theory in the embodied sensory experiences of everyday life it seeks to explain and generalise from. Its inability to achieve this integration of image and word and ethnography and theory is one of the limitations of film. This does not mean that anthropologists should not make films but that film may not be the most effective way to combine or challenge written anthropology with the visual. The potential of hypermedia is in fact to bypass the challenge and to use the visual to enlarge the scope and impact of the theoretical on the ethnographic and vice versa.

Summing up: interweaving theory, moving images and words

Women's Worlds is an experimental project, awaiting feedback, and part of a larger project of exploring ways to resolve both wider issues related to ethnographic/anthropological representation and of the relationship between moving images, spoken words and written text. In *Women's Worlds* I have sought to appropriate some of the qualities of different existing ethnographic media, in this case video and writing, to create a text that might communicate visual and verbal knowledge.

Goals

- Combine video and words to represent the ethnography:

  1   Juxtaposing a 'deep' (video) and 'explanatory', after the event, (writing) reflexivity, each of which provides different types of information about how ethnographic knowledge was produced.
  2   Communicating ethnographic information about the everyday experiences, practices, aspirations and feminine identities of my informants (using words and video).
  3   Comparing my informants' unique everyday housework and home decoration ideas and practices (using words and video) to each other's and to the culturally and academically defined models and housewifely femininity (using words).

- Combine words and video to make anthropological arguments about how gender identities are constituted through everyday practices in the home:

  1   Producing conventional written essays to discuss (a) gender performativity and the housewife through housework and home decoration, and (b) the embodied sensory experience of the home and domestic practices in it (in words, using video clips, quotations and description as examples that root the theory in the fieldwork).
  2   Connecting the theoretical with the ethnographic, and the abstract with the individual by embedding individual (video and writing) experiences in anthropological discussion (writing).

- Make explicit the relationship between the production of ethnographic knowledge (represented in the case studies) and the anthropological understandings of these ethnographic materials:

  1   Using hypermedia and cross-referencing to indicate how the same video clips might be situated in different theoretical and ethnographic narratives.

- Exploit the potential of digital hypermedia to produce a text that both references and departs from written and visual anthropology in its design and content:

  1   Creating a multimedia text that includes images and words in ways familiar to the existing genres in visual anthropology and writing but that combines these.
  2   Creating a multilinear text that uses hyperlinks to suggest and facilitate the making of meaningful connections between different narratives.
  3   Creating a design and structure that uses colour, font, layout and narratives not possible in writing or film.

- Create a text that is conversant with mainstream gendered and visual anthropology by using:

  1 Video clips that have the reflexive and descriptive qualities of ethnographic film
  2 Montage-style case studies that tell ethnographic stories
  3 Written anthropological essays

Anthropological writing and film are successful and appropriate media for anthropological representation. I am not suggesting they should be abandoned. However there is also space for anthropological representations that reference and depart from these forms. *Women's Worlds* is an experiment in how this might be achieved in ways that are informed by the creative possibilities offered by new media, that respond to existing debates on anthropological representation, and that both refer to and depart from existing forms.

Acknowledgements

The research that *Women's Worlds* is based on was funded by Unilever Research and designed in collaboration with Katie Deverell.

References

Banks, M. (1994) 'Interactive multimedia and anthropology: a sceptical view', at http://rsl.ox.ac.uk/isca/marcus.banks.01.htm
—— (2001) *Visual Methods in Social Research*, London: Sage.
Barbash, I. and Taylor, L. (1997) *Cross Cultural Film-making: A Handbook for Making Documentary and Ethnographic Films and Video*, London: University of California Press.
Biella, P. (1994) 'Codifications of ethnography: linear and nonlinear', at http://www.usc.edu/dept/elab/welcome/codifications.html
—— (1997) 'Mama Kone's possession: scene from an interactive ethnography', *Visual Anthropology Review* 12(2): 59–95.
Chaplin, E. (1994) *Sociology and Visual Representations*, London: Routledge.
Cornwall, A. and Lindisfarne, N. (1994) *Dislocating Masculinity*, London: Routledge.
del Valle, T. (1993) *Gendered Anthropology*, London: Routledge.
Gilmore, D. (ed.) (1985) *Sex and Gender in Southern Europe: Problems and Prospects* special issue no. 3 of *Anthropology*, May–Dec. vol. 9, nos. 1 and 2.
—— (1987), *Aggression and Community: Paradoxes of Andalusian Culture*, New Haven: Yale University Press.
Goddard, V. (ed.) (2000) *Gender, Agency and Change*, London: Routledge.
Grimshaw, A. (2001) *The Ethnographer's Eye: Ways of Seeing in Anthropology*, Cambridge: Cambridge University Press.
Hendry, J. (1998) *An Introduction to Social Anthropology: Other People's Worlds*, London and Basingstoke: Macmillan.

Henley, Paul (2000). 'Ethnographic film: technology, practice and anthropological theory', *Visual Anthropology* 13: 207–26.

Hughes-Freeland, F. (ed.) (1998) *Ritual, Performance, Media*, London: Routledge.

Loizos, P. (1992), 'User-friendly ethnography?', in J. da Pina Cabral and J. Campbell (eds), *Europe Observed: Anthropological Fieldwork in Southern Europe*, London: Macmillan.

MacDougall, D. (1997) 'The visual in anthropology', in M. Banks and H. Morphy (eds), *Rethinking Visual Anthropology*, London and New Haven: Yale University Press.

—— (1998) *Transcultural Cinema*, Princeton: Princeton University Press.

—— (2001) 'Renewing ethnographic film: is digital video changing the genre?', *Anthropology Today* 17(3): 15–21.

Marcus, G. (1995) 'The modernist sensibility in recent ethnographic writing and the cinematic metaphor of montage', in L. Devereaux and R. Hillman (eds), *Fields of Vision*, Berkeley: University of California Press.

Martínez, A. (ed.) (2000) *Taller de las Cuatro Estaciones*, Cordoba: Alas de colibrí ediciones.

Marvin, G. (1988) *Bullfight*, Oxford: Blackwell.

Mason, B. and Dicks, B. (2001) 'Going beyond the code', *Social Science Computer Review* 19(4): 445–57.

Moore, H. (1994) *A Passion for Difference*, Oxford: Polity Press.

Moore, H. (1999) 'Anthropology at the turn of the century', in H. Moore (ed.), *Anthropological Theory Today*, Oxford: Polity Press.

Morley, D. (2000) *Home Territories: Media, Mobility and Identity*, London: Routledge.

Pink, S. (1997) *Women and Bullfighting: Gender, Sex and the Consumption of Tradition*, Oxford: Berg.

—— (1999) *Romance de Valentía*, S. Herman Dolz, reviewed for *Visual Anthropology* 12(4): 87–9.

—— (2001) *Doing Visual Ethnography: Images, Media and Representation in Research*, London: Sage.

—— (2003) 'Representing the sensory home: ethnographic experience and ethnographic hypermedia', in G. Bloustien (ed.), *En-visioning Ethnography: Exploring the Complexity of the Visual Methods in Ethnographic Research*, a special issue of *Social Analysis*, 47(3).

—— (forthcoming) *Home Truths*, Oxford: Berg.

Ruby, J. (2000a) *Picturing Culture: Explorations of Film and Anthropology*, Chicago: University of Chicago Press.

—— (2000b) 'Some Oak Park stories: experimental ethnographic videos', paper presented at the Visible Evidence Conference, Oxford.

—— (2001) 'From ethnographic film to hypertext ethnography', unpublished commentary.

Sanchíz, P. (ed.) (1992) *Mujer Andaluza: la caida de un mito?* Spain: Muñoz Moya y Montraveta Editores. Biblioteca Andaluza.

Thuren, B. (2000) 'Out of the house – to do what? Women in the Spanish neighbourhood movement', in V. Goddard (ed.), *Gender, Agency and Change*, London: Routledge.

Films

Herman Dolz, S. (1994) *Romance de Valentía*

A Buen Común (2000) *Mujeres invisibles*

Chapter 12

Working with images, images of work

Using digital interface, photography and hypertext in ethnography

Roderick Coover

Au sein d'une vigne	From the middle of a vine
Je reçus le jour	I was given birth
Cette mère est digne	This mother is worthy
De tout mon amour.	Of all my love
Depuis la naissance	Since birth
Elle me nourrit	She has fed me
Par reconnaissance	In gratitude
Mon coeur la chérit.	I love her with all my heart.

('Joyeux Enfants de la Bourgogne', verse 1)[1]

Cantata

Winemaking in Burgundy begins in the first millennium AD[2] and significantly shapes the cultural development of the region. In the Middle Ages, the Church plays a central role in developing winemaking techniques and advancing the notion of *cru* by which plots of vines are distinguished and classified. This knowledge of the land, or *terroir*, is a result of generations of experiments in growing techniques, grape varieties and production methods. This medieval 'renaissance' (Dion 1959: 285–300) in winemaking is also supported by favourable economic conditions brought about by the rise of Burgundy as a wealthy European commercial power under the Valois Dukes in the fourteenth and fifteenth centuries (ibid.). The trading system contributes to the increasingly central role that wine merchants, or *negoçiants*, play in the growth of the region. By the eighteenth and nineteenth centuries, they dominate the wine industry. More than just distributors, the *negoçiants* buy the grapes from growers, make the wine, and ship it by barrel and bottle to the emerging middle and upper class French and foreign markets. Independent wineries begin to form in the early half of the twentieth century, and they flourish after World War II. The rise of independent wineries occurs in large part due to increasing global trade opportunities presented by foreign distributors that would buy wine directly from the wineries as well as a growing foreign market for French wines in Europe, North American and elsewhere; to the formation of the Appellations

Figure 12.1.1 Signs to Bouzeron © Roderick Coover.

Figure 12.1.2 A porter resting © Roderick Coover.

d'Origine Contrôlées (AOC) in the 1930s that guarantee wine quality and origins; and to technological innovations such as the straddler-tractor and temperature-control devices that give winemakers greater control in the vines and winery. While there are numerous books about wine and its history, there are far fewer studies about the labour practices associated with winemaking and the cultural ideas surrounding these practices.[3]

To study cultural aspects of winemaking in Burgundy, I begin by working as a harvester in several winemaking villages in the prestigious Côte d'Or – a region comprised of the Côte de Nuits and the Côte de Beaune – and in the more modest Côte Chalonnaise to its south. My project investigates the relationship between the language used to describe wine and the practices that go into its production: how descriptions are embedded in a synesthetic cultural experience. The work includes studying the impact of winemaking on local history, geography, and cultural practices in villages and towns that have grown over the centuries around the vineyard plots. The fortunes of these worlds have closely paralleled those of the wine trade.

I am particularly interested in how actions, events and the use of objects help one to understand the work and the world in which they are an integral part. My process includes looking at the work alongside those *with* whom I am working. Participant observation introduces the ethnographer to a lived experience. In taking images and collecting data, one looks for strategies that will bring back the diverse qualities of that experience. At the same time, looking at the world alongside one's informants helps one circumvent objectifying aspects of ethnographic photography.[4] I combine traditional techniques of participant observation, interviews and archival research with photo studies and video recordings, and I use digital editing and hypertext programs to work with the materials. This process takes place over two years and results in the production of a 60-minute documentary, *La Bourgogne et le langage du vin* (2003).

I use photo studies primarily as a way of training my eye to see. I find the constraints of working with a still camera help me identify evolving stories, moods and motifs; the photos serve as catalysts for further research and visual studies that shape the shooting of the documentary film. After digitising these images, I analyse both the content and my image-gathering strategies. I compare the images with my written notes and recorded interviews. The digital platform allows me to analyse and critique some of the conventions of documentary representation found in other media and to juxtapose materials constructed through differing media, thus highlighting their unique advantages, conventions and constraints. Juxtaposing data collected with a range of media shows how each medium shapes its message and helps to evoke what lies between; a composite representation derives meaning both from the content of the ethnographic materials and the links by which the reader learns to read and combine them. By preparing to make the documentary, *Bourgogne et le langage du vin*, in this way, I end up creating a second work that can only exist on a digital platform. The work develops as a 50-photo study of a harvest which unfolds across an 18,750-pixel-wide Webpage. This horizontal format permits the layering of the fifty images above bands of text about the shooting experience, the harvest and the winemaker (see Figure 12.5.2). The reader scrolls back and forth across the images and writing. Links lead to further notes, images and video clips.

This essay reflects upon that electronic work to consider how new media tools can contribute to visual ethnography. The electronic work that emerges from an ethnographic film-making practice is one that reveals its processes. Through the use of an electronic interface and hypertextual links, it provides a synesthetic experience that maximises the role of the reader–viewer in connecting information provided through sound, image and language.

Taking photos is a process of learning to look. Images, like words, evoke worlds; they propose views[5] shaped by the technology and image-making choices such as those of framing, focus selection, focal range, subject choice, colour, tone, contrast, light quality and grain. The act of presenting a place through pictures is one of linking images to some idea that they both refer to and help articulate. Images can evoke the moods and expressions that define a moment; but if the images are not grounded in a web of references – whether through visual knowledge or language – viewers are left to rely on preconceptions and generalisations in order to make sense of the visual data. In an interactive, multimedia environment, the reader–viewer must actively look for clues as to how differing kinds of data may be understood, and a reader–viewer must choose a point of view by which to connect a piece of information to an idea or a narrative event. In this way, the position of the reader–viewer is analogous to that of the ethnographer looking for ways to connect a particular experience to broader questions about the culture.

In his essay, 'The subjective voice in ethnographic film', David MacDougall writes:

> Anthropologists, by and large, have wished film to make increasingly accurate, complete, and verifiable descriptions of what can be seen–that is, of behavior, ritual, and technology–whereas filmmakers have shown a growing interest in precisely those things that cannot be seen. It was never the physical body that was felt to be missing in ethnographic films. The body was always constantly and often extravagantly before us in its diversity of faces, statures, costumes, and body decorations. It was all too easy to present such images with their accompanying exoticism. What was missing was not the body but the experience of existing in it.
>
> There is thus in ethnographic filmmaking not only a journey of discovery from the abstract to the personal but from representation to evocation.
>
> (MacDougall 1995: 249)

Digital media present opportunities for confronting this ironic disjunction that has grown between anthropologists and film-makers. Hyperlinks and juxtapositions allow for the combination of differing modes of cross-cultural representation

Figure 12.2.1 Subject and object: a harvester with an empty bucket © Roderick Coover.

Figure 12.2.2 Subject and object: a bucket of grapes © Roderick Coover.

and expression. Images can present factual data and point to cultural ideas and the circumstances in which they were made depending on the contexts by which the image is examined.

I shoot the photos in this essay in 1996 during a harvest in Burgundy at the vineyards of Aubert and Pamela de Villaine in the village of Bouzeron. The village is located in the Côte Chalonnaise. The vineyards of the Côte Chalonnaise, which also includes the towns of Givry, Mercurey and Rully, stretch across the hills above the Saône river south of Chagny. Aubert de Villaine is also a co-owner and winemaker of the famous Domaine de la Romanée Conti (DRC) in the Côte d'Or where he succeeded his father and grandfather. He and his wife bought their own vineyard in Bouzeron in 1970.

A winemaker's vocation

Au printemps, ma vigne en sa fleur,	In the spring my vine in flower,
D'une fillette a la pâleur;	Has the pale whiteness of a little girl;
L'été, c'est une fiancée	In the summer, it's a fiancée
Qui fait craquer son corset vert;	Who bursts out of her green corset;
A l'automne tout s'est ouvert;	In the fall, everything has shown itself;
C'est la vendange et la pressée;	It's the harvest and the pressing;
En hiver, pendant son sommeil,	In winter, during her slumber,
Son vin remplace le soleil.	Her wine replaces the sun.

('Ma Vigne', verse 2)[6]

In the vines one day, de Villaine tells me that for him, 'Wine is an image', by which he means, as he goes on to say, that each aspect of winemaking is part of a process of working towards an *ideal form*. The image, he tells me, is 'based on the wines that he has known in the past'. His goal is to make wine in 'the simplest ways possible' to yield a product that is pure. This is his vocation.

This 'image' of the wine is a reflection of de Villaine's taste, memory and knowledge of what different soils, grapes and conditions might provide. It is a reflection of cultural ideals he holds about balance, structure and elegance. Such an image cannot be rendered by a single picture – it is rather formed through an accumulation of ideas and experiences held in relation to each other. If a significant part of the ethnographer's job is to *translate* the meaning of objects, the ethnographer must also find ways to describe relationships, for a description of an object, event or person, whether through writing, imagery or other form, can explain little without drawing connections to the worlds of which it is a part.[7]

Take the word *clos*, for example. A common term on wine bottles, *clos* designates a walled enclosure that has been distinguished from other plots. The term often suggests that the plot has been valued for its grapes – enough at least to build the wall. As de Villaine tells me, a winemaker in the more prestigious villages is born into a world of walls, of named designations, and of precise traditions. The villages may lord over the vines, but they are also walled in by them. De Villaine explains:

> In Vosne-Romanée there is a fantastic history of the invention of *cru* by the monks in the eleventh century to which the village has been entirely dedicated. For eight centuries we've made the same wine on the same plots with the same names. The growth of the village has always had a vertical growth. There has never been a horizontal growth. It has always had a fixed area of vines that is impossible to expand. The village is both a servant and a prisoner to that history.

De Villaine envisions himself as participating in a long history of winemaking. He reads logs from past winemakers to learn about prior knowledge of the soil and climate conditions, and he keeps a log of his own experiences. De Villaine believes he makes his wines to fulfil a certain ideal he has, based on what he believes a *terroir* can yield. His role is to assist in a natural process. This includes moderating negative forces, such as those of frost and mildew, which can diminish the health of the vine and the positive qualities of grapes. For de Villaine, a wine made as simply as possible with maximum reduction of chemical and biological treatments is one most likely to reflect the qualities of the *terroir*. The qualities are defined by natural elements such as aspect, drainage, bedrock and soil, all of which determine the potential quality of grapes grown on that land. The steepness of the slope effects waterflow, airflow, temperature changes and the amount of sunlight that hits the vine leaves and grapes; an east-facing aspect (Côte d'Or refers to the oriental, or eastern, direction of the valley slopes) will warm slowly with the rising sun. Soils determine water retention and influence the balance of nutrients that the grapes receive, while the grapes also benefit from a minimal top soil that will force the plant roots to reach deep into cracks in the bedrock from which grapes will gain much of their mineral characteristics. De Villaine explains:

> I believe that in Burgundy, the talent – the talent which produces the great wine – is in the *terroir*. The reputation of the wine from Burgundy was made over the past several centuries and it comes from the quality of wine that the (particular) *terroir* can provide. That is the talent. The role of the winemaker is to enable the *terroir* to be in the best condition possible – to help bring forward (like a midwife) the product of the exceptional land. The role is to listen to the *terroir*. One listens always to the *terroir* to understand what to do to achieve an equilibrium in the soil, what to use as vegetal material, how to prune, how to treat the vines. There is always a selection of the best methods so that the *terroir* is in its best disposition possible to make a good wine.

De Villaine frequently describes how the winemakers and winemaking villages are shaped by that 'talent' in the *terroir*. The wines that they produce are a

Figure 12.3.1 Framing and light: a porter with a full pannier © Roderick Coover.

Figure 12.3.2 Framing and light: faces at lunch © Roderick Coover.

reflection of a *relationship* by which each winemaker expresses his or her own character, tastes and decision-making.

The Côte Chalonnaise was never known for great Pinots or Chardonnays. However, in researching archives in Mâcon and elsewhere, de Villaine discovered that there was a tradition of growing the less-regarded Aligoté grape in this valley of the village of Bouzeron where he lives. Around the village the soil is particularly poor. De Villaine believes this helps intensify the flavours of the Aligoté, which is a vigorous vine. At the same time the conditions are more challenging than in the Côte d'Or, and the local wines will never sell for sums that can support the more expensive production techniques and equipment used in more prestigious areas. Not only do the soils present certain difficulties, so, too, do the meteorological conditions offer more problems such as frost, which arrives more frequently in Bouzeron than in the vineyards of the Côte d'Or. A qualitative balance sought in a product is also determined by financial circumstances; an ideal image of a wine coexists with that determined by temporal, economic or even cultural circumstances.

A village is shaped by the histories of *cru* and *terroir*. The relatively wealthy villages in the Côte d'Or, literally, are walled in as a result of this history and new, expanding generations must find homes elsewhere. Old roads in the region snake about the prized land while faster roads must pass lower in the valley to connect the vineyard villages to the merchant towns such as Nuits-St-Georges and Beaune. When cheap wine began arriving by rail from the south of France in the nineteenth century, it reduced the economic viability of wine production in less prized areas of Burgundy. After the outbreak of phylloxera, which destroyed French winemaking at the end of the nineteenth century, villages like Bouzeron did not replant vines. Instead many of its residents took industrial jobs in the nearby cities. The recent growth of Bouzeron calls upon both the medieval and recent history, and signs point to the valley's historical markers and many new vineyards (Figure 12.1.1). Signs may reflect this past but their image is more about expectations held about the present and future. They are placed on the roadside to promote an idea some villagers have about the village, its winemaking and a profitable future. They demonstrate how winemaking has been restored as the village's primary identity.

A sense of time

Puisque tout succombe	Because everything dies
Un jour je mourrai	One day so will I
Jusque dans ma tombe	Even in my tomb
Pourtant je boirai	I will drink
Je veux dans la terre	I hope that in the ground
Au pied de mon corps	At the foot of my corpse
Qu'on mette mon verre	My glass will be placed
Rempli jusqu'au bord.	Full to the rim.

('Joyeux Enfants de la Bourgogne', verse 5)

The moment de Villaine announces the harvest, the winemaker is gambling with nature and money. Bring forty harvesters to your property too early, you pay for them to sit about; if they come too late, you might lose the harvest to rain or hail. The problem is complicated by growing three different varieties – the Chardonnay, Pinot Noir, and Aligoté – which ripen at different times. Hail in the next village is ominous: for those winemakers just over the crest of the hill, the hail has caused the loss of a year's work.

For the harvester, one day falls into the next. In a routine of working between the vines buried in one's thoughts, rising up to see the wide vistas, stopping for conversations, water or wine, or sharing songs and words between the grape leaves, the fortnight can begin to seem like a single long day. The day is punctuated by highs and lows, shifting moods and changing weather.

The pickers select the grapes, and the panniers haul them to the tractor where they are checked for quality. Vineyards in less affluent areas usually cannot justify the cost of a sorting table, and, instead, the harvest workers must be trained to sort as they pick. Red grapes should not be cut too green, or with too much leaf. Rotten grapes should be cut away. Best are the tiny concentrated grapes of older vines whose roots reach far into the bedrock from where they extract richer mineral content. Gloves wear through quickly. Without them, the sugars and acids moistness of the grapes helps to bring on blisters. The gloves, clippers and grapes become intimate objects – extensions of the flesh.

The anticipation of the lunch break and dinner is fuelled by occasional bottles of the wine and water passing between the vines. Before lunch, we wash the mud from our clothes with a garden hose. At the dining table there is a kind of weary revelry (Figure 12.3.2). The dining tables are in a cavernous room beneath the house and dormitories. The room is dark and comforting to eyes that have come in from hours in the sun. The space is damp and has a rich smell of the meat stews we are served. The soft, thick and crumbling stone walls fall into darkness illuminated only by the small beams of light that come from the door and small deep windows. In the vines we begin thinking of lunch ahead. In the dining hall, there is a desire to remain suspended between the memory and anticipation of the work outside.

Visually, when one is working in the vines, the world seems either very near or very distant; it is a world of close-ups and landscape vistas. The presence of the fellow workers comes by way of the sounds and conversations which pass through the thicket. You feel your body in parts: your hands, your knees, or your back, and you catch the occasional glimpse of other workers in fragments through the leaves, posts and wires (Figure 12.4.1).

Working with text and photos I find I have a similar visual experience of imagining wholes from parts. From an image-fragment (a cap, a hand, a face) I remember the person that was on the other side of the vines, and the dark concentrated images within that space contrast with the open shots above. In the 50-image sequence, stills of the woman in the billed cap (Figures 12.2.1, 12.5.1) appear on several occasions. As a subset, they describe a person and

Figure 12.4.1 Fragments: a worker in the vines © Roderick Coover.

Figure 12.4.2 Shifts in perspective: dumping the grapes in a vat © Roderick Coover.

her work. This may be complemented by text, her voice, or other biographical information. When juxtaposed with other images in the series, the same very images may say something else about the vineyard, work, tools, the narrative moments – such as the image of workers at a moment of rest (Figure 12.5.1) – or even about the plants, soil or weather. Shifting focus also can function in this way by moving attention from the people or broad landscape views to the space of the vines between. The use of grain, shifting focus, and framing by the photographer is not unlike a writer's use of adjectives, adverbs, well chosen verbs, metaphors, irony or other figures of speech. These are devices that help identify specific qualities and link ideas together.[8] Formal connections between images such as between the static signs and the stationary and almost pole-like stance of the tired porter in Figure 12.1.2 with his socks pulled high might also suggest an ironic position between the commercial idea and the hard work. A metonymic connection is suggested both in the focal shift within the frame and across frames, such as in the photos of a porter and the close-up of his hand (Figure 12.3.2). The close-up of the hand concentrates our attention on one part of the action. The hand is not only a place of contact between body, scarf and bucket; it is a stress point – a pivot in the action. Working with how parts describe wholes, the ethnographer finds multiple ways of describing the same images based on the kind of action they present, the narratives they point to, or the kinds of sets and series to which objects in the image might belong.

So, too, do ideas associated with images change in time. In Figure 12.2.1, a harvest worker is shown before an empty bucket, and, in Figure 12.2.2, her hand rests on the full bucket, the result of her work. Placed in relation to an image of the grapes or vines the photo of the bucket may offer an alternative statement such as one about the relationship between the small cluster and the grapes in mass. Walking in the vines before harvest, I find the clusters have a beauty as discrete, natural objects that later metamorphose into the red and white juices in that other object, the bottle. In the course of the harvest, the image of the grape cluster in my mind becomes replaced by a sensual idea that marries the single cluster with the truckload and the image with sticky touch and tannic taste. Like the intimacy of views from working in the vines, the grapes are both an idea and a substance. Cut, and piling up in the buckets and trucks, the grapes lose their identity as emblems of a product. In mass, they are only a substance: stories, histories and images revolve about them.

As with words like *clos* and *terroir*, so too do images of a wall, vine, soil, grapes or, indeed, a person, carry different and multiple meanings for each viewer–reader. Image-processing tools like Adobe Photoshop maximise some techniques already available to photographers while the digital interface provides a readerly experience of the images less easily attained in print media; words and pictures revolve about identified ideas and motifs. No such work can be neutral or all-encompassing. There is always something left out, material inside the frame not focused or commented upon. As the anthropologist Clifford Geertz once wrote, 'Cultural analysis is intrinsically incomplete. And, worse than that, the more deeply it goes the less complete it is' (Geertz 1973: 29). Rather, identifying relationships in a world pictured though images and language is a matter of directing attention to fragments to show how their meanings may be diverse and demand further exploration.

That relationships shift, as do moods and modes, is an important and often missing part of cross-cultural representations. The image of an object is important for what the object is but also for how the object *might* be used or what it *might* mean to one or another particular person. An individual's presence in a scene is exciting for what they *might* say or do; and a scene is alive because of what *could* happen. So, too, might an image lead to any other one in such a set; looking for connections, visual tropes can unfold into narratives. While the images cannot be restored to the actual moment of their being made, in a series they can be returned to what John Berger describes as a 'context of experience' (Berger and Mohr 1982: 289). The process evokes the ways by which meanings are generated through the roles objects and actions play in their original environments. This approach to cross-cultural image-making builds relationships between images as well as between differing viewing conditions to create *an experience of context.* In this production of context, the ethnographers offer parameters that shape the kinds of choices that a reader–viewer might make. These routes through the material are often based on the ethnographer's original experience as well as on other primary texts. They are also based on the constraints of production which becomes revealed in this process. As with lived experience, there is no single true reading; the rightness – what Nelson Goodman describes as 'worldmaking' (Goodman 1978) – corresponds to the coherency of the vision presented seen from a wide range of perspectives and modes of analysis and the validity of the data supporting it. The process of placing images and other materials in a context will suggest ways images, words and sounds interconnect. For the reader–viewer, the process parallels, though cannot duplicate, participation in the original moment; the reader–viewer, like the ethnographer, is asked to test assumptions about the materials or events and their meanings.

Fragments restored

Joyeux enfants de la Bourgogne	Happy children of Burgundy
Je n'ai jamais eu de guignon	I've never had any bad luck
Et quand je vois rougir ma trogne	And when I see my face becoming red
Je suis fier d'être Bourguignon.	I am proud to be a Burgundian.

('Joyeux Enfants de la Bourgogne', refrain)

Here, and this is no longer true at all vineyards, the harvest ends with the *paulée*, a harvest feast and party. The dinner is held in the same cavern beneath the main house and dormitories where we have spent two weeks of meals. Tonight

Figure 12.5.1 Changing mood: harvesters at a moment of rest © Roderick Coover.

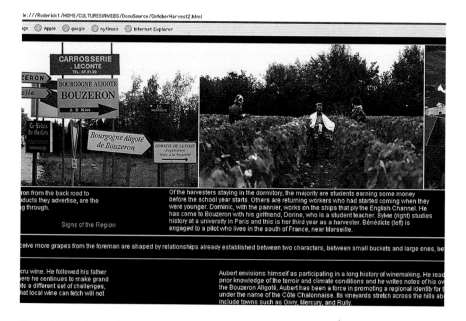

Figure 12.5.2 Example of hypertext interface from *Cultures In Webs* © Roderick Coover.

it is warmed with candlelight, music and a meal rich in meats and cheeses. The tables are arranged in a large and royal 'U' with Aubert and Pamela de Villaine at the head table. The de Villaines make an effort to hire friends and their families through generations. The children, cousins and nephews of past workers help construct a sense of community and a lore surrounding a low-paying work that is both miserable and memorable. During the feast, the workers present gifts to the winemakers and the cook. There are ritualised songs, toasts, jokes, gifts and impromptu performances. The winemakers are given a large dish, the stew-cooking chef is given a recipe book for salads. By noon tomorrow, all the harvesters will have left and an almost unfamiliar calm will return to the vineyard and village. With the goodbyes, harvesters say – 'until the next one'. *A la prochaine*. Memory is a route toward anticipation; the present is replete with concealed and awaited narratives. The harvest now past is gathered into the memory of harvests, each with its particular conditions and its new and returning characters.

For me the work of harvesting grapes, of talking for hours with the other workers in the vines, and of taking photos of the harvest leads to the next process of developing a documentary work. Sifting through the collection I reflect on my own act of looking, on the events at the vineyard, and on how the research relates to my experiences in other vineyards in Burgundy where I am also working. The web environment mirrors this experience and promotes the inclusion of reflexive thoughts, synesthetic materials and diverse perspectives. What happens in this series in a static, readerly environment will be transformed again when I return with a film crew to work in a time-based medium, further unravelling the motifs through montage studies and interviews.

I find myself looking for ways to compare the data from this harvest experience with field notes, images and interviews I gathered in other parts of the region. Images that fit in this sequence tell a story about a harvest and its participants. The same photos are included in other sets and series about the region. In studies of roads and towns, for example, the large promotional signs on the highway marketing Bouzeron compete with those pointing to other winemaking towns. These signs are designed to attract visitors and build name recognition, as wines from Burgundy are named based on their AOC-rated *cru*; a wine's label will state in large print its region, village or plot of origin, and only in much smaller print will it give the individual winemaker's name. A sign for Bouzeron reads, 'Un petit village, un gran vin', for Meursault 'Les meilleurs vins blancs du monde', for St Aubin-Gamay, 'Son site/ses vins fins', and at Chambertin, 'Roi des vins'. The competition between villages presented by the many road signs is an indication of similarities between villages in the region; the signs are the result of shared histories and economic aspirations tied to the wine trade.

Working in digital media with this data not only allows one to integrate visual and audio recordings, it also allows one to incorporate differing approaches to writing. In this case, I have field notes, archival research notes, reading notes, camera logs, songs and poems I have collected, text from conversations I have had, overheard or transcribed from tapes, and drafts of several essays I have been developing about the region. I find myself using differing writing styles to explain the circumstances under which the images were taken, the choices that went into their production, and issues or ideas to which the images pertain. When I organise the photos into a series and interconnect them in various alternative series and subgroups, I find it helpful to organise my text in similar ways. Soon I have distinct bands of text that interconnect with the images and each other.

Started as a means of developing a documentary film, the electronic analyses of this project reveal choices made in the act of taking pictures and writing notes. They help one see how images and text can work together to describe cultural ideas and the cross-cultural, ethnographic practices. In such a work, the research and production strategies are exposed in the product. The reader–viewer can examine the ethnographic process, image-making choices and intellectual arguments at the same time. Viewed horizontally, such a page (Figure 12.5.2) can be read in a linear fashion. Or, the reader–viewer may proceed vertically moving across the photos and bands of text to simultaneously follow the differing text and images. One can view how arguments are derived from notes and recorded materials. Similar approaches might allow the reader–viewer to change the order in which material is compiled, or allow informants and/or reader–viewers to add their own text and images in response to the material. The original moments of production conjoin with those of reader–viewership; the ethnographer and the reader–viewer alike can find themselves linking back and forth through the material to look for traces of alternative sequences and sub-stories, and where this linking reveals gaps, the process also provokes further questions and research.

In moving into the dynamic video and DVD formats, I will be able to integrate interviews with interpretive audio and visual studies. Organised in relation to words associated with the work of winemaking in Burgundy, sound and montage studies will evoke differing moods and modes of the synaesthetic experience. Presenting the material in a time-based format will help provoke questions how spontaneous responses to sound and images are formed and how they relate to language, conscious thought and reflection.

For de Villaine, the warm days that linger on bring the unhappy realisation that this year he might have waited longer and made a yet better wine. In the few harvests of a lifetime, he remarks, one has few chances to make something truly exceptional and he worries that an opportunity was missed. He explains, by visual analogy, the predicament:

> In a winemaker's life, one makes a wine thirty, forty, or if you are lucky, fifty times, but usually more like forty times, which is not a lot. And, even if one has experience and knowledge, one is always before a blank sheet. You only know what nature has written after the fact. All the year, you follow a page that is written before you, and you participate, but you never know where you are and what is nature's design.

De Villaine hadn't trusted a record from over a hundred years previously that advised waiting on harvesting the Aligoté in years, like this one, when cool winds blow from the north. The cool summer and fall sunshine meant that the Aligoté ripened later than the Chardonnay and Pinot Noir. Waiting might have achieved a greater sugar content and a richer wine. However, any change in weather and the advantage would have been more than lost and waiting adds a significant cost when harvesters who have arrived for the collection of other varieties must be kept about without work until the Aligoté is ready.

He gathers samples from the vines, clusters of grapes that were left uncut, and tests them. Although the wine that will be made from this harvest will be a good one, these remaining grapes provide an image of a potential that went unrealised – an image unfulfilled. Next time these conditions arise, he will take the risk and delay the Aligoté harvest.

Notes

Sections of the text are included in the CD-ROM *Cultures in Webs: Working in Hypermedia with the Documentary Image* (Cambridge: Eastgate 2003) and are reprinted with permission of the publisher. Interview text with Aubert de Villaine previously appeared in the documentary, *La Bourgogne et le langage du vin / Burgundy and the Language of Wine* (Roderick Coover 2003).

1 'Joyeux Enfants de la Bourgogne' is a traditional Burgundian song written by Henry Pary 1831 to the tune of 'Le petit vin blanc d'Argenteuil'.

2 Wines from the Côte d'Or were transported along trade routes of the Roman empire. Winemaking in the region dates to at least the third century AD (Lachiver 1988: 35–56).

3 Landmark French-language works about cultural aspects of winemaking include texts by Gilbert Garrier (1995) and Roger Dion (1959). In the English-language press, perhaps the most intimate description of daily life in a Burgundian winemaking village is found in the non-academic *Puligny-Montrachet: Journal of a Village in Burgundy*, by Simon Loftus (1993), while important cultural ethnographies and geographies of French winemaking include works by Robert Ulin (1996) and Tim Urwin (1991) and an insightful collection of interviews with winemakers edited by Leo A. Loubère *et al.* (1985).

4 For a discussion about objective and reflective approaches to ethnographic photography see Pink 2001: esp. 23–4 and 49–76; and MacDougall 1995.

5 For an introductory discussion about how images function as *propositions* see John Berger's essay, 'Appearances', in John Berger and Jean Mohr, *Another Way of Telling* (1982: 81–130).

6 'Ma Vigne' was written by Pierre Dupont in the nineteenth century. Lyrics and music are printed in *Le Livre d'or de la chanson française*, vol. 2, ed. Clement Marot, Paris: Les Editions Ouvrières, 1972.

7 As with the use of tropes in the translation of poetry, they representation of visual, auditory and other syneasthetic qualities are often evoked through recording and editing strategies. Just as such verbal or visual rhetoric provides the means of evocation, so, too, do digital media shape how conditions can be evoked due to the code and programs, the characteristics of the interface, and the speed of the processors.

8 For a further discussion of language and images and related sources see Coover (2001: 415–38).

References

Abric, L. (1993) *Le Vin de Bourgogne au XIXe siècle: aspects économiques, sociaux, culturels*, Précy-sous-Thil: Editions de l'Armançon.

Amiel, C. (1985) *Les Fruits de la vigne: représentations de l'environnement naturel en Languedoc*, Paris: Editions de la Maison des sciences de l'homme.

Bellour, R. (1996) 'The double helix', in Tim Druckrey (ed.), *Electronic Culture: Technology and Visual Representation*, New York: Aperture.

Berger, J. and Mohr, J. (1982) *Another Way of Telling*, New York: Pantheon Books.

Bousquet, A. and Lepage, J. (1996) *Vins, vignes, vignerons dans la peinture Française*, Narbonne: Musée d'Art et d'Histoire de Narbonne.

Brennan, T. E. (*c*.1997) *Burgundy to Champagne: The Wine Trade in Early Modern France*, Baltimore: Johns Hopkins University Press.

Coover, R. (2001) 'Worldmaking, metaphors, and montage', *Visual Anthropology* 14(4): 415–33.

—— (2003) *Cultures in Webs: Working in Hypermedia with the Documentary Image*, Cambridge: Eastgate. Online. http://www.eastgate.com

—— (2003) *La Bourgogne et le langage du vin / Burgundy and the Language of Wine*.

Dermody, S. (1995) 'The pressure of the unconscious upon the image: the subjective voice in documentary', in L. Devereaux and R. Hillman (eds), *Fields of Vision: Essays in Film Studies, Visual Anthropology, and Photography*, Berkeley: University of California Press.

Devereaux, L. (1995) 'Experience, re-presentation, and film', in L. Devereaux and R. Hillman (eds), *Fields of Vision: Essays in Film Studies, Visual Anthropology, and Photography*, Berkeley: University of California Press.

Dion, R. (1959) *Histoire de la vigne et du vin en France des origines au XIXe siècle*, Paris.

Edwards, E. (ed.) (1992) *Anthropology and Photography 1860–1920*, New Haven: Yale University Press.

Eisenstein, S. (1997) *Film Form*, ed. and trans. by Jay Leyda, New York and San Diego: Harcourt Brace.

Fernandez, J. (1986) *Persuasions and Performances: The Play of Tropes in Culture*, Bloomington: Indiana University Press.

—— (ed.) (1991) *Beyond Metaphor: The Theory of Tropes in Anthropology*, Stanford: Stanford University Press.

Garrier, G. (1995) *Histoire sociale et culturelle du vin*, Paris: Bordas.

Geertz, C. (1973) *The Interpretation of Cultures: Selected Essays*, New York: Basic Books.

Goodman, N. (1978) *Ways of Worldmaking*, Indianapolis: Hackett.

Hockings, P. (ed.) (1995) *Principles of Visual Anthropology*, New York: Mouton de Gruyter.

Johnson, H. (1989) *Vintage: The Story of Wine*, New York: Simon and Schuster.

Lachiver, M. (1988) *Vins, vignes et vignerons: histoire du vignoble Français*, Paris: Fayard.

Loftus, S. (1993) *Puligny-Montrachet: Journal of a Village in Burgundy*, New York: Knopf.

Loizos, P. (1993) *Innovation in Ethnographic Film: From Innocence to Self-Consciousness*, Chicago: University of Chicago Press.

Loubère, L. A. *et al.* (1985) *The Vine Remembers: French Vignerons Recall their Past*, Albany: State University of New York Press.

MacDougall, D. (1994) 'Whose Story is it?' in L. Taylor (ed.), *Visualizing Theory: selected essays from V.A.R., 1990–1994*, New York: Routledge.

—— (1995) 'The subjective voice in ethnographic film', in L. Devereaux and R. Hillman (eds), *Fields of Vision: Essays in Film Studies, Visual Anthropology, and Photography*, Berkeley: University of California Press.

Marcus, G. E. (1994) 'The modernist sensibility in recent ethnographic writing and the cinematic metaphor of montage', in L. Taylor (ed.), *Visualizing Theory: Selected Essays from V.A.R., 1990–1994*, New York: Routledge.

Marker, C. and Resnais, A. (1953) *Les Statues Muerent Aussi*. Distributed by Tadie and Arte Video. France.

Nichols, B. (1994) 'The ethnographer's tale', in L. Taylor (ed.), *Visualizing Theory: selected essays from V.A.R., 1990–1994*, New York: Routledge.

Paul, H. W. (1996) *Science, Vine, and Wine in Modern France*, Cambridge and New York: Cambridge University Press.

Pink, S. (2001) *Doing Visual Ethnography: Images, Media and Representation in Research*, London: Sage.

Sapir, D. and Crocker, C. (eds) (1997) *The Social Use Of Metaphor*, Philadelphia: University of Pennsylvania Press.

Tomaselli, K. G. (1996) *Appropriating Images: The Semiotics of Visual Representation*, Højbjerg, Denmark: Intervention Press.

Ulin, Robert C. (1996) *Vintages and Traditions: An Ethnohistory of Southwest French Wine Co-operatives*, Washington, DC: Smithsonian Institution Press.

Unwin, T. (1991) *Wine and the Vine: An Historical Geography of Viticulture and the Wine Trade*, London: Routledge.

Veltman, K. H. (1996) 'Electronic media: the rebirth of perspective and the fragmentation of illusion', in T. Druckrey (ed.), *Electronic Culture: Technology and Visual Representation*, New York: Aperture.

Chapter 13

Working images

Epilogue

Felicia Hughes-Freeland

This chapter sums up key issues and themes raised in this book, and suggests what their implications are for contemporary and future visual research and representation. In particular it addresses the implications for visual anthropology. Given the far-reaching scope of this book, it is to be hoped that it will refresh and develop arguments for the critical role of the visual in anthropology produced over many years in both Europe and the United States to some who are less familiar with them. There is much in the book that is not routinely explored in visual anthropology books, which are often dedicated either to film or to photography. As such it offers a wider range of arguments and approaches than are usually brought together in a single volume, and provides a powerful case for the importance of using a wider range of methods and forms of representation in anthropological practice than is currently the norm in most doctoral and post-doctoral research projects, in Britain if less so in the United States.

Visual anthropology

For many years now, a relatively small number of anthropologists have been battling to gain academic recognition for visual work, ethnographic film in particular.[1] Neither this battle nor the notion that anthropologists need to attend to the visual dimension of social relations in their research and the representation of their findings is new. The precise origins of visual anthropology remain contentious, but the 1970s marked the start of a more systematic academic engagement (Ruby 2000; Hockings 1975/1995). However, in the opening session of the meeting from which this book (among other publications) has sprung, László Kürti and Janos Tari reminded us of an important earlier connection between anthropology and ethnographic film, the Hungarian film-maker Paul Fejos (1887–1963), who subsequently became director of the Wenner-Gren Foundation (which provided a major source of funding for the meeting which produced this book), and encouraged a young anthropologist to produce an early and neglected anthropological ethnography of Hollywood (Powdermaker 1951).[2] In the ensuing five decades, increasing numbers of academic anthropologists have trained in both practical and theoretical aspects of visual work and arguments have been made to diversify the scope of the visual within anthropology (such as Taylor 1994; Devereaux and Hillman 1995; Banks and Morphy 1997), two high-profile international journals, *Visual Anthropology* and *Visual Anthropology Review* have been published in the USA, but despite these efforts and developments, the mainstream logocentrism of academe results in such work being classed as subordinate to the written analysis and presentation of research results (Ginsburg 1998).[3]

I travelled to 'Working Images', a joint meeting of the Teaching Anthropology Network and Visual Anthropology Network of the EASA in September 2002, soon after the attack on New York's World Trade Center, equipped with a list of quotations from John Berger's *Another Way of Telling* (1982). This was intended for use in my summing up of the meeting, because it still remains a central and radically *visual* source for thinking about pictures, and for teaching others to realise what differentiates images from writing. In this chapter I will consider this polarisation, and argue that we need further differentiations in our thinking about what it is that words and pictures do. An image-based lyrical poem is closer to a photograph than it is to an academic paper. The contrast between word and image is only powerful if crudely argued, although in the world at large crude oppositions seem increasingly to sway the public regardless of finer points of reasoning produced by academics. And yet ironically, academics protect their traditions of thought and analysis by producing the kind of simplified arguments against images that they would deplore in other contexts. This stance, interestingly, is maintained as distance learning or life-long learning increase exponentially through the use of e-universities and a rapidly emerging domain of virtual learning packages – packages which rely on the visual presentation of ideas, packages in which texts become part of a process of knowledge acquisition which is structured spatially and temporally in a very different way from printed books. At the heart of these new texts are unexamined assumptions about the importance of images and our ability to interpret them – assumptions that sit alongside academic denials about the importance of images in themselves. The new 'discipline' of 'visual culture' may be entering university curricula and publishers' lists, but, ironically, its medium remains words. These pessimistic ruminations I carried with me to the conference were rapidly dissipated on arriving at Lisbon. I didn't need to invoke Berger, and the papers suggested that we had moved on further than I had thought, but as these conclusions will show, while there is cause for optimism in the face of such inventiveness and creativity, we still need to watch our backs.

The chapters in this book are divided into methods and representations, but I will address my comments to the implications of working with images for anthropological practices, because a continuing concern within anthropology is the extent to which we reveal our workings in the way we represent our findings. During 2001 SAGE alone published three books on visual methods, all of which are amply referred to by the contributors. But there is the risk of a polarisation or isolation of visual methods from other methods, or alternatively of failing to recognise their distinctiveness.[4] This book represents a range of positions. Some contributors tend to equate image with the visual, while other go beyond that understanding, bringing together words and pictures in a manner which is both rigorous and innovative.

In praise of simplicity

It is usually imagined that working with images requires expensive technology and training. A crucially important message in this book is that this is not necessarily the case. During our meeting in Lisbon the room was dauntingly equipped with every modern visual technological provision, but all that Cristina Grasseni (Chapter 2) needed to elaborate her concept of 'skilled vision' was an overhead projector. Means of delivery apart, Grasseni's chapter demonstrates that responses to the materially visible dimension of social life – in this instance aesthetic distinctions employed in cattle-breeding in North Italy – form a crucial object *of* research, as well as playing an important part in communicating research findings about subjects which may or may not be constituted as 'visual anthropology'. Having long argued against the ghetto-isation of the visual in anthropology, I welcome the fact that Grasseni, herself trained in film-making at Manchester's Granada Centre and now working as an academic anthropologist, nonetheless makes a strong argument for how the visual can enlighten us on matters other than the visual *per se*. She rightly identifies observation as a practice which requires further thought, both in what she describes as 'the anthropology of vision', and beyond. The aesthetic dimension pervades social experience in varying degrees of explicitness. While Grasseni urges us to work with ecological dynamics, I see no reason why this should supersede semiotic or tropic dynamics of the kind raised by Coover (Chapter 12). Grasseni's chapter provides a strong statement, and should remind anthropologists that the current interest in the materiality of culture necessitates attention to the social understandings of that materiality, and appearance, while not being the whole story, is a critical part of what is experienced, communicated and referred to by the people we work with. Anthropologists now research animals, landscape, ecologies, media and medicine, as well as longer-established subfields. Anthropologists working in these fields all have the potential to make the visual dimension of experience and its interaction with the non-visual a more important and respectable part of the research process and its subsequent forms of representation and dissemination.

A second key point in relation to technology and image production in anthropology is the value of drawing (and painting) as a method and as a means of representing findings. As a student at the National Film and Television School I was struck by the advice of the well-known film-maker Richard Leacock that we should draw every day to enhance our ability to look. There is nothing like drawing to train the powers of observation, and to assist the remembering of what was seen. Drawing transforms the event of seeing into the structure of memories. Two chapters invoke that most humble of visual technologies, the pencil: a low-tech, low-priced and widely available visual resource for teaching and learning. Ana Afonso (Chapter 5) reminds us of the usefulness of sketching as a means of documentation in research, and in so doing notes the potential of what she calls 'graphic anthropology', still in its infancy. But the use of mark-making by anthropologists (and subjects) in the research situation is not limited to pencils, nor are the ethical dilemmas and issues of communicability familiar to all social scientists limited to visual images such as film, video and photography. In an unusual field story, Ramos (Chapter 9) narrates the fate of some paintings he was commissioned to do when in Addis Ababa. The tale of the paintings of the Queen of Sheba is a salutary reminder of images that become unusable for whatever reason, in this case for political ones. Ramos is a talented artist as well as anthropologist, and these two chapters should inspire students and professionals who will never handle a camera to turn their hand to image-making and trading with low-tech tools.[5] And for those who think that images are of necessity pictorial, we should not forget too that non-linear representations of verbal symbols provide images which are standard in our publications and classrooms: maps, diagrams and tables (Postill 2002). These visually defined structures of information are fundamental to the 'scientific' nature of how we represent and contextualise our research or how we communicate the research of others. A book without figures and tables is somehow less 'serious' than one that has a profusion of visual summations of findings (as, for instance, in Bourdieu's (1984) *Distinction*). General information can be presented in a structured way out of a narrative context in the form of a map or a table, a use of images poles apart from particularity of filmic images, which is nonetheless also of relevance in thinking about the visual in anthropology.

Technical skill as a means to understanding

This book also raises questions about technology in research and the representation and dissemination of its results. Photography is a field that has finally become respectable for research but remains relatively marginal pedagogically. And yet photographic images which pervade the exchanges and transactions of everyday life also become 'cultural texts', sedimenting into the durable images of history and cultural representation, as Kürti's exploration of postcards (Chapter 4) explains. 'Banal' and 'simple' though postcards be, they nonetheless resist gratuit ous decipherment. Kürti explores the hidden history of the humble postcard, with reference to Lajosmizse, a Hungarian town south-east of Budapest. He describes the founding of the Historical Cultural Association in 1999, the creation of a Digital Photo Archive which among other activities republished old postcards, demonstrating how postcards interact with built environment, social institutions, social occasions, as well as family events. Importantly, the postcard is treated not just as a photograph but as the 'coexistence of the written text and image' which brings together two kinds of narrative (of the implications of this, see below). Kürti's essay is quintessentially anthropological in its attention to specific locality and the uniqueness of a particular case which nonetheless can highlight issues of a general relevance. Just as drawing an object or scene can inscribe it in the memory of the individual who draws, so the transacting of postcards inscribes memory in the collectivity of the community, facilitating the transmission of history and, in the case of Lajosmizse, a pride in the fact that things have changed. Kürti's contribution describes an innovative application of visual anthropology, and attests to the potential of the new digital technologies in research. In order to extend this kind of recognition of the value of photographs in understanding social relations and dynamics, teachers of anthropology should remember the usefulness of asking students to produce photo-essays (Olechnicki 2001) or take photographs (Bowman 2001) as a means to transmit a wide range of research tools and also encourage students to think actively and reflexively about what anthropological practice entails.

For purposes of research, another means of working with images is collaboration with professional image-makers. In Chapter 10 Olivia da Silva's intriguing ethnographic photographic project work with fishermen and stallholders in markets in Portugal and England is mediated by Sarah Pink's anthropological perspective on photography. Anthropologists are invited to consider how innovations in documentary photography might suggest new ways of representing ethnography photographically. This vein of creativity in anthropology also has the potential to reach a wider audience, in the way that collaborations between film-makers and anthropologists did in Granada's *Disappearing World* series, and more recently as artists and anthropologists have attempted to do.[6] In the case of da Silva's project, the ethnographic integrity of her imagework is enhanced by the number of stages to the project, which is based on a genuine sense of collaboration with the subjects, and a strong process of feedback. This explicit degree of collaboration is exemplary, and sets a high standard for future practice.

The chapters by da Silva, Pink (Chapter 11) and Coover (Chapter 12) provide stimulating models for how visual and verbal information can be combined; in other words, we are *not* in the domain of visual anthropology only, although there is some slippage between 'image' and 'visual image'. To combine different forms of information beyond the merely illustrative is not simple. Anthropologists need to think carefully about design and the reading of images: navigating a hypertext is not only a new kind of reading: it requires a new way of thinking about writing, a writing that uses pictures and words in a non-illustrative relationship. Pink's chapter explains her research into uses of domestic space, and concentrates on two case studies and her own mediation of those studies (so two women become three), and in particular emphasises the importance of colour symbolism in constructing non-linear texts. In her case, the colour pink provides an iconographic theme to the gendering of the material in question. Deliberate and skilled artistry is also evident in Coover's presentation of his study into the practices of wine-making in Burgundy, artistry in the use of photography. In contrast to Pink, Coover works in black and white in this project, retaining a classicism and continuity with pre-digital forms of representation and conceptualisation.

Indeed, Coover's project is closely referenced to John Berger, and despite the highly innovative methods he uses to communicate his research, his explanatory discourse is carefully embedded in important discussions about images which sometimes are not given their due in other parts of this book. There is a tendency for images to be treated as visual or non-verbal, which creates a false contrast with language. Everyone who makes films knows that a film is a sound-image. But while photographic images may speak to us in a different way from a verbal description, the visual-in-the-verbal, in the form of rhetorical tropes such as metaphors, is often forgotten. The message of the 1980s arguments about writing ethnography concerned precisely this issue: that language in anthropology is not used scientifically, but evocatively. Ramos discusses 'ekphrasis', 'a description with great visual content' (Chapter 9), and Coover, to my great relief, recognises that 'images, *like words*, evoke worlds' (Chapter 12, my emphasis). Representation concerns more than visual images. In the late 1970s and early 1980s, a semantic turn in anthropology compelled many of us to explore the metaphoricity of social action as well as our representations of it, and at that point Nelson Goodman's constructivism (1978) seemed the way forward from an anthropology which overdid meaning, by emphasising the delimitation of meaning. Coover rediscovers Goodman in his attempt to consider precisely what the relationship (rather than the difference) is between words and pictures. He notes that 'identifying relationships in a world pictured through images and language is a matter of directing attention to fragments to show how their meanings may be diverse and demand further exploration' (Coover, Chapter 12), and inverts Berger's claims for photography to provide the context of experience (Berger 1982: 289) by suggesting that anthropologists should use verbal and visual images to convey the experience of context.

This is a slightly different approach from that taken by MacDougall's discussion of the challenge of images in 'Transcultural Cinema' when he remarks that 'Although it would be mistaken to deny the possibility of access to sensory experience in anthropological writing, visual anthropology opens more directly onto the sensorium than written texts and creates psychological and somatic forms of intersubjectivity between viewer and social actor' (1998: 262). Although MacDougall recognises the power of metaphor, this is in the context of anthropological understanding; for his purposes, the image is the visual, which undermines writing (1998: 264). In the broadest take on imagework in anthropology, we might reconsider the reification of experience-in-the-visual which of course visual anthropology has defensively implied in its battle against logocentrism. Kürti's chapter already takes issue with MacDougall's contrast in his discussion of that miniature incarnation of verbal and visual images, the postcard. Coover further challenges the demarcation, and by implication proposes a new poetics of anthropology which recognises both non-verbal images and the sensory, non-linear, non-denotational performative potential of language. It could be argued that the way in which Coover writes his chapter makes this point very well, without even needing to show us his pictures, although having seen more of the winemaking CD-ROM, I would not argue that his contribution to this book in any way subsumes that project – rather, it is another way of world-making, or a differently inflected context of experience. It is also significant that Coover's chapter ends with an ethnographic, not analytical point – the distinguishing mark of the anthropological style.

The key case of this book could be seen not as one for pictures versus words, but one which reaffirms the polyvalent character of anthropology as a science and a humanity, and the role of the imagination and its images in *both* those domains. What the contributors to the present volume do is to reassert the representational relationship between verbal and visual images, in order to carry forward the work of anthropology, both visual and general. MacDougall has proposed that visual work logically brings us into the field of what he calls 'experiential studies' with a concern with the anthropology of consciousness which might turn out to be 'nothing less than the empirical arm of phenomenology' (1998: 272). Embodiment and experience are themes in this present book, but they are not addressed through the discourse of phenomenology. For instance, Pink states that 'the visual is actually incorporated into the written texts to anchor the theory in the embodied sensory experiences of everyday life it seeks to explain and generalise from' (Chapter 11). Here, unlike MacDougall's visual take on the image, the verbal has the last word. It would be interesting for anthropologists to take MacDougall's claims for the visual image from the field of film to that of making hypermedia, to explore his challenge to start from the (visual) image, and to think about how we might develop image-led learning. Some of the starting points for how this might be done are found in this chapter and others in this book.

Images are not always what they seem

A further surprising conclusion to be drawn from this collection is that images may be *invisible*. To pursue the line that image is not just visual, and the future not just hi-tech, I turn to examples of the humanistic and creative use of image-making in anthropology in another style. Orobitg and Edgar both raise questions about how to work inside the black box, and to elicit representations of invisible images to reconstruct the imaginary world. Orobitg's study of dreams among the Pumé (Chapter 3) would have been impossible without such imagework.[7] A similar method in a context closer to home is Edgar's account of imagework, a process by which images are produced in the mind's eye to release various unconscious elements in therapeutic contexts (Chapter 6). Here, images become a means to elicit and evoke self-knowledge and self-identities of participants in a way other methods cannot. Images thus elicit verbal narratives, rather than constituting them. This approach emphasises the importance of the role of the imagination as well as the construction of narratives. It is a means, not an end, just as other therapies such as dance and drama therapy, which also reference pre-modern ritual practices, are performed to achieve wellbeing and personal integration and could be perceived as forms of amplification of imagework in which the process is inherent in imagery which goes on the move rather than transforming into words to complete the work. At a time when the notion of 'data-sets' determines how many social scientists are having to represent their results to themselves and to funding councils, these approaches bring anthropological imagework closer to the domain of art therapy, and hint at other ways for anthropologists working visually to also be 'unruly' (à la Ginsburg, 1998) and to resist some of the normative homogenisation in the professionalisation of research.

Films do still matter even if they are not the whole story

Although an important yet recognised conclusion to be drawn from this book is that film-making is only one way of using images in anthropology, a complementary conclusion must be that the acquisition of anthropological knowledge (or understanding) and cinematic pleasure are less mutually exclusive than is sometimes argued (Ruby 2000: 36). Although this book does not include the strand of the meeting which dealt with images in museum archives and exhibitions, I wish to mention here Caterina Alves Costa's (another former student of Manchester's Granada Centre) highly pleasurable film, *Ora rindo ora chorando* (No Suffering, No Song) commissioned by the Ethnographic Museum at Lisbon as part of its exhibition on *fado*. This is one of many innovative projects in the museum, and it is to be hoped that the path-breaking visual practices developed by the director, Joaqim Pais de Brito and his staff, will provide a model for other museums in Europe. This is the kind of practice which directly tackles anthropology's interface with the public and shapes how anthropology is understood outside the academy.

This book has focused on visual images, visible and invisible, pictorial and verbal. It proves indisputably that visuality lies at the heart of researching, teaching and learning, and that anthropology will remain 'a discipline of words' (Mead 1975/1995), using 'words' in an anti-imagistic sense, at its peril. Two contributions about film (Henley, and Camas Baena *et al.*) provide powerful arguments against those who might think that narrative cinema has been made redundant through hypermedia and post-narrative forms. Henley (Chapter 7) summarises the principles of observational cinema, and argues that despite critiques (notably Nichols 1991), this kind of film-making remains particularly appropriate for anthropological research. It is possible to quibble about the use of 'observational' in the light of David MacDougall's influential film/writing practice, which would suggest 'participant observational' cinema as a more accurate label for what Henley and others trained under Colin Young's regime at the National Film and Television School at Beaconsfield in the 1980s actually do. Of crucial importance here is the use of exchanges of dialogue during filming between the subjects and the crew: such participatory engagement in fact brings film-making even closer to what anthropologists do in traditional fieldwork. Henley's latest film, *The Legacy of Antonio Lorenzano*, is a moving portrait of a subject who died before the necessary funding could be obtained to travel to the Amazon, and an example of what could be called participant-observational cinema, or even post-observational cinema.

In explaining observational cinema, Henley invokes Geertz's 'experience-near' and 'experience-distant' categories (1983) which for Geertz were part of the process at arriving at empathy *through* the interpretive work, rather than being a precondition for interpretation. For Henley, extraneous commentary is categorised as 'experience-distant', but the technological apparatus of film and video production is also not 'near' to all subjects, as the well-known argument between James Faris and Terence Turner about the appropriateness of training Kayapo people to make videos has shown (Turner 1992, Faris 1993). Image-making of course may be compared to Geertz's 'thick description' because the image itself is already an intepretation, albeit at a lower level of distance than a verbal commentary. All the images discussed in this book combine actuality and artifice, which is precisely what continues to produce anxiety in a discipline which cannot always appreciate the liberating effect on science in general of Thomas Kuhn's 'paradigm shift'. Verbal communication is still regarded as the domain of rationality, despite the fact that, ultimately, the stuff of communication and expression most susceptible to manipulation is, of course, language. However much we need to claim a place for images in anthropological practice, we have to remember that the visual exists in the verbal though images tropes. And in film and video, what the 'viewer' responds to are in fact *sound*-images. To repeat, images are not purely visual.

If 'ethnographic' film used to bring back home images of the 'other' for consumption by an audience differentiated from film subjects in space as well as time, and shown in a spirit of liberal education, the locality of film-making is increasingly 'at home'. For students of anthropological film-making, this is due to constraints of time and money, as well as the current trend in British and European anthropology to research parochial issues in the name of 'relevance'. The applied face of anthropology has moved from a purely overseas development context to the 'other' at home. In Chapter 9, we learn about the work of the *A Buen Común*, which produces documentaries to influence policy, albeit by the rather diffused means of influencing opinion within a particular set of networks. Films such as *Mujeres invisibles* (Invisible Women), a visual document about marginal and 'invisible' women living in Cordoba, in which they speak of poverty and illiteracy, play a role in the community by revealing painful things otherwise hidden to local citizens of Cordoba. Ethnographic film brings the 'other' home, and brings film out of the classroom or film festival into the domain of public policy. Given the dependence of policy-related research on verbal data collection, often carried out by commercial companies, this intensely ethnographic approach is to be welcomed. While it is likely to be an uphill battle to persuade policy researchers and funding agencies to follow this example, the attention drawn to this group's work here will provide some ammunition for anyone interested in applying film in this manner. Of course, there is the possibility of pushing the practice further, by involving the participants in what would be more of a 'shared' anthropology, in which both image-production and verbal interpretation and framing were produced in dialogue through the entire phase of the work.

This is an issue which is implied but not always explicit in this volume, although it is most evident in Chapter 10, where the photographer's ethnographic project demonstrates an enviably complete series of feedback and development in collaboration with the subjects. Henley's film referred to above is also the result of collaboration with another anthropologist as well as the community explored in the film. It is precisely this processual and dialectical aspect which breaks down the hard boundary between method and representation, because in image work, representation becomes methodological, and accountability to those who become images is of prime importance. This is because the hallowed ethical procedure of anonymisation cannot be sustained when pictorial images are used (unless one chooses to blur or break down the image to mask the face). The production of images and their deployment intensifies the increasingly stringent ethical concerns in social sciences with the proliferation of ethics committees, if only because that key ethical gambit, anonymisation, becomes problematic when the person is shown. Within ethnographic film, the issue of privacy and consent continues to challenge film-makers of all ranks, and it is ironic perhaps that in an age where the making, taking and displaying of images is so ubiquitous, legitimacy in this enterprise becomes more and more problematic. It is concerns such as these that have resulted in a number of contributors rejecting the Internet as the appropriate site for their representations. To protect their images from abuse or misuse, Pink and Coover have both chosen to present their multimedia work in the form of CD-ROMS or DVDs, and not as websites. It is also the case that sections of Coover's CD-ROM are available on the distributor's website, but because they are inscribed in a material form with clear boundary, it means that these images are not available for appropriation and re representation by anyone, but are transacted subject to the same constraints as images in books.

In Britain in 2002, a moral panic about child pornography on the Internet has made any visual image production involving children even more complex to negotiate than previously. For film-makers especially, the question of obtaining signed releases is a major part of the practice, but as has been pointed out, people might not fully realise what they are giving their consent to, and for what purposes (Winston 1995). When images are unleashed on the public, effects are unpredictable, whether on the subject of 'home' based institutions such as the police force on television (Graef 1989) or a more 'traditional' anthropological topic in a public screening (Holtedahl 1993). The way our images go out into the world remains problematic. It is now a crucial time for anthropologists to address this issue, not only for reasons of ethics and unintended political consequences of representation, but also, in the case of Britain, for representing anthropological relevance to an increasingly ignorant and indifferent public (Sillitoe 2003; Mills 2003). How we enable others to imagine us through our imagework is critical for the very survival of the subject in some countries.

Techno-phobia and the cruelty of institutions

A final conclusion, demonstrated in this volume but not represented in it, concerns the gap between technological potential and institutional management; I need to refer to some papers presented at the original meeting which are published elsewhere. At the Lisbon workshop we were all impressed by what the participants had achieved, given the enormous amount of time it takes to learn the techniques and produce the material electronically. Technological potential is not matched by the limited resources provided by most universities, and using these new technologies requires major investment of time and money within universities (Dracklé 2001).[8] We are in a period of transition. Our gold standard (the written text) is under attack from more complex means of exploring and communicating new ideas. Our institutions present policies about IT and virtual learning, but as Dracklé reminds us, these policies are under-resourced. An important conclusion is that despite the potential of the latest visual technologies to realise the power of the visual dramatically in *all aspects of anthropological practice*, there are many problems for us in *realising* this potential. There is an alarming gap between what we could be doing, and what the motivation is to do it.

There are also major training issues. If we aspire to create visual designs from our research on CD-ROMs or on web pages, we should be able at least to make a drawing, take a photograph, or produce a decent photo-essay. This point has been made many times, but what still needs to be made clear is that not only is visual literacy an area of training in anthropology where there is much work to do, but that a prerequisite for it is that an awareness of its importance be given proper recognition within institutions. The redundancy of research photography and the divergence between anthropological and commercial film-making has been the subject of recent comment (see Ruby 2000: Introduction), but if students learn to use these visual technologies early on, the chances of them using them more strategically and effectively in later research or employment are strengthened. For other methods and forms of representation to become legitimate within anthropological practice and equal in the race for funding to more traditional methods and means of representation, the next generation of anthropologists needs to be trained properly. It is my long-held view that doing practical visual work in undergraduate courses is an invaluable means to develop anthropological insights in students, as well as helping them to appreciate the work of others, and for many years I used a free-standing series of ethnographic films to cultivate visual literacy. Since then I have set up courses specifically addressed to appreciating ethnographic film, and I also use digital film-making with undergraduates at Swansea to force them to understand the realities of interacting with subjects in the field. I say 'force' because having a camera tempts them to control the situation, and inevitably results in situations beyond their control, making them appreciate the situated nature of understanding, and the serendipitous nature of research (Hughes-Freeland 1999). Film-making becomes a way of driving home to students the importance of patience and humility in anthropological interactions and practice. Nonetheless, it remains the case that in this multimedia age, most assessment at undergraduate level takes the form of the traditional written essay, so in 2002–3 I set up a project to explore different means of using visual work and the criteria for assessing it through C-SAP,[9] to provide training in digital editing for the film-making course, and also scanning training for students doing the 'history of anthropological theory' course to create resources for other students in the form of CD-ROMS (Hughes-Freeland n.d.). The benefit to the students in terms of providing them with variety in their ways of thinking about anthropology and transferable skills for the job market is evident, but they do also raise complex resourcing and logistical issues.

Why invest hours of unpaid extra work to develop new resources and new representations of research, if these are not given the credit in the interminable audits and assessments we all now undergo? A film, CD-ROM or website produced from research does not have the kudos of a printed monograph. The skill and labour it takes to produce on-line, CD-ROM or DVD materials for students are not adequately resourced or recognised in career development. And yet our students expect their learning to include such resources. The technological aspect of many exciting new developments in education presents a problem within universities of recognition and also of role: the old divide between technician and academic is no longer so simple, and many of us are expected to become our own technicians, on top of the other roles we take on. The problem is not simply finding time to process data in electronic media, but how to create appropriate conditions for work and access within these new communicative fields. Dracklé's worst-case scenario is that in hyperspace we risk becoming slaves to our institutions and students, unable to control our privacy. This is the downside of images becoming miraculously accessible, and we need to remember this as we become punch-drunk with the possibilities that lie ahead. It is indisputable that, given the proper resourcing and contracts, making photographic archives (for instance) available on the web or CD-ROM will be of immense benefit to researchers, though it is also the case that new ways of cataloguing data will be needed. The potential for becoming lost, or simply overwhelmed, is enormous. It is important for even better systems facilitating navigation and retrieval to be developed because our human memories cannot compete with electronic ones.

People, not technology

From attempting to persuade students to take up their pencils (and I have since the workshop in Lisbon tried to convince singularly unimpressed post-graduates of the virtue of this humble method – but they were also unimpressed by photo-elicitation, still wedded to the power of the word), to persuading university administrators of the relevance of open-access labs with editing software (another battle in train), we will come up against institutional structures which in the case of visual resources inevitably seem to manifest themselves as structures of resistance. This is the case in museums as well as universities, even though in museum practice, visuality is paramount. This is why I have referred to the admirable work of the ethnographic museum in Lisbon above. Whatever the strength of the cases for the methods and theories advocated in this book, the truth of the matter is that it is never simple to introduce innovations.

Ultimately, then, just as anthropology is always about social relations regard-less of its particular subfields, I can only conclude that whatever resources have been identified in this book, and however strong the cases for introducing new methods, it is always human interactions, negotiations and creativity which will carry us forward – and always human power strategies and equivocations which will hold us back. As I write this, it would appear that we have a double struggle on our hands: to preserve anthropology in its widest forms of diversity with its greatest range of methods and objectives, and to preserve anthropology in any form at all. As we argue our cases for working images, let us try to make sure that we do not simply become technical adjuncts to other disciplines which some would have us believe are valuable and relevant because the market makes them so. We need to preserve the human face of image-making in all techno-logies, and to do this, we need to ensure that anthropology will survive to keep us being human.

And now, dear reader...

Books remain the most portable and compact medium for bearing information, but for those of us working with visual material, particularly moving images, books have their limitations. Indeed, the papers here can describe and theorise the issues of visual images, but they do not perform the arguments as they were enacted in our meeting. You, the reader, will need to follow through the links to websites, or obtain the CD-ROMs, DVDs and films cited in particular chapters. A full appreciation of these chapters requires you to work with the polyvalent images, be they visual or visual/verbal. If you do not, you will limit this book to being a compromise with the status quo, despite its convincing arguments for making the conservative majority change their attitudes.

Notes

1 My own work with images has ranged from making films, videos, websites and photographs through to writing about film, photography, dance, performance, ritual, media and installation art. I have not published most of my work in the usual 'visual anthropology' contexts because I feel that visuality is part of anthropology and needs to be integrated into general practice.

2 It is revealing that I first heard about this book, not from an anthropologist, but from the film-maker Roy Boulting. He said that it was by Margaret Mead, ensuring that it took me a few more years to track down.

3 Ginsburg refers to the 'minimal recognition of visual anthropology's contributions and potential, and a lack of power in the academy' (1998: 173–4).

4 For instance, in the latest volume in the ASA Research Methods in Social Anthropology series in Britain, visual materials are compared to interview transcripts (Davies 1999: 117).

5 Drawing may also be used to elicit data, as Armin Prinz showed with reference to an Azande boy's drawings of witchcraft; Prinz and others from the Institute for the History of Medicine at Vienna also presented very interesting posters at the Lisbon meeting (*Viennese Ethnomedicine Newsletter* 2001).

6 For example, the Royal Anthropology Institute's International Ethnographic Film Festival at Goldsmiths College, London included a conference at which artists also spoke in 1997. A similar but larger-scale meeting was 'Fieldworks: Dialogues between Art and Anthropology', a conference at the Tate Modern, London in September 2003.

7 A similar approach was used by Tsing in her work with a Meratus shaman in Indonesian Borneo (1993).

8 This and two other papers about the pros and cons of developing distance-learning schemes in anthropology (Ardevol 2001; Trias i Valls 2001) have been published in a special edition of the *Journal for Applied Anthropology in Policy and Practice* entitled *Visual Learning, Virtual Learning.*

9 As I write these conclusions I am completing a project on visual technologies and their assessment at undergraduate level, funded by C-SAP, Birmingham University, as part of the Teaching and Learning Support Network in Britain. See http://www.swan.ac.uk/visualanthropology

References

Ardevol, E. (2001) 'Teaching anthropology virtually: learning communities at work', *Visual Learning, Virtual Learning, Journal for Applied Anthropology in Policy and Practice* 9(2): 32–42.

Banks, M. and Morphy, H. (eds) (1997) *Rethinking Visual Anthropology*. New Haven: Yale University Press.

Berger, J. (1982) *Another Way of Telling*, London: Writers and Readers Publishing Co-operative Society.

Bourdieu, P. (1984) *Distinction: A Social Critique of the Judgement of Taste*, London: Routledge and Kegan Paul.

Bowman, G. (2001) 'Elicitation versus illustration: a perennial problem in the teaching of visual anthropology', unpublished paper presented to 'Working Images', Lisbon, September 2001.

Davies, C. (1999) *Reflexive Ethnography*, London and New York: Routledge.

Devereaux, L. and Hillman, R. (eds) (1995) *Fields of Vision: Essays in Film Studies, Visual Anthropology and Photography*, Berkeley: University of California Press.

Dracklé, Dorle (2001) 'Teaching and learning multimedia', *Visual Learning, Virtual Learning, Journal for Applied Anthropology in Policy and Practice* 9(2): 24–31.

Faris, J. (1993) 'A response to Terence Turner', *Anthropology Today* 9(1): 12–14.

Geertz, C. (1983) 'From the natives' point of view . . .', in *Local Knowledge: Further Essays in Interpretive Anthropology*, New York: Basic Books.

Ginsburg, F. (1998) 'Instituting the unruly: a charter for visual anthropology', *Ethnos* 63(2): 173–201.

Goodman, N. (1978) *Ways of Worldmaking*, Indianapolis: Hackett.

Graef, R. (1989) 'Privacy and ethnographic film', *Anthropology Today* 5(2): 1–2.

Hockings, P. (ed.) (1975/1995) *Principles of Visual Anthropology*, Berlin and New York: Mouton de Gruyter.

Holtedahl, L. (1993) 'Communication problems in social research', in P. I. Crawford (ed.), *The Nordic Eye*, Aarhus: Intervention Press.

Hughes-Freeland, F. (1999) 'Dance on film: strategy and serendipity', in T. J. Buckland (ed.), *Dance in the Field: Theory, Methods and Issues in Dance Ethnography*, Basingstoke: Macmillan.

—— (n.d.) 'Moving images', paper to the panel 'Beyond Observational Cinema – Again', the ASA Decennial 'Anthropology and Science', 14–18 July 2003.

MacDougall, D. (1998) 'Transcultural cinema', in L. Taylor (ed.), *Transcultural Cinema*, Princeton: Princeton University Press.

Mead, M. (1975/1995) 'Visual anthropology in a discipline of words', in P. Hockings (ed.), *Principles of Visual Anthropology*, Berlin and New York: Mouton de Gruyter.

Mills, D. (2003) 'Quantifying the discipline', *Anthropology Today* 19(3): 19–22.

Nichols, B. (1991) *Representing Reality*, Bloomington and Indianapolis: Indiana University Press.

Olechnicki, K. (2001) 'Teaching and learning the photo-essay: theory and practice', *Visual Learning, Virtual Learning, Journal for Applied Anthropology in Policy and Practice* 9(2): 17–22.

Postill, J. (2002) 'Using maps and diagrams to teach a region-based anthropology: a Balkan experience', *Visual Learning, Virtual Learning, Journal for Applied Anthropology in Policy and Practice* 9(2): 6–16.

Powdermaker, H. (1951) *Hollywood the Dream Factory: An Anthropologist Looks at the Movie-Makers*, London: Secker and Warburg.

Ruby, J. (2000) *Picturing Culture: Explorations of Film and Anthropology*, Chicago: The University of Chicago Press.

Sillitoe, P. (2003) 'Time to be professional?', *Anthropology Today* 19(1): 1–2.

Taylor, L. (ed.) (1994) *Visualizing Theory: Selected Essays for VAR 1990–1994*, London and New York: Routledge.

Trias i Valls, Ma Angels (2001) 'Online teaching: the role of visual media in the delivery of anthropology online', *Visual Learning, Virtual Learning, Journal for Applied Anthropology in Policy and Practice* 9(2): 43–51.

Tsing, A. L. (1993) *In the Realm of the Diamond Queen*, Princeton: Princeton University Press.

Turner, T. (1992) Forman lecture on Kayapo project, *Anthropology Today* 8(9): 5–16.

Viennese Ethnomedicine Newsletter (2001) 4(1), October.

Winston, B. (1995) *Claiming the Real*, London: British Film Institute.

Index